FLUID POWER SYSTEMS AND INDUSTRIAL AUTOMATION

MR3591 ANNA UNIVERSITY

ANAND JAYAKUMAR ARUMUGHAM

Dedicated to my mother Mrs Jeevalakshmy Arumugham

Contents

Contents

Preface

Welcome to the dynamic world of Fluid Power Systems and Industrial Technology, where the forces of fluid mechanics converge with cutting-edge industrial applications to drive innovation and efficiency. This comprehensive textbook is designed to serve as a guide and companion for students, engineers, and professionals seeking a profound understanding of the principles, components, and applications that constitute the backbone of modern industrial systems.

Fluid power, encompassing both hydraulics and pneumatics, plays a pivotal role in a myriad of industrial processes, ranging from manufacturing and construction to aerospace and beyond. The ability to harness and control the power of fluids is fundamental to the advancement of technology, providing the muscle behind countless machines and systems that propel our modern society.

This book is crafted to cater to a diverse audience, from those taking their first steps in the study of fluid power systems to seasoned professionals seeking to deepen their knowledge and stay abreast of the latest advancements. It combines theoretical foundations with practical insights, offering a balanced approach that empowers readers to grasp the underlying principles while appreciating their real-world applications.

Key features of this book include:

Fundamental Concepts: A thorough exploration of the fundamental principles of fluid mechanics, providing the necessary groundwork for understanding fluid power systems.

Component Analysis: In-depth discussions on the components that constitute fluid power systems, including pumps, valves, actuators, and control systems, offering a holistic view of their design, functionality, and interdependence.

System Design: Practical insights into the design considerations and methodologies involved in developing efficient and reliable fluid power systems, ensuring that readers are well-equipped to tackle real-world engineering challenges.

Applications Across Industries: Case studies and examples spanning a diverse range of industries, demonstrating how fluid power systems are integral to the functioning of machinery in manufacturing, agriculture, construction, and beyond.

Emerging Technologies: Exploration of the latest trends and innovations in fluid power systems and industrial technology, including the integration of smart sensors, automation, and digital controls.

I believe that this book will serve as a valuable resource for educators, students, and professionals alike, fostering a deep appreciation for the role of fluid power in shaping the technological landscape. As the realms of engineering and industrial technology continue to evolve, this text aims to be a reliable companion, providing a solid foundation for understanding and navigating the exciting and ever-changing field of fluid power systems.

This book is written in tune with the latest syllabus of Anna University and the syllabus has been taken as a guide for the organization of this text.

The author's responsibility here is to stress abundantly that he lays no claim to the original research in preparing this book. Many of the subject matters that are available in the works of eminent authors have been made available freely. Perhaps what I may claim, in all modesty, is that I have tried to fashion the vast amount of materials available from primary and secondary sources into coherent body of description and analysis.

Although every care has been taken to make the text error free, yet the author shall feel obliged if errors present are brought to his notice. Constructive criticism of the book will be warmly received.

Anand Jayakumar Arumugham
jay4upeople@gmail.com

Acknowledgements

The satisfaction and euphoria of successful completion of any task could be incomplete without mentioning the people who made it possible, whose constant guidance and encouragement crown my efforts with success.

I take this opportunity to express my sincere gratitude to the chairman Shri.V. LAKSHMINARAYANASAMY MBA, the chairman, Suguna collage of engineering, for providing me with a successful environment and his encouragement in the right path to develop a fine book.

I am thankful to my Director Dr. PRAKASAM, M.E, Ph.D., for his constant encouragement and support throughout the preparation of the book.

I are also very much grateful and would like to express my sincere thanks to our Principal Dr.R.MAGUDEESWARAN, M.E, Ph.D., who provided me with constant support and encouragement in preparing this book.

I would like to extend my sincere thanks to all the faculty members and lab technicians for their constant support and coordination in bringing out this book.

Above all I thank my beloved mother and brother for their moral support, encouragement and their prayers during the preparation of this book.

MR3591 FLUID POWER SYSTEMS AND INDUSTRIAL AUTOMATION
UNIT – I FLUID POWER SYSTEM GENERATION AND ACTUATORS
Need For Automation, Classification of Drives - Hydraulic, Pneumatic and Electric –Comparison –
ISO Symbols for their Elements, Selection Criteria. Generating Elements- Hydraulic Pumps and
Motor Gears, Vane, Piston Pumps – Motors - Selection and Specification - Drive Characteristics –
Utilizing Elements - Linear Actuator – Types, Mounting Details, Cushioning – Power Packs –
Accumulators.

UNIT – II CONTROL AND REGULATIING ELEMENTS
Control and Regulating Elements — Direction, Flow and Pressure Control Valves -Methods of
Actuation, Types, Sizing of Ports. Spool Valves - Operating Characteristics -Electro Hydraulic
Servo Valves - Types - Characteristics and Performance.

UNIT – III CIRCUIT DESIGN FOR HYDRAULIC AND PNEUMATICS
Typical Design Methods – Sequencing Circuits Design - Combinational Logic Circuit Design -
Cascade Method – KV Mapping - Electrical Control of Pneumatic and Hydraulic Circuits - Use of
Relays, Timers, Counters and PLC in pneumatics and hydraulics

UNIT – IV PROGRAMMABLE LOGIC CONTROLLER
Industrial Automation - Programmable Logic Controller - Functions of PLCs - Features of PLC -
Selection of PLC - Architecture – IEC61131-3 programming standard and types - Basics of PLC
Programming – Ladder Logic Diagrams – Communication in PLC – Programming Timers and
Counters – Data Handling - PLC modules – Advanced motion controlled Multi Axis PLC

UNIT – V DATA COMMUNICATION AND SUPERVISORY CONTROL SYSTEMS
Industrial Data Communications -– Modbus – HART – DeviceNet – Profibus – Fieldbus – RS232-
RS485- Modbus/ Modbus TCP/IP - mechatrolink – CAN – EtherCAT - Introduction to Supervisory
Control Systems – SCADA - Distributed Control System (DCS) – Safety Systems – human
machine interfaces - Total Integrated Automation (TIA) – Industry 4.0.

Fluid Power System Generation and Actuators

Need For Automation, Classification of Drives - Hydraulic, Pneumatic and Electric –Comparison – ISO Symbols for their Elements, Selection Criteria. Generating Elements- Hydraulic Pumps and Motor Gears, Vane, Piston Pumps – Motors - Selection and Specification - Drive Characteristics – Utilizing Elements - Linear Actuator – Types, Mounting Details, Cushioning – Power Packs – Accumulators.

Need For Automation

The need for automation has become increasingly apparent in today's rapidly evolving world. Automation refers to the use of technology to perform tasks without human intervention, and it has become a crucial element in various industries and aspects of daily life. In this essay, we will explore the reasons behind the growing demand for automation, examining its impact on efficiency, productivity, safety, and overall societal progress.

1. Efficiency and Productivity:

One of the primary drivers for the adoption of automation is the significant boost in efficiency and productivity it offers. Automated systems can perform tasks at a much faster rate and with a higher level of precision compared to their human counterparts. This is particularly evident in manufacturing, where robotic arms and automated assembly lines can produce goods at a speed and consistency that would be impossible for humans to match. In industries like automotive manufacturing, for example, automation has revolutionized production processes, leading to increased output and reduced costs.

2. Precision and Accuracy:

Automation ensures a high level of precision and accuracy in various tasks. Machines and software are programmed to follow specific instructions meticulously, eliminating the margin of error that is inherent in human work. This is especially crucial in industries such as healthcare, where precision in diagnosis and treatment is of utmost importance. Automated medical equipment, for instance, can perform surgeries with unparalleled accuracy, minimizing the risks associated with human error.

3. Cost Reduction:

Automation often leads to cost reduction in the long run. While the initial investment in automation technology can be substantial, the operational cost savings over time are significant. Automated systems can work 24/7 without the need for breaks, vacations, or overtime pay. This continuous operation results in increased output and lower per-unit production costs. In industries like logistics and warehousing, automated systems for sorting and packaging can lead to substantial cost savings.

4. Safety:

Automation plays a crucial role in improving safety, particularly in hazardous or high-risk environments. Dangerous tasks, such as handling toxic substances, working in extreme temperatures, or performing repetitive and physically demanding activities, can be assigned to automated systems. This not only protects human workers from potential harm but also enhances overall workplace safety. In the mining industry, for example, automated drilling and extraction systems reduce the risk of accidents and exposure to harmful conditions.

5. Consistency and Quality:

Automated systems can consistently deliver high-quality output. By eliminating variations in human performance, automation ensures that each product or service meets the same standards. This is vital in industries like food production, where consistency in flavor, texture, and safety is paramount. Automated quality control systems can quickly and accurately identify defects or deviations from standards, preventing subpar products from reaching consumers.

6. Adaptability to Complex Tasks:

Automation is not limited to simple, repetitive tasks; it can also handle complex and intricate processes. Advanced technologies such as artificial intelligence and machine learning enable automation systems to adapt to changing conditions, learn from experience, and make decisions in real-time. This adaptability is particularly valuable in fields like finance, where automated algorithms can analyze vast amounts of data to make investment decisions or detect fraudulent activities.

7. Time Savings:

Automation can save valuable time by expediting tasks that would take humans much longer to complete. This time savings is crucial in today's fast-paced business environment, where timely decision-making and rapid responses to market changes are essential. In the realm of customer service, for instance, chatbots and automated response systems can handle routine inquiries, allowing human agents to focus on more complex and personalized customer interactions.

8. Economic Competitiveness:

Countries and businesses that embrace automation gain a competitive edge in the global economy. The efficiency and cost-effectiveness achieved through automation contribute to the overall competitiveness of industries. Nations that invest in automation technologies can enhance their economic growth, attract foreign investments, and create a skilled workforce capable of managing advanced technologies. The strategic adoption of automation is thus a key driver for long-term economic success.

9. Innovation and Technological Advancement:

The pursuit of automation fosters innovation and technological advancement. As industries seek to optimize processes and enhance efficiency, they invest in research and development to create cutting-edge automation technologies. This continuous cycle of innovation not only improves existing processes but also opens doors to entirely new possibilities. The development of autonomous vehicles, for example, represents a paradigm shift in transportation and logistics, with potential implications for safety, efficiency, and environmental sustainability.

10. Addressing Labor Shortages:

Automation can help address challenges related to labor shortages, which are becoming increasingly prevalent in certain industries and regions. In sectors where finding skilled labor is a challenge, automation provides a viable solution. For instance, in agriculture, where there is a growing shortage of farm labor, automated harvesting machines can mitigate the impact of workforce shortages and ensure timely crop harvesting.

11. Environmental Sustainability:

Automation can contribute to environmental sustainability by optimizing resource usage and reducing waste. Smart technologies and automated systems can monitor and control energy consumption, leading to more efficient use of resources. In manufacturing, for example, automation can minimize material waste and energy consumption, promoting sustainable and eco-friendly practices. Additionally, the development of cleaner technologies, often associated with automation, can help mitigate the environmental impact of various industries.

12. Enhanced Data Analysis:

Automation facilitates the collection and analysis of vast amounts of data in real-time. This capability is particularly valuable in sectors like healthcare, finance, and marketing. Automated data analysis can uncover patterns, trends, and insights that would be challenging for humans to identify manually. In healthcare, for instance, automated analysis of patient data can assist in early disease detection and personalized treatment plans.

13. Adaptation to Changing Demographics:

As demographics shift, with an aging population in many parts of the world, automation can play a crucial role in addressing the challenges associated with an aging workforce. Automated systems can handle tasks that may be physically demanding for older workers, allowing them to remain active in the workforce for longer. This adaptation is essential for maintaining a skilled and diverse workforce in the face of demographic changes.

14. Global Health Crises and Resilience:

Events like the COVID-19 pandemic have underscored the importance of automation in maintaining essential services and economic activities during crises. Automated systems, including remote work tools, online services, and robotic solutions, have played a pivotal role in ensuring business continuity and resilience. The ability of automation to operate with minimal human contact is particularly relevant in situations where social distancing and safety measures are imperative.

15. Ethical Considerations and Human Well-being:

While automation offers numerous benefits, it also raises ethical considerations related to job displacement and the impact on the well-being of workers. As certain tasks become automated, there is a need for society to address the potential consequences, such as job retraining and the creation of new opportunities. Striking a balance between automation and human involvement is essential to ensure that technological advancements contribute to overall societal well-being.

In conclusion, the need for automation is multifaceted and extends across various industries and societal domains. From improving efficiency and productivity to enhancing safety, addressing labor shortages, and fostering innovation, automation plays a pivotal role in shaping the present and future of human endeavors. While the adoption of automation brings about numerous benefits, it is essential to navigate its implementation ethically, considering the broader impact on individuals, communities, and the global economy. As technology continues to advance, the strategic and responsible integration of automation will be key to unlocking its full potential for the betterment of society.

Classification of Drives

The classification of hydraulic, pneumatic, and electric drives is essential for understanding the different mechanisms used to transmit power in various industrial applications. These drives serve as the backbone of machinery, providing the necessary force to move, lift, or manipulate objects. In this comprehensive exploration, we will delve into each type, examining their working principles, applications, advantages, and disadvantages.

Introduction:

1. Overview of Drives:

Drives are systems that convert energy into mechanical motion to accomplish specific tasks. The choice of drive type depends on factors such as the required force, speed, precision, and environmental considerations. Hydraulic, pneumatic, and electric drives are the three main categories, each utilizing distinct principles for power transmission.

Hydraulic Drives:

1. Working Principle:

Hydraulic drives operate based on the principles of fluid dynamics, employing incompressible fluids like oil to transmit power. The system typically consists of a pump, hydraulic fluid, valves, cylinders, and a reservoir. The pump pressurizes the hydraulic fluid, and this pressurized fluid is then directed to cylinders, where it acts on a piston to generate mechanical motion.

2. Applications:

Hydraulic drives find widespread use in heavy-duty applications where high force is required. Industries such as construction, mining, and manufacturing utilize hydraulic systems for tasks like lifting, pressing, and bending. Hydraulic systems are also common in aircraft for functions such as landing gear operation and brake systems.

3. Advantages:

High force capability: Hydraulic systems can generate substantial force, making them suitable for heavy-duty applications.

Precise control: Hydraulic systems can provide precise control over speed and force, allowing for intricate movements.

Overload protection: Hydraulic systems are less prone to damage from overloading due to their incompressible fluid nature.

4. Disadvantages:

Fluid leaks: Hydraulic systems may experience fluid leaks, which can lead to environmental concerns and maintenance challenges.

Temperature sensitivity: The efficiency of hydraulic systems can be affected by temperature variations, necessitating cooling mechanisms.

Complex maintenance: Hydraulic systems may require more intricate maintenance procedures compared to other drive types.

Pneumatic Drives:

1. Working Principle:

Pneumatic drives utilize compressed air to transmit power. The system comprises a compressor, air reservoir, valves, and actuators. Compressed air is generated by the compressor and stored in the reservoir. When needed, the compressed air is directed to actuators, such as cylinders, causing mechanical motion.

2. Applications:

Pneumatic drives are commonly employed in applications where rapid and repetitive movements are required. Industries like manufacturing, packaging, and automotive assembly lines use pneumatic systems for tasks such as gripping, pushing, and lifting. Pneumatic drives are also found in robotics and various handheld tools.

3. Advantages:

Rapid response: Pneumatic systems can achieve fast response times, making them suitable for applications requiring quick and repetitive movements.

Clean operation: Pneumatic systems do not involve oil or other fluids, resulting in cleaner operation and reduced environmental impact.

Cost-effective: Pneumatic components are often more affordable than their hydraulic or electric counterparts.

4. Disadvantages:

Limited force: Pneumatic systems may have limitations in generating high force, restricting their use in heavy-duty applications.

Lack of precision: Compared to hydraulic or electric drives, pneumatic systems may have lower precision in controlling speed and position.

Noisy operation: Pneumatic systems can produce noise during operation, which may be a consideration in certain environments.

Electric Drives:

1. Working Principle:

Electric drives utilize electrical energy to produce mechanical motion. The system typically consists of an electric motor, a power supply, and a control unit. The electric motor converts electrical energy into rotational motion, and this motion is then transmitted to the load through gears, belts, or other mechanical linkages.

2. Applications:

Electric drives are versatile and find applications in a wide range of industries. From small household appliances to large industrial machinery, electric drives power an array of devices. Electric drives are commonly used in conveyor systems, pumps, fans, and precision machinery due to their ability to provide consistent and controllable motion.

3. Advantages:

High precision: Electric drives can achieve precise control over speed, position, and torque, making them suitable for applications demanding accuracy.

Clean operation: Electric drives do not involve fluids, reducing the risk of leaks and making them environmentally friendly.

Broad applicability: Electric drives are suitable for various applications, ranging from low-power household devices to high-power industrial machinery.

4. Disadvantages:

Limited force density: Electric drives may have limitations in generating high force compared to hydraulic systems, particularly in heavy-duty applications.

Dependency on power supply: Electric drives rely on a stable and continuous power supply, making them susceptible to disruptions in the electrical grid.

Initial cost: The initial investment in electric drive systems, including motors and control units, may be higher than that of hydraulic or pneumatic systems.

Comparison and Selection:

1. Force and Power:

Hydraulic drives excel in applications requiring high force, making them suitable for heavy-duty tasks.

Pneumatic drives are adept at providing rapid and repetitive motion but may be limited in force compared to hydraulic systems.

Electric drives offer a balance between force and precision, making them versatile for a wide range of applications.

2. Precision and Control:

Hydraulic and electric drives provide precise control over speed, position, and force, making them suitable for applications demanding accuracy.

Pneumatic drives may have limitations in precision compared to hydraulic or electric systems.

3. Environmental Impact:

Hydraulic systems may pose environmental concerns due to fluid leaks, while pneumatic and electric systems are generally cleaner and more environmentally friendly.

4. Application Considerations:

The choice between hydraulic, pneumatic, and electric drives depends on the specific requirements of the application, considering factors such as force, speed, precision, and environmental considerations.

Conclusion:

In conclusion, the classification of hydraulic, pneumatic, and electric drives provides a framework for understanding the diverse mechanisms employed in power transmission. Each type has its strengths and weaknesses, making them suitable for different applications based on specific requirements. Hydraulic drives excel in heavy-duty applications, pneumatic drives offer rapid and repetitive motion, and electric drives provide a versatile solution with high precision. The selection of the appropriate drive type requires a careful consideration of the application's demands, environmental factors, and economic considerations, ensuring optimal performance and efficiency in various industrial settings.

Comparison of Drives

The comparison of hydraulic, pneumatic, and electric drives is crucial for understanding the strengths, weaknesses, and applications of each technology. These drive systems serve as the backbone for various industrial processes, offering different advantages and limitations. In this comprehensive exploration, we will delve into the key aspects of hydraulic, pneumatic, and electric drives, including their working principles, applications, efficiency, environmental impact, and economic considerations.

Introduction:

1. Purpose of Drives:

Drives are integral components in machinery and industrial systems, responsible for converting energy into mechanical motion to perform specific tasks. Hydraulic, pneumatic, and electric drives are the primary categories, each utilizing unique principles for power transmission. A detailed comparison of these drives is essential for making informed decisions in industrial design and system implementation.

Hydraulic Drives:

1. Working Principle:

Hydraulic drives harness the principles of fluid dynamics to transmit power. The system typically includes a hydraulic pump, fluid reservoir, valves, cylinders, and hydraulic fluid (usually oil). The pump pressurizes the hydraulic fluid, and this pressurized fluid is directed to cylinders, where it acts on a piston, generating mechanical motion.

2. Applications:

Hydraulic drives are prevalent in heavy-duty applications where high force is a prerequisite. Industries such as construction, mining, and manufacturing rely on hydraulic systems for tasks such as lifting, pressing, and bending. Aircraft use hydraulic systems for landing gear operation and brake systems, highlighting the versatility of hydraulic drives.

3. Advantages:

High Force Capability: Hydraulic systems excel in generating substantial force, making them suitable for applications involving heavy loads.

Precise Control: Hydraulic drives offer precise control over speed and force, enabling intricate movements.

Overload Protection: The incompressible nature of hydraulic fluids provides inherent overload protection, minimizing the risk of damage.

4. Disadvantages:

Fluid Leaks: Hydraulic systems may experience fluid leaks, posing environmental concerns and requiring maintenance.

Temperature Sensitivity: Variations in temperature can affect the efficiency of hydraulic systems, necessitating cooling mechanisms.

Complex Maintenance: Maintenance procedures for hydraulic systems can be intricate compared to other drive types.

Pneumatic Drives:

1. Working Principle:

Pneumatic drives utilize compressed air to transmit power. The system comprises a compressor, air reservoir, valves, and actuators (typically cylinders). Compressed air, generated by the compressor and stored in the reservoir, is directed to actuators when needed, inducing mechanical motion.

2. Applications:

Pneumatic drives find prominence in applications requiring rapid and repetitive movements. Industries such as manufacturing, packaging, and automotive assembly lines leverage pneumatic systems for tasks like gripping, pushing, and lifting. Pneumatic drives are also common in robotics and various handheld tools.

3. Advantages:

Rapid Response: Pneumatic systems exhibit fast response times, making them suitable for applications demanding quick and repetitive movements.

Clean Operation: Pneumatic systems do not involve oil or other fluids, resulting in cleaner operation and reduced environmental impact.

Cost-Effectiveness: Pneumatic components are often more affordable than their hydraulic or electric counterparts.

4. Disadvantages:

Limited Force: Pneumatic systems may have limitations in generating high force, restricting their use in heavy-duty applications.

Lack of Precision: Precision in controlling speed and position may be lower in pneumatic systems compared to hydraulic or electric drives.

Noisy Operation: Pneumatic systems can produce noise during operation, which may be a consideration in certain environments.

Electric Drives:

1. Working Principle:

Electric drives utilize electrical energy to produce mechanical motion. The system typically consists of an electric motor, a power supply, and a control unit. The electric motor converts electrical energy into rotational motion, which is then transmitted to the load through gears, belts, or other mechanical linkages.

2. Applications:

Electric drives are versatile and find applications in a wide range of industries. From small household appliances to large industrial machinery, electric drives power an array of devices. Conveyor systems, pumps, fans, and precision machinery commonly rely on electric drives due to their ability to provide consistent and controllable motion.

3. Advantages:

High Precision: Electric drives can achieve precise control over speed, position, and torque, making them suitable for applications demanding accuracy.

Clean Operation: Electric drives do not involve fluids, reducing the risk of leaks and making them environmentally friendly.

Broad Applicability: Electric drives are suitable for various applications, ranging from low-power household devices to high-power industrial machinery.

4. Disadvantages:

Limited Force Density: Electric drives may have limitations in generating high force compared to hydraulic systems, especially in heavy-duty applications.

Dependency on Power Supply: Electric drives rely on a stable and continuous power supply, making them susceptible to disruptions in the electrical grid.

Initial Cost: The initial investment in electric drive systems, including motors and control units, may be higher than that of hydraulic or pneumatic systems.

Comparison and Selection:

1. Force and Power:

Hydraulic drives excel in applications requiring high force, making them suitable for heavy-duty tasks.

Pneumatic drives are adept at providing rapid and repetitive motion but may be limited in force compared to hydraulic systems.

Electric drives offer a balance between force and precision, making them versatile for a wide range of applications.

2. Precision and Control:

Hydraulic and electric drives provide precise control over speed, position, and force, making them suitable for applications demanding accuracy.

Pneumatic drives may have limitations in precision compared to hydraulic or electric systems.

3. Environmental Impact:

Hydraulic systems may pose environmental concerns due to fluid leaks, while pneumatic and electric systems are generally cleaner and more environmentally friendly.

4. Application Considerations:

The choice between hydraulic, pneumatic, and electric drives depends on the specific requirements of the application, considering factors such as force, speed, precision, and environmental considerations.

Efficiency and Energy Consumption:

1. Efficiency:

Hydraulic systems can have high efficiency due to the incompressible nature of hydraulic fluids, but losses can occur in pumps and valves.

Pneumatic systems may experience energy losses due to air compressibility, impacting overall efficiency.

Electric drives can achieve high efficiency, especially with the advancement of energy-efficient motor technologies and control systems.

2. Energy Consumption:

Hydraulic systems may consume more energy due to pump operation and fluid viscosity.

Pneumatic systems may be less energy-efficient due to air compressibility and leakage.

Electric drives are often more energy-efficient, with the ability to control power consumption based on demand.

Environmental Impact:

1. Fluids and Emissions:

Hydraulic systems involve the use of hydraulic fluids, and leaks can result in environmental contamination.

Pneumatic systems, using compressed air, have a cleaner operation with no fluid involvement.

Electric drives are environmentally friendly as they do not involve fluids or emissions during operation.

2. Environmental Considerations:

Hydraulic and pneumatic systems may require careful management to prevent fluid leaks and minimize environmental impact.

Electric drives are often considered more environmentally sustainable, especially with the increasing use of renewable energy sources.

Economic Considerations:

1. Initial Costs:

Hydraulic systems may have moderate to high initial costs, including pumps, valves, and hydraulic fluid.

Pneumatic systems are generally more cost-effective in terms of initial investment.

Electric drives may have higher initial costs due to the procurement of motors, controllers, and associated equipment.

2. Maintenance Costs:

Hydraulic systems may incur higher maintenance costs due to the complexity of components and the potential for fluid leaks.

Pneumatic systems may have lower maintenance costs as they involve simpler components.

Electric drives typically have moderate maintenance costs, and advancements in motor technologies contribute to longer service life.

3. Operational Costs:

Hydraulic systems may have higher operational costs due to energy consumption and fluid replacement.

Pneumatic systems generally have lower operational costs, especially with efficient compressor technologies.

Electric drives can have competitive operational costs, and the increasing efficiency of electric motors contributes to overall cost-effectiveness.

Future Trends and Innovations:

1. Integration of Technologies:

Future trends involve the integration of technologies, such as the use of smart sensors and automation, to enhance the efficiency and performance of all three drive types.

The development of intelligent control systems will contribute to better adaptability and energy optimization in hydraulic, pneumatic, and electric drives.

2. Sustainability and Energy Efficiency:

Ongoing efforts are directed toward making hydraulic and pneumatic systems more environmentally sustainable by reducing fluid leaks and optimizing energy efficiency.

Electric drives are witnessing advancements in energy-efficient motor technologies and the integration of renewable energy sources for a more sustainable operation.

Conclusion:

In conclusion, the comparison of hydraulic, pneumatic, and electric drives highlights the diverse characteristics of each technology. Hydraulic drives excel in heavy-duty applications requiring high force, pneumatic drives are suitable for rapid and repetitive motion, and electric drives offer versatility and precision. The choice of drive type depends on specific application requirements, considering factors such as force, speed, precision, environmental impact, and economic considerations. As technological advancements continue, the integration of smart systems and a focus on sustainability will shape the future of hydraulic, pneumatic, and electric drives, contributing to more efficient and environmentally friendly industrial processes.

ISO Symbols

ISO (International Organization for Standardization) symbols are standardized graphical representations used to depict different components and functions in hydraulic, pneumatic, and electric systems. These symbols provide a universal language for engineers, technicians, and designers to communicate and understand the configuration and operation of systems. Let's explore the ISO symbols for hydraulic, pneumatic, and electric components in detail.

Hydraulic ISO Symbols:

1. Hydraulic Pump (ISO 1219-1 Symbol: 03):

Hydraulic Pump

The hydraulic pump is represented by a circle with an arrow indicating the direction of fluid flow. The symbol includes additional details such as the type of pump (gear, vane, piston) and specific features.

2. Hydraulic Motor (ISO 1219-1 Symbol: 04):

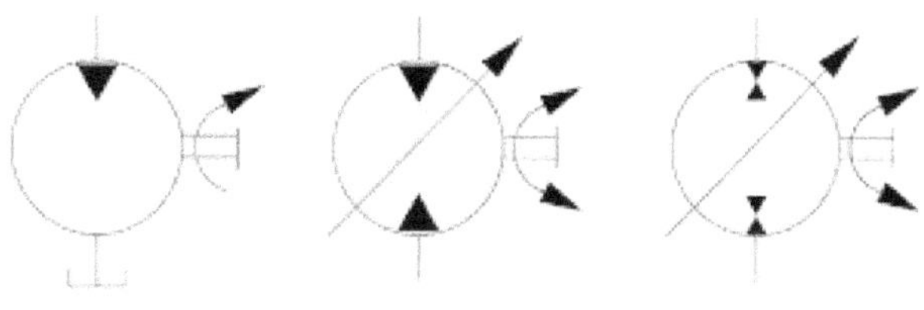

Hydraulic Motor

A hydraulic motor is depicted by a circle with an arrow pointing in the opposite direction of fluid flow. Like the hydraulic pump, additional information about the type of motor may be included in the symbol.

3. Hydraulic Cylinder (ISO 1219-1 Symbol: 05):

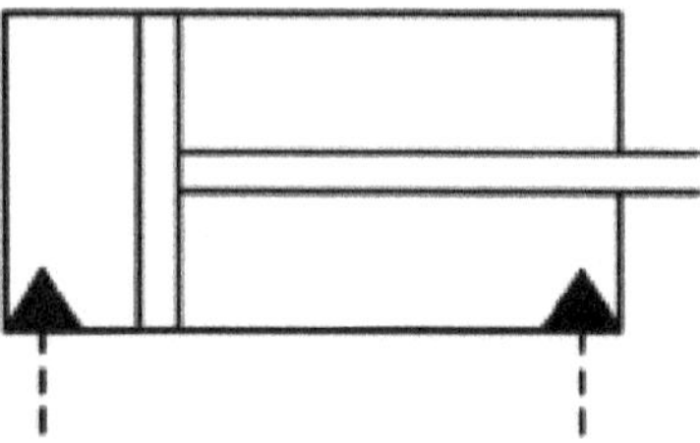

Hydraulic Cylinder

The hydraulic cylinder is represented by a rectangle with an arrow indicating the direction of the piston movement. The symbol includes details such as the number of acting directions and the type of cylinder (single-acting, double-acting).

4. Hydraulic Control Valve (ISO 1219-1 Symbol: 07):

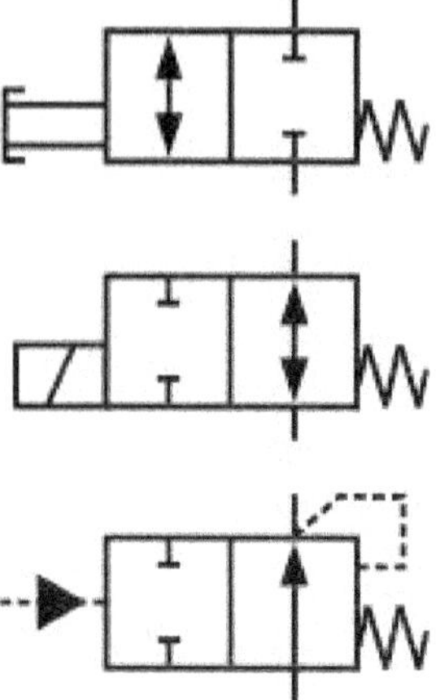

Hydraulic Control Valves

Hydraulic control valves are depicted by various symbols, including rectangles, circles, and arrows, representing different types of valves such as directional control valves, pressure control valves, and flow control valves.

5. Hydraulic Reservoir (ISO 1219-1 Symbol: 10):

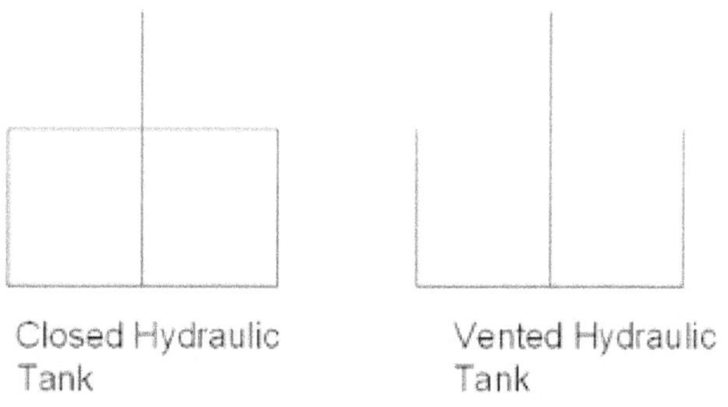

Hydraulic Reservoir

The hydraulic reservoir is represented by an open-topped rectangle. It may include additional symbols inside to indicate features such as a breather, filter, or level indicator.

Pneumatic ISO Symbols:

1. Pneumatic Compressor (ISO 1219-1 Symbol: 20):

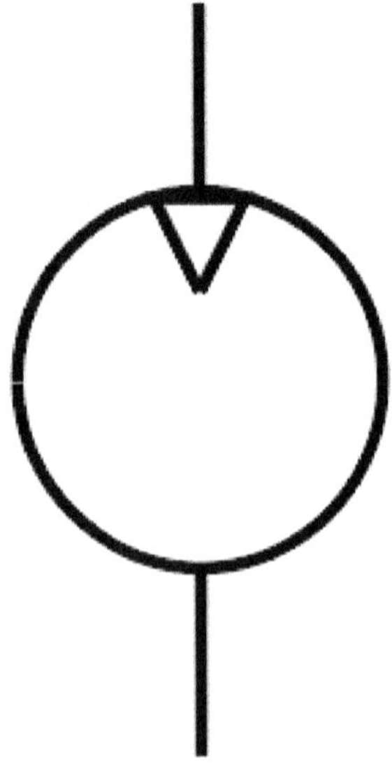

Pneumatic Compressor

The pneumatic compressor is represented by a circle with a triangle inside, indicating the compression of air. Additional details may be included to specify the type of compressor.

2. Pneumatic Motor (ISO 1219-1 Symbol: 21):

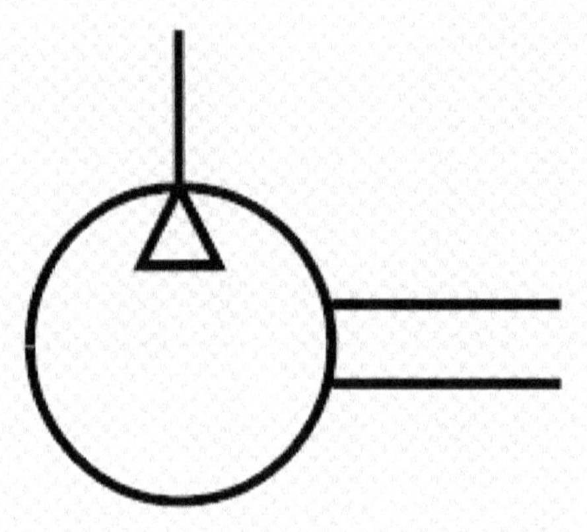

Pneumatic Motor

A pneumatic motor is represented by a circle with a triangle inside, similar to the compressor symbol. The arrow indicates the direction of air flow.

3. Pneumatic Cylinder (ISO 1219-1 Symbol: 22):

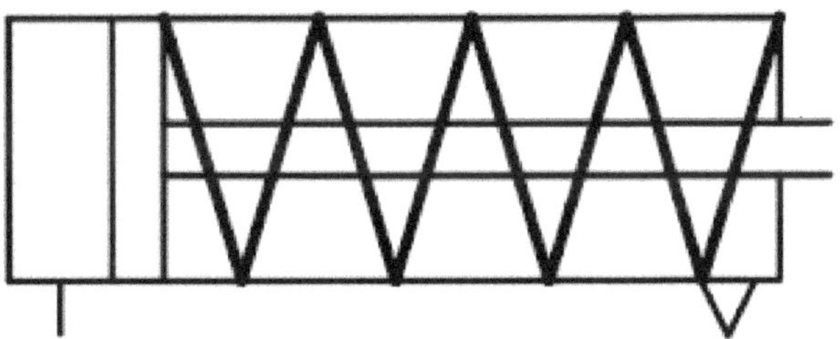

Pneumatic Cylinder

Pneumatic cylinders are represented by a rectangle with an arrow indicating the direction of the piston movement. The symbol may include details about the number of acting directions and whether it is a single-acting or double-acting cylinder.

4. Pneumatic Control Valve (ISO 1219-1 Symbol: 23):

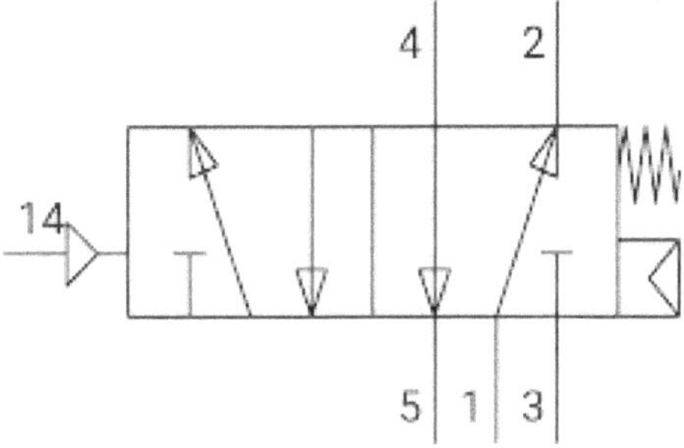

Pneumatic Direction Control Valve

Pneumatic control valves are depicted by various symbols, including rectangles, circles, and arrows, similar to hydraulic control valves. They represent directional control valves, pressure control valves, and other types of valves.

5. Pneumatic Reservoir (ISO 1219-1 Symbol: 24):

Pneumatic Reservoir

The pneumatic reservoir is represented by an open-topped rectangle, similar to the hydraulic reservoir symbol. It may include additional symbols to indicate features such as a breather or filter.

Electric ISO Symbols:

1. Electric Motor (ISO 1219-1 Symbol: 18):

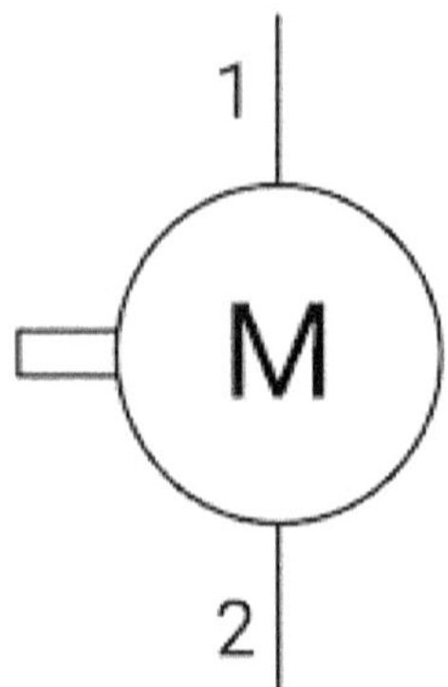

Electric Motor

The electric motor is represented by a circle with an "M" inside. The symbol may include additional details indicating the type of motor.

2. Electric Generator (ISO 1219-1 Symbol: 19):

Electric Generator

An electric generator is depicted by a circle with a zigzag line inside, indicating the generation of electrical power.

Conclusion:

ISO symbols for hydraulic, pneumatic, and electric components provide a standardized visual language for engineers and technicians across the globe. Understanding these symbols is crucial for effective communication in the design, maintenance, and troubleshooting of systems. Whether dealing with hydraulic pumps, pneumatic cylinders, or electric motors, these symbols facilitate a common understanding of the components and their functions in diverse engineering applications.

Selection Criteria

Selecting the right components for hydraulic, pneumatic, and electric systems is crucial for the optimal performance and efficiency of industrial machinery and processes. Each type of system has its unique characteristics and considerations when it comes to component selection. In this detailed exploration, we will delve into the criteria for selecting hydraulic, pneumatic, and electric components, covering aspects such as performance requirements, environmental considerations, maintenance considerations, and cost factors.

Hydraulic Components Selection Criteria:

1. Performance Requirements:

Force and Power: Consider the required force and power for the application. Hydraulic systems are known for their ability to generate high forces, making them suitable for heavy-duty tasks.

Speed and Precision: Evaluate the speed and precision needed for the application. Hydraulic systems can provide precise control over speed and force, making them suitable for applications requiring accuracy.

2. Fluid Compatibility:

Fluid Type: Select hydraulic fluids based on their compatibility with system components and operating conditions. Consider factors such as temperature range, viscosity, and potential for contamination.

3. Component Type:

Pumps, Motors, and Cylinders: Choose hydraulic pumps, motors, and cylinders based on the specific requirements of the application. Consider factors such as pump type (gear, vane, piston), motor type, and cylinder type (single-acting, double-acting).

4. Valve Selection:

Directional, Pressure, and Flow Control Valves: Select hydraulic valves based on the application's control requirements. Directional control valves, pressure control valves, and flow control valves are crucial components that should be chosen based on the specific needs of the system.

5. Sealing and Material Considerations:

Seals and Materials: Consider the compatibility of seals and materials with the hydraulic fluid and operating conditions. The choice of materials for components such as seals, valves, and cylinders is essential for long-term reliability.

6. Environmental Considerations:

Temperature and Environmental Conditions: Evaluate the temperature range and environmental conditions in which the hydraulic system will operate. Choose components that can withstand the intended operating environment, including exposure to harsh weather or corrosive substances.

7. Maintenance and Reliability:

Maintenance Requirements: Assess the maintenance requirements of hydraulic components. Components with accessible maintenance points and straightforward procedures may contribute to ease of maintenance and reduced downtime.

8. Cost Factors:

Initial Costs and Lifecycle Costs: Consider both initial costs and lifecycle costs. While high-quality components may have a higher upfront cost, they may offer better reliability and longevity, reducing overall lifecycle costs.

Pneumatic Components Selection Criteria:

1. Performance Requirements:

Force and Speed: Evaluate the required force and speed for the application. Pneumatic systems are known for their rapid response and are suitable for applications requiring quick and repetitive movements.

2. Compressor and Motor Selection:

Compressor Type: Choose the type of compressor based on the application's air supply requirements. Different compressor types, such as reciprocating, rotary screw, and centrifugal, have varying capabilities.

Pneumatic Motor Type: Select pneumatic motors based on the application's speed and power requirements. Pneumatic motors are commonly used in applications where electric motors may not be suitable.

3. Cylinder Selection:

Pneumatic Cylinder Type: Choose pneumatic cylinders based on the application's requirements for force, speed, and stroke length. Consider whether a single-acting or double-acting cylinder is more suitable.

4. Control Valve Selection:

Directional Control Valves: Select directional control valves based on the required motion control. Pneumatic systems often use various types of valves, such as 3/2-way, 4/2-way, and 5/2-way valves, to control the direction of air flow.

5. Air Treatment Components:

Air Filters, Regulators, and Lubricators (FRL): Include air treatment components in the system to ensure clean, regulated, and lubricated air supply. FRL units are critical for maintaining the performance and longevity of pneumatic components.

6. Environmental Considerations:

Humidity and Contaminant Sensitivity: Consider the sensitivity of pneumatic components to humidity and contaminants. Pneumatic systems may require additional filtration and drying components in environments with high humidity or dust.

7. Maintenance and Reliability:

Maintenance Requirements: Assess the maintenance requirements of pneumatic components. Regular inspection and maintenance of air filters, regulators, lubricators, and other components are essential for system reliability.

8. Cost Factors:

Initial Costs and Lifecycle Costs: Consider the initial costs and lifecycle costs of pneumatic components. While pneumatic systems are often cost-effective, selecting components with good durability and efficiency contributes to long-term savings.

Electric Components Selection Criteria:

1. Performance Requirements:

Power and Speed: Evaluate the power and speed requirements for the application. Electric systems offer precise control over speed, position, and torque, making them suitable for a wide range of applications.

2. Motor Selection:

Electric Motor Type: Choose the type of electric motor based on the application's power requirements and efficiency considerations. Common types include AC motors (induction, synchronous) and DC motors (brushed, brushless).

3. Control System:

Control Unit and Programmable Logic Controller (PLC): Select a control unit or PLC that meets the application's requirements for automation, sequencing, and precision control. The control system is critical for managing the operation of electric components.

4. Sensor Integration:

Sensors: Integrate sensors to provide feedback on parameters such as position, speed, and temperature. Sensors contribute to the precision and accuracy of electric systems.

5. Transmission Elements:

Gears, Belts, and Couplings: Choose transmission elements based on the required mechanical linkage between the electric motor and the load. The selection of gears, belts, and couplings influences the efficiency and performance of the system.

6. Environmental Considerations:

Temperature and Environmental Conditions: Assess the operating temperature range and environmental conditions for electric components. Some electric motors may require additional cooling mechanisms in high-temperature environments.

7. Maintenance and Reliability:

Maintenance Requirements: Evaluate the maintenance requirements of electric components. Proper lubrication, periodic inspection of transmission elements, and attention to the control system contribute to the reliability of electric systems.

8. Cost Factors:

Initial Costs and Lifecycle Costs: Consider both initial costs and lifecycle costs when selecting electric components. While electric systems may have a higher initial investment, their efficiency and controllability often result in long-term cost savings.

General Considerations for All Systems:

1. Integration and Compatibility:

System Integration: Ensure that selected components are compatible with each other and can be seamlessly integrated into the overall system. Compatibility between hydraulic, pneumatic, and electric components may be crucial in certain hybrid systems.

2. Safety and Standards:

Safety Standards: Adhere to safety standards relevant to the industry and application. Ensure that selected components meet or exceed safety requirements to protect operators and equipment.

3. Space and Weight Constraints:

Space Efficiency: Consider space constraints when selecting components. Hydraulic, pneumatic, and electric systems may have different space requirements, and selecting compact components may be essential in certain applications.

Weight Considerations: Evaluate weight constraints, especially in applications where weight is a critical factor, such as aerospace or automotive applications.

4. Energy Efficiency:

Energy Consumption: Consider the energy efficiency of the selected components. Choose components that contribute to overall system energy efficiency, taking into account factors such as motor efficiency and transmission losses.

5. Lifecycle Considerations:

Service Life and Replacement: Assess the service life of components and factor in considerations for replacement and maintenance. Selecting components with longer service life can contribute to reduced downtime and maintenance costs.

6. Environmental Impact:

Environmental Regulations: Comply with environmental regulations and consider the overall environmental impact of the selected components. Choose materials and fluids that align with environmental sustainability goals.

7. Training and Skill Levels:

Operator Training: Consider the training and skill levels of operators and maintenance personnel. Select components that align with the expertise available in the workforce to ensure efficient operation and maintenance.

8. Cost-Benefit Analysis:

Total Cost of Ownership: Conduct a thorough cost-benefit analysis that includes initial costs, operating costs, and maintenance costs. Evaluate the total cost of ownership over the expected lifespan of the system.

Conclusion:

In conclusion, the selection criteria for hydraulic, pneumatic, and electric components are multifaceted, encompassing performance requirements, environmental considerations, maintenance factors, and cost considerations. A systematic approach to component selection involves a careful assessment of the specific needs of the application, adherence to safety standards, and consideration of factors such as space constraints, energy efficiency, and environmental impact. By weighing these criteria and conducting a comprehensive analysis, engineers and decision-makers can make informed choices that lead to the efficient and reliable operation of industrial systems.

Gear Pumps

Gear pumps are a type of positive displacement pump widely used for transferring fluids in various industrial applications. They operate on the principle of using meshing gears to create a continuous flow of fluid. In this comprehensive exploration, we will delve into the working principles, types, applications, advantages, and limitations of gear pumps.

I. Introduction to Gear Pumps:

1. Basic Working Principle:

Gear pumps belong to the category of positive displacement pumps, which means they displace a fixed amount of fluid for each revolution of the pump's gears. The fundamental working principle involves the meshing of gears within a pump housing. As the gears rotate, they trap and displace fluid from the inlet to the outlet, creating a continuous flow.

2. Types of Gear Pumps:

There are two primary types of gear pumps:

a. External Gear Pumps:

In external gear pumps, two gears (an external gear and an internal gear) rotate externally to each other.

Fluid is trapped between the gear teeth and the pump housing, creating a seal and promoting fluid movement from the inlet to the outlet.

External gear pumps are widely used in various industries due to their simplicity and efficiency.

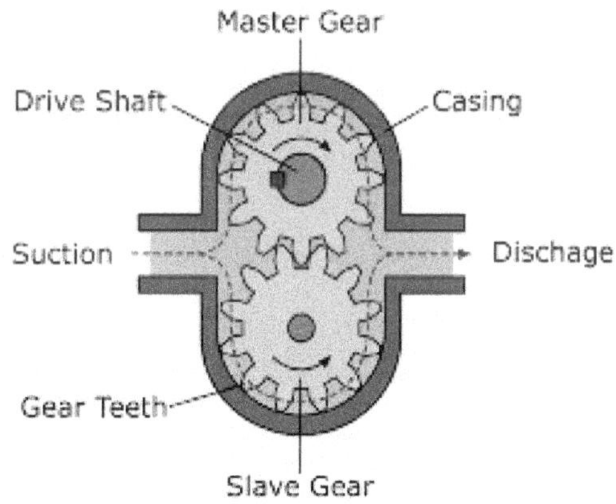

External Gear Pump

b. Internal Gear Pumps:

Internal gear pumps have an external gear that drives an internal gear.

Fluid is trapped between the gears and the pump housing, similar to external gear pumps.

Internal gear pumps are known for their ability to handle a wide range of viscosities and maintain efficiency.

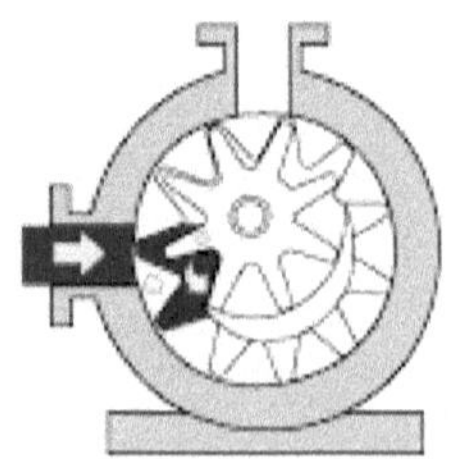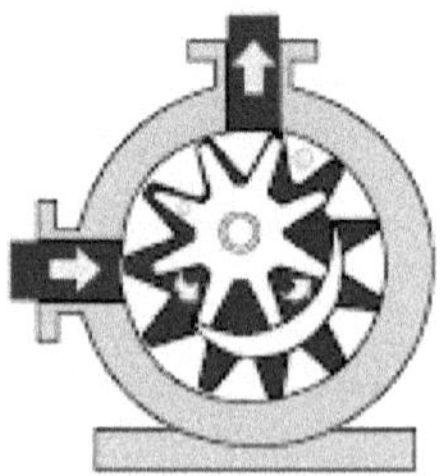

Internal Gear Pump

3. Operating Characteristics:

Gear pumps are known for their ability to provide a constant and smooth flow of fluid, making them suitable for applications where precision is crucial.

They are particularly effective in applications requiring moderate pressure and relatively low to moderate flow rates.

II. Components and Construction:

1. Basic Components:

Gears: The gears are the central components responsible for creating the pumping action. In a gear pump, you typically have two gears – a driving gear and a driven gear.

Pump Housing: The pump housing contains the gears and facilitates the fluid flow. It is designed to ensure proper alignment and sealing to prevent leakage.

Inlet and Outlet Ports: Gear pumps have dedicated ports for fluid entry (inlet) and exit (outlet). The design of these ports contributes to the efficiency and functionality of the pump.

2. Construction Materials:

Gear pumps can be constructed from various materials, including cast iron, aluminum, bronze, or stainless steel.

The choice of materials depends on the application requirements, such as the type of fluid being pumped, the operating environment, and considerations for durability.

III. Working Mechanism:

1. Fluid Flow Cycle:

The cycle begins when the gears start to rotate. The fluid is drawn into the pump through the inlet port as the gears separate.

As the gears rotate, the fluid is trapped between the gear teeth and the pump housing, creating a sealed chamber.

The fluid is carried around the gears and is forced out through the outlet port as the gears mesh and reduce the volume of the chamber.

This process repeats with each revolution of the gears, creating a continuous and consistent flow of fluid.

2. Seal Design:

The effectiveness of a gear pump relies on maintaining a good seal between the gears and the pump housing.

Gears in gear pumps are designed with close tolerances to minimize backflow and improve overall efficiency.

The design of the seals and clearances is crucial to prevent leakage and maintain the pump's volumetric efficiency.

IV. Applications of Gear Pumps:

1. Industries and Sectors:

Automotive: Gear pumps are commonly used in automotive applications, such as lubrication systems and hydraulic systems in vehicles.

Agriculture: They find applications in agricultural machinery for tasks like fluid transfer and crop spraying.

Industrial Manufacturing: Gear pumps are utilized in various manufacturing processes, including injection molding, metalworking, and chemical processing.

Oil and Gas: In the oil and gas industry, gear pumps play a role in transferring fluids and maintaining lubrication in machinery.

Marine: Gear pumps are employed in marine applications for fluid transfer, hydraulic systems, and fuel transfer.

2. Specific Applications:

Hydraulic Systems: Gear pumps are commonly used in hydraulic systems, providing a reliable and consistent flow of hydraulic fluid to power various hydraulic components.

Lubrication Systems: They are employed for lubricating components in machinery, ensuring smooth operation and reducing friction.

Fuel Transfer: Gear pumps play a crucial role in transferring fuel in vehicles, aircraft, and industrial machinery.

Chemical Processing: In the chemical industry, gear pumps handle the transfer of various chemicals, both viscous and non-viscous.

Metering and Dosing: Gear pumps are suitable for applications where precise metering and dosing of fluids are required, such as in pharmaceutical manufacturing.

V. Advantages of Gear Pumps:

1. Simple Design:

Gear pumps have a straightforward design, making them easy to manufacture and maintain.

The simplicity of their design contributes to their reliability and cost-effectiveness.

2. Compact Size:

Gear pumps are often more compact than some other types of pumps, making them suitable for applications where space is limited.

3. Efficient Operation:

Gear pumps provide a consistent and efficient flow of fluid, ensuring reliable performance in various applications.

4. Versatility:

Gear pumps are versatile and can handle a wide range of viscosities, making them suitable for applications with varying fluid characteristics.

5. Cost-Effective:

The simplicity of the design, ease of manufacturing, and reliability contribute to the cost-effectiveness of gear pumps.

VI. Limitations and Considerations:

1. Viscosity Sensitivity:

Gear pumps may experience efficiency issues with highly viscous fluids. The effectiveness of the pump can be affected if the viscosity of the fluid is too high.

2. Pressure Limitations:

Gear pumps are generally suitable for moderate-pressure applications. High-pressure requirements may necessitate the use of other pump types.

3. Noise Levels:

Gear pumps can generate significant noise during operation, which may be a consideration in applications where noise is a concern.

4. Wear and Tear:

The close tolerances required for effective sealing can lead to wear over time, particularly if the pump handles abrasive fluids.

5. Temperature Sensitivity:

Gear pumps can be sensitive to temperature fluctuations, and extreme temperatures may affect the viscosity of the pumped fluid, impacting pump performance.

VII. Maintenance and Troubleshooting:

1. Regular Inspection:

Regular inspection of the pump, gears, and seals is essential to identify any signs of wear or damage.

2. Lubrication:

Proper lubrication is crucial for maintaining the efficiency of gear pumps. Lubricants help reduce friction and prevent premature wear of components.

3. Seal Replacement:

Seals may need periodic replacement to ensure effective sealing and prevent fluid leakage.

4. Troubleshooting:

Troubleshooting may involve diagnosing issues such as reduced flow, noise, or leaks and addressing them promptly to avoid further damage.

VIII. Future Trends and Innovations:

1. Material Advances:

Ongoing research focuses on developing advanced materials that enhance the durability and wear resistance of gear pump components.

2. Smart Technologies:

Integration of smart technologies, such as sensors and monitoring systems, is expected to improve the efficiency and predictive maintenance of gear pumps.

3. Energy Efficiency:

Innovations in design and materials aim to improve the energy efficiency of gear pumps, reducing overall operational costs.

4. Industry-Specific Solutions:

Manufacturers are likely to develop gear pumps tailored to specific industries, considering the unique challenges and requirements of each sector.

IX. Conclusion:

In conclusion, gear pumps are fundamental components in fluid transfer systems across various industries. Their simple yet effective design, compact size, and versatility make them suitable for a wide range of applications, from hydraulic systems in vehicles to chemical processing in industrial settings. Understanding the working principles, advantages, limitations, and maintenance requirements of gear pumps is crucial for efficient operation and longevity. As technology continues to advance, gear pumps are expected to evolve with innovations aimed at improving efficiency, reliability, and adaptability to the diverse needs of modern industries.

Vane Pumps

Vane pumps are a type of positive displacement pump that employs vanes or blades to move fluid through the pump. They are widely used in various industrial applications for their efficiency, reliability, and versatility. In this comprehensive exploration, we will delve into the working principles, types, construction, applications, advantages, limitations, maintenance, and future trends of vane pumps.

I. Introduction to Vane Pumps:

1. Basic Working Principle:

Vane pumps operate on the principle of positive displacement, where a fixed volume of fluid is displaced with each rotation of the pump's vanes. These vanes are typically mounted on a rotor that is eccentrically positioned within a cam ring or housing. As the rotor turns, centrifugal forces cause the vanes to extend and retract, trapping and displacing fluid in the process.

2. Types of Vane Pumps:

There are primarily two types of vane pumps:

a. Unbalanced (Overhung) Vane Pumps:

In unbalanced vane pumps, the rotor is positioned eccentrically, leading to unequal forces on the vanes.

This design is simpler but may result in higher side loads and increased wear on the vanes and housing.

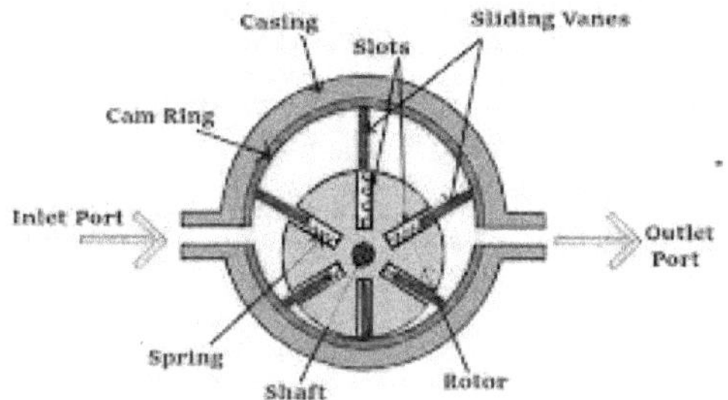

Enter Caption

b. Balanced Vane Pumps:

Balanced vane pumps address the side load issues by incorporating counterweights or balance springs.

This design reduces wear on components and enhances the overall efficiency of the pump.

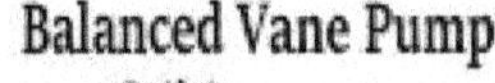

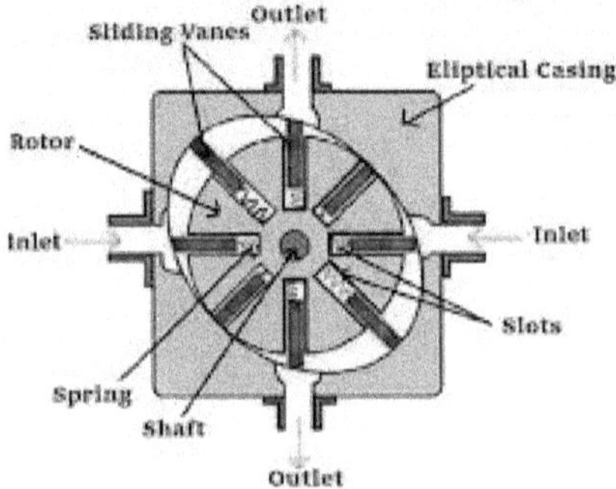

Enter Caption

II. Components and Construction:

1. Basic Components:

Rotor with Vanes: The rotor, often eccentrically positioned, contains vanes that move in and out as the rotor rotates.

Cam Ring or Housing: The housing provides a path for the vanes to move within, shaping the pumping chambers.

Inlet and Outlet Ports: Vane pumps have dedicated ports for fluid entry (inlet) and exit (outlet), allowing for the continuous flow of fluid.

2. Construction Materials:

Vane pumps can be constructed from materials such as cast iron, aluminum, or stainless steel, depending on the application's requirements and the type of fluid being pumped.

III. Working Mechanism:

1. Fluid Flow Cycle:

The fluid flow cycle begins as the rotor starts to turn within the housing.

Centrifugal forces cause the vanes to slide outward, creating expanding chambers that draw in fluid from the inlet.

As the rotor continues to rotate, the vanes retract due to the eccentric motion, compressing the fluid within the chambers.

The compressed fluid is then pushed through the outlet port, creating a continuous flow.

2. Seal Design:

The efficiency of vane pumps depends on maintaining a good seal between the vanes and the housing.

Close tolerances between the vanes and the housing are essential to prevent fluid from leaking back into the inlet.

IV. Applications of Vane Pumps:

1. Industries and Sectors:

Automotive: Vane pumps find applications in power steering systems and automatic transmissions in vehicles.

Aerospace: They are used in aircraft hydraulic systems for functions such as landing gear actuation.

Industrial Manufacturing: Vane pumps play a role in various industrial processes, including hydraulic presses and machine tools.

Marine: In marine applications, vane pumps are used for hydraulic steering systems and cargo handling.

2. Specific Applications:

Hydraulic Systems: Vane pumps are common in hydraulic systems, providing a reliable and efficient means of fluid transfer and pressure generation.

Fuel Transfer: They are employed in fuel transfer applications in both automotive and industrial settings.

Power Steering Systems: Vane pumps are integral components in power steering systems, providing the necessary hydraulic assistance for steering.

Chemical Processing: Vane pumps can handle a variety of fluids, making them suitable for chemical processing applications.

Printing Presses: Vane pumps are used in printing presses for ink circulation and transfer.

V. Advantages of Vane Pumps:

1. Efficiency:

Vane pumps are known for their high volumetric efficiency, providing a consistent and reliable flow of fluid.

2. Versatility:

They can handle a wide range of fluids, including both low and high viscosity liquids, making them versatile in various applications.

3. Compact Design:

Vane pumps are often more compact than some other positive displacement pumps, making them suitable for applications with limited space.

4. Balanced Operation:

Balanced vane pump designs help reduce side loads, leading to less wear on components and improved overall reliability.

5. Smooth Operation:

The continuous and smooth flow of fluid in vane pumps results in less pulsation and noise compared to some other pump types.

VI. Limitations and Considerations:

1. Temperature Sensitivity:

Vane pumps can be sensitive to temperature changes, and extreme temperatures may affect the viscosity of the pumped fluid, impacting pump performance.

2. Viscosity Limitations:

While vane pumps can handle a range of viscosities, they may not be as effective with extremely high viscosity fluids as some other pump types.

3. Wear and Tear:

The vanes and housing in vane pumps can experience wear over time, particularly if the pump handles abrasive fluids.

4. Pressure Limitations:

Vane pumps may not be suitable for high-pressure applications compared to certain other pump types.

5. Maintenance Requirements:

Regular inspection and maintenance are necessary to address wear on vanes and housing, ensuring the pump's continued efficiency.

VII. Maintenance and Troubleshooting:

1. Regular Inspection:

Routine inspection of the pump, vanes, and housing is crucial to identify signs of wear or damage.

2. Lubrication:

Proper lubrication is essential to minimize friction and wear on moving parts, ensuring the longevity of the pump.

3. Vane Replacement:

Vanes may need periodic replacement to maintain effective sealing and prevent fluid leakage.

4. Troubleshooting:

Troubleshooting may involve addressing issues such as reduced flow, noise, or leaks promptly to avoid further damage.

VIII. Future Trends and Innovations:

1. Materials and Coatings:

Advances in materials and coatings aim to enhance the wear resistance of vane pump components, extending their service life.

2. Smart Technologies:

Integration of smart technologies, such as condition monitoring and predictive maintenance, is expected to improve the efficiency and reliability of vane pumps.

3. Energy Efficiency:

Ongoing research focuses on design modifications and materials to improve the energy efficiency of vane pumps, reducing operational costs.

4. Adaptability to New Fluids:

Innovations may lead to vane pump designs that can effectively handle a broader range of fluids, including those with unique characteristics.

IX. Conclusion:

Vane pumps play a vital role in various industries, offering efficient and reliable fluid transfer solutions. Their positive displacement design, coupled with versatility and compactness, makes them well-suited for applications ranging from automotive power steering systems to industrial hydraulic machinery. Understanding the working principles, advantages, limitations, and maintenance requirements of vane pumps is essential for ensuring their optimal performance and longevity. As technology continues to advance, ongoing research and innovations are likely to further enhance the efficiency, reliability, and adaptability of vane pumps to meet the evolving needs of diverse industries.

Piston Pumps

Piston pumps are a type of positive displacement pump commonly used in various industrial applications to move fluids. These pumps utilize reciprocating pistons to displace fluid, creating a continuous flow. In this comprehensive exploration, we will delve into the working principles, types, construction, applications, advantages, limitations, maintenance, and future trends of piston pumps.

I. Introduction to Piston Pumps:

1. Basic Working Principle:

Piston pumps operate on the principle of positive displacement, where a fixed volume of fluid is displaced with each stroke of the piston. The reciprocating motion of the piston within a cylinder creates suction and discharge phases, allowing fluid to enter and exit the pump, resulting in a continuous flow.

2. Types of Piston Pumps:

There are various types of piston pumps, with axial piston pumps and radial piston pumps being the most common:

a. Axial Piston Pumps:

In axial piston pumps, pistons move parallel to the axis of rotation.

These pumps are known for their efficiency and ability to handle high-pressure applications.

Axial piston pumps can be further classified into swashplate and bent-axis designs.

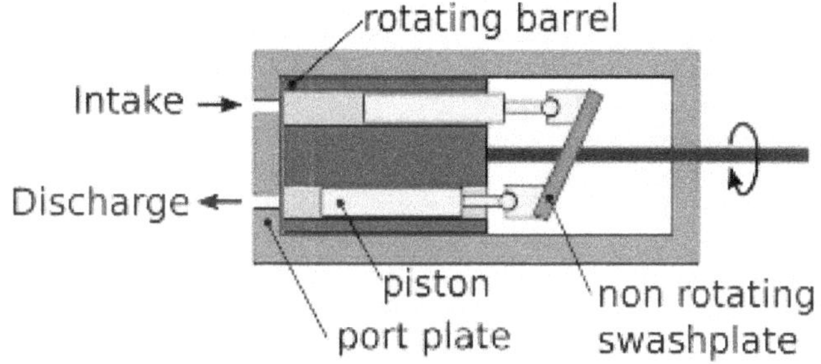

Axial Piston Pump

b. Radial Piston Pumps:

Radial piston pumps have pistons that move radially outward from or inward toward the axis of rotation.

They are often used in applications where high pressure and compact design are crucial.

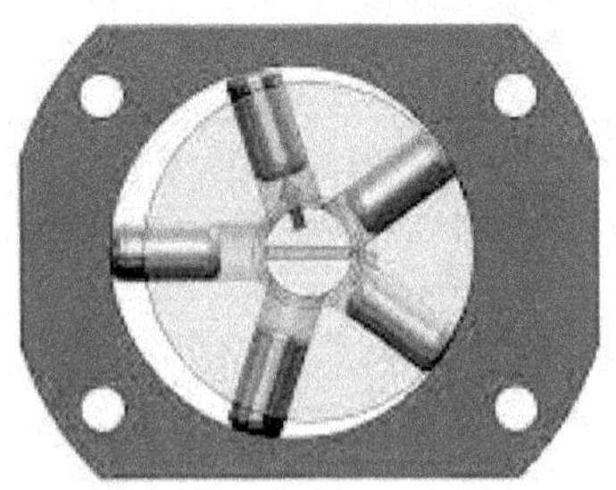

Radial Piston Pump

II. Components and Construction:

1. Basic Components:

Piston and Cylinder: The piston reciprocates within a cylinder, creating the pumping action.

Cylinder Block: The cylinder block houses multiple cylinders, each with its piston, creating a compact and efficient pump design.

Inlet and Outlet Ports: Piston pumps have dedicated ports for fluid entry (inlet) and exit (outlet), allowing for the continuous flow of fluid.

2. Construction Materials:

Piston pumps can be constructed from materials such as cast iron, aluminum, or stainless steel, depending on the application's requirements and the type of fluid being pumped.

III. Working Mechanism:

1. Fluid Flow Cycle:

The fluid flow cycle begins as the piston retracts within the cylinder, creating a low-pressure area that allows fluid to enter the pump through the inlet port.

As the piston advances, the fluid is compressed within the cylinder, reaching high pressure.

The compressed fluid is then pushed out through the outlet port, creating a continuous and pressurized flow.

2. Seal Design:

The efficiency of piston pumps depends on maintaining a good seal between the piston and the cylinder.

Seals and gaskets are employed to prevent fluid leakage and ensure effective compression and discharge.

IV. Applications of Piston Pumps:

1. Industries and Sectors:

Hydraulics: Piston pumps are extensively used in hydraulic systems for applications such as heavy machinery, construction equipment, and industrial presses.

Oil and Gas: They find applications in oil and gas exploration and production for fluid transfer and hydraulic control systems.

Aerospace: Piston pumps are utilized in aircraft hydraulic systems for functions like landing gear actuation and flight control.

Automotive: They are employed in automotive power steering systems and hydraulic braking systems.

2. Specific Applications:

Hydraulic Presses: Piston pumps play a crucial role in hydraulic presses, providing the high pressure needed for material forming processes.

Injection Molding Machines: They are used in injection molding machines for the precise and controlled movement of molds and injection units.

Mobile Equipment: Piston pumps power hydraulic systems in mobile equipment such as excavators, loaders, and forklifts.

Marine: In marine applications, piston pumps are used for hydraulic steering systems and cargo handling.

V. Advantages of Piston Pumps:

1. High Pressure Capability:

Piston pumps are known for their ability to generate high pressures, making them suitable for applications that require substantial force.

2. Efficiency:

They exhibit high volumetric efficiency, providing a consistent and reliable flow of fluid.

3. Variable Displacement:

Many piston pumps offer variable displacement, allowing for the adjustment of fluid flow and pressure based on the application's requirements.

4. Compact Design:

Piston pumps can be designed in a compact form, making them suitable for applications with limited space.

5. Precise Control:

The reciprocating motion of the piston allows for precise control over fluid flow and pressure, contributing to accurate and controlled movements in various applications.

VI. Limitations and Considerations:

1. Complexity:

Some piston pump designs can be more complex than other pump types, requiring careful engineering and maintenance.

2. Cost:

Piston pumps, especially those with advanced features, may have a higher initial cost compared to some other pump types.

3. Maintenance Requirements:

Regular maintenance is crucial to address wear on pistons, cylinders, and seals, ensuring the pump's continued efficiency.

4. Noise Levels:

The reciprocating motion of pistons can generate noise during operation, which may be a consideration in applications where noise is a concern.

5. Temperature Sensitivity:

Piston pumps can be sensitive to temperature changes, and extreme temperatures may affect the viscosity of the pumped fluid, impacting pump performance.

VII. Maintenance and Troubleshooting:

1. Regular Inspection:

Routine inspection of the pump, pistons, cylinders, and seals is crucial to identify signs of wear or damage.

2. Lubrication:

Proper lubrication is essential to minimize friction and wear on moving parts, ensuring the longevity of the pump.

3. Seal Replacement:

Seals may need periodic replacement to maintain effective sealing and prevent fluid leakage.

4. Piston and Cylinder Wear:

Monitoring and addressing wear on pistons and cylinders is essential to maintain the efficiency and reliability of the pump.

VIII. Future Trends and Innovations:

1. Materials and Coatings:

Advances in materials and coatings aim to enhance the wear resistance of piston pump components, extending their service life.

2. Smart Technologies:

Integration of smart technologies, such as condition monitoring and predictive maintenance, is expected to improve the efficiency and reliability of piston pumps.

3. Energy Efficiency:

Ongoing research focuses on design modifications and materials to improve the energy efficiency of piston pumps, reducing operational costs.

4. Digitalization and Automation:

Increased integration with digital control systems and automation is likely to enhance the precision and adaptability of piston pumps in various applications.

IX. Conclusion:

Piston pumps are integral components in a wide range of applications, providing the necessary fluid flow and pressure for hydraulic systems across various industries. Their ability to generate high pressures, precise control, and variable displacement makes them suitable for tasks ranging from industrial machinery to automotive systems. Understanding the working principles, advantages, limitations, and maintenance requirements of piston pumps is crucial for ensuring their optimal performance and longevity. As technology continues to advance, ongoing research and innovations are likely to further enhance the efficiency, reliability, and adaptability of piston pumps to meet the evolving needs of diverse industries.

Motors

Hydraulic motors are devices that convert hydraulic energy (the flow and pressure of hydraulic fluid) into mechanical energy (rotary motion). They are essential components in various industrial applications where precise and powerful rotational motion is required. In this comprehensive exploration, we will delve into the working principles, types, construction, applications, advantages, limitations, maintenance, and future trends of hydraulic motors.

I. Introduction to Hydraulic Motors:

1. Basic Working Principle:

Hydraulic motors operate on the principle of fluid power conversion. The hydraulic fluid, usually oil, is pressurized and directed into the motor, creating a flow that drives the motor's rotor or piston, generating mechanical output in the form of rotary motion.

2. Types of Hydraulic Motors:

There are several types of hydraulic motors, with the most common being:

a. Gear Motors:

Gear motors use a set of gears to convert hydraulic energy into mechanical energy.

They are known for their simplicity and cost-effectiveness.

Gear Motor

b. Vane Motors:

Vane motors utilize vanes mounted on a rotor to generate rotary motion.

These motors are compact and suitable for applications requiring moderate speed and torque.

Vane Motors

c. Piston Motors:

Piston motors use pistons reciprocating in cylinders to create rotary motion.

Axial piston motors and radial piston motors are two common subtypes with distinct design characteristics.

Piston Motors

3. Operating Characteristics:

Hydraulic motors exhibit features such as variable speed and torque, making them versatile for a wide range of applications.

They can operate bidirectionally, allowing for reversible rotational motion.

II. Components and Construction:

1. Basic Components:

Rotor or Piston: The rotor (in gear and vane motors) or pistons (in piston motors) is the primary component that receives the force from the hydraulic fluid, generating rotary motion.

Cylinder or Housing: The cylinder or housing contains the rotor or pistons and facilitates the fluid flow, directing it to create the necessary motion.

Inlet and Outlet Ports: Hydraulic motors have ports for the entry and exit of hydraulic fluid, ensuring a continuous flow.

2. Construction Materials:

Hydraulic motors can be constructed from materials like cast iron, aluminum, or stainless steel, depending on factors such as application requirements and fluid compatibility.

III. Working Mechanism:

1. Fluid Flow Cycle:

The fluid flow cycle begins as pressurized hydraulic fluid is directed into the motor.

The fluid interacts with the rotor or pistons, creating a force that drives the rotary motion.

The spent fluid is then returned to the hydraulic reservoir to complete the cycle.

2. Variable Displacement:

Some hydraulic motors, particularly piston motors, offer variable displacement, allowing for the adjustment of speed and torque based on the application's requirements.

IV. Applications of Hydraulic Motors:

1. Industries and Sectors:

Construction and Heavy Machinery: Hydraulic motors power various components in construction equipment, such as excavators and loaders.

Agriculture: They are used in agricultural machinery for tasks like driving irrigation systems and operating tractors.

Marine: Hydraulic motors play a crucial role in marine applications, powering winches, cranes, and propulsion systems.

Manufacturing: Hydraulic motors drive machinery in manufacturing processes, providing precise control and high torque.

2. Specific Applications:

Conveyor Systems: Hydraulic motors drive conveyor belts in industries such as mining and material handling.

Rotary Actuators: Hydraulic motors are employed in rotary actuators for tasks like controlling the movement of robotic arms.

Automotive: Hydraulic motors are used in convertible car roofs and power steering systems.

Mining: They power various equipment in mining operations, including crushers and drilling machines.

V. Advantages of Hydraulic Motors:

1. High Power Density:

Hydraulic motors offer high power density, delivering substantial power output relative to their size and weight.

2. Variable Speed and Torque:

Many hydraulic motors provide variable speed and torque, allowing for precise control in diverse applications.

3. Bidirectional Operation:

Hydraulic motors can operate in both directions, making them suitable for applications requiring reversible rotational motion.

4. Compact Design:

Hydraulic motors can be designed in a compact form, making them suitable for applications with limited space.

5. High Efficiency:

Hydraulic motors can achieve high efficiency, especially when matched with the appropriate pump, leading to energy savings.

VI. Limitations and Considerations:

1. Fluid Contamination:

Hydraulic motors are sensitive to fluid contamination, and the presence of contaminants can lead to wear and damage.

2. Maintenance Requirements:

Regular maintenance, including fluid checks and filter replacements, is crucial to ensure the longevity and efficiency of hydraulic motors.

3. Temperature Sensitivity:

Hydraulic motors can be sensitive to temperature changes, and extreme temperatures may affect the viscosity of the hydraulic fluid, impacting motor performance.

4. Complexity in Variable Displacement Motors:

Variable displacement hydraulic motors, especially piston motors, can be complex, requiring careful engineering and maintenance.

5. Cost:

Hydraulic motors, especially those with advanced features, may have a higher initial cost compared to some other types of motors.

VII. Maintenance and Troubleshooting:

1. Regular Inspection:

Routine inspection of the motor, rotor or pistons, and seals is crucial to identify signs of wear or damage.

2. Fluid Checks:

Regular checks of the hydraulic fluid, including monitoring cleanliness and fluid levels, are essential for optimal motor performance.

3. Filter Replacements:

Filters should be replaced as recommended to prevent contaminants from affecting motor components.

4. Seal Replacement:

Seals may need periodic replacement to maintain effective sealing and prevent fluid leakage.

VIII. Future Trends and Innovations:

1. Materials and Coatings:

Advances in materials and coatings aim to enhance the wear resistance of hydraulic motor components, extending their service life.

2. Smart Technologies:

Integration of smart technologies, such as condition monitoring and predictive maintenance, is expected to improve the efficiency and reliability of hydraulic motors.

3. Energy Efficiency:

Ongoing research focuses on design modifications and materials to improve the energy efficiency of hydraulic motors, reducing operational costs.

4. Digitalization and Automation:

Increased integration with digital control systems and automation is likely to enhance the precision and adaptability of hydraulic motors in various applications.

IX. Conclusion:

Hydraulic motors play a crucial role in numerous industrial applications, providing powerful and precise rotational motion. Their versatility, high power density, and ability to operate in diverse conditions make them indispensable in sectors ranging from construction to marine and manufacturing. Understanding the working principles, advantages, limitations, and maintenance requirements of hydraulic motors is essential for ensuring their optimal performance and longevity. As technology continues to advance, ongoing research and innovations are likely to further enhance the efficiency, reliability, and adaptability of hydraulic motors to meet the evolving needs of diverse industries.

Selection and Specification of Motors

The selection and specification of hydraulic motors are critical steps in designing hydraulic systems for various industrial applications. The right hydraulic motor must be chosen based on the specific requirements of the application, taking into consideration factors such as speed, torque, efficiency, environmental conditions, and compatibility with the overall hydraulic system. In this comprehensive exploration, we will delve into the key considerations, criteria, and steps involved in the selection and specification of hydraulic motors.

I. Introduction to Hydraulic Motor Selection:

1. Understanding the Application:

Before delving into the selection process, a thorough understanding of the application is essential. Consider the following aspects:

Load Characteristics: Determine the load type, whether constant, intermittent, or variable, and the corresponding torque and speed requirements.

Environmental Conditions: Consider factors such as temperature, humidity, and exposure to contaminants or corrosive substances.

Space Limitations: Evaluate the available space for the hydraulic motor, considering both physical dimensions and installation requirements.

2. Key Performance Parameters:

Identify and define the critical performance parameters for the hydraulic motor based on the application requirements:

Speed Requirements: Specify the desired rotational speed of the hydraulic motor, taking into account both minimum and maximum speed requirements.

Torque Requirements: Determine the torque needed to drive the load, considering variations in load conditions.

Power Requirements: Calculate the power required, considering both speed and torque, to meet the application's demands.

II. Hydraulic Motor Types and Characteristics:

1. Types of Hydraulic Motors:

Understand the different types of hydraulic motors, such as gear motors, vane motors, and piston motors. Each type has unique characteristics and is suitable for specific applications. Consider the following:

a. Gear Motors:

Simple and cost-effective.

Suitable for low-speed, high-torque applications.

Limited in terms of efficiency and speed capabilities.

b. Vane Motors:

Compact design with moderate efficiency.

Suitable for applications with moderate speed and torque requirements.

Offers good overall performance in various conditions.

c. Piston Motors:

Provides high efficiency and power density.

Available in axial and radial piston designs.

Suitable for high-speed and high-torque applications.

Offers variable displacement options for greater control.

2. Efficiency and Power Density:

Consider the efficiency and power density characteristics of the hydraulic motor types in relation to the application's requirements:

Efficiency: Evaluate the overall efficiency of the hydraulic motor under different operating conditions. Consider factors such as volumetric efficiency, mechanical efficiency, and overall system efficiency.

Power Density: Assess the power density of the hydraulic motor, which is crucial for applications with space constraints.

III. Hydraulic System Considerations:

1. System Pressure and Flow:

Understand the hydraulic system parameters that will influence the motor's performance:

System Pressure: Consider the maximum and minimum pressure levels the hydraulic motor will experience during operation.

Flow Requirements: Evaluate the flow rate needed to meet the application's demands.

2. Fluid Compatibility:

Ensure that the hydraulic motor is compatible with the hydraulic fluid used in the system. Consider factors such as fluid viscosity, temperature stability, and potential for fluid contamination.

3. System Dynamics:

Consider the dynamic characteristics of the hydraulic system:

Acceleration and Deceleration: Assess how quickly the hydraulic motor needs to accelerate or decelerate based on the application's requirements.

Inertia and Load Characteristics: Evaluate the system's inertia and the load's dynamic characteristics to determine the motor's response to changes in speed and torque.

IV. Environmental and Operational Conditions:

1. Temperature and Environmental Factors:

Consider the environmental conditions in which the hydraulic motor will operate:

Temperature Range: Ensure that the hydraulic motor can operate within the specified temperature range without compromising performance.

Corrosion Resistance: Evaluate the need for corrosion-resistant materials if the motor will be exposed to corrosive environments.

2. Duty Cycle:

Understand the duty cycle of the application, including factors such as intermittent operation, continuous operation, and peak load conditions. This information is crucial for selecting a hydraulic motor that can withstand the expected operating conditions.

3. Mounting and Installation:

Consider the mounting and installation requirements of the hydraulic motor:

Mounting Orientation: Determine whether the hydraulic motor will be mounted vertically, horizontally, or in another orientation.

Space Constraints: Ensure that the selected motor fits within the available space and aligns with the installation requirements.

V. Selection Process:

1. Preliminary Selection:

Based on the gathered information, conduct a preliminary selection of hydraulic motor types that seem suitable for the application's requirements.

2. Detailed Analysis:

Perform a detailed analysis of the potential hydraulic motor options:

Comparison of Motor Types: Evaluate the advantages and disadvantages of each type of hydraulic motor based on the application's requirements.

Performance Curves: Examine the performance curves provided by manufacturers to understand how the hydraulic motor performs under different conditions.

Efficiency Maps: Analyze efficiency maps to determine the efficiency of the hydraulic motor across the operating range.

3. Manufacturer Specifications:

Review manufacturer specifications and technical data for each potential hydraulic motor:

Torque-Speed Characteristics: Examine torque-speed characteristics to ensure they align with the application's requirements.

Pressure and Flow Ratings: Verify that the hydraulic motor can handle the maximum pressure and flow rates of the hydraulic system.

4. Consideration of Additional Features:

Evaluate additional features offered by hydraulic motor manufacturers, such as:

Integrated Valves: Some hydraulic motors come with integrated valves for enhanced control.

Variable Displacement: Consider hydraulic motors with variable displacement options for applications requiring variable speed and torque.

VI. Sizing and Calculations:

1. Torque and Speed Calculations:

Perform torque and speed calculations based on the application's requirements:

Torque Calculation: Use the formula Torque = Power / Speed to calculate the required torque.

Speed Calculation: Determine the desired speed based on the application's specifications.

2. Pressure and Flow Calculations:

Calculate the required pressure and flow based on the torque and speed calculations:

Pressure Calculation: Use the formula Pressure = Torque / (Motor Displacement × Motor Efficiency) to determine the required pressure.

Flow Calculation: Calculate the necessary flow rate using the formula Flow = Motor Displacement × Speed.

3. Verification:

Verify that the selected hydraulic motor meets the calculated torque, speed, pressure, and flow requirements.

VII. Documentation and Specifications:

1. Creation of Specifications:

Compile a detailed specification document that includes:

Application Requirements: Outline the specific requirements of the application, including torque, speed, and power.

Environmental Conditions: Specify the environmental factors the hydraulic motor must withstand.

System Parameters: Include system pressure, flow, and fluid compatibility requirements.

Mounting and Installation Details: Provide information on mounting orientation, space constraints, and installation requirements.

2. Manufacturer Consultation:

Consult with hydraulic motor manufacturers to validate the selection and specifications. Manufacturers can provide additional insights and recommendations based on their expertise.

3. Cost Analysis:

Conduct a cost analysis, considering both the initial purchase cost and the long-term operating costs, including maintenance requirements and energy consumption.

VIII. Future Trends and Innovations:

1. Smart Technologies:

Monitor advancements in smart technologies, such as embedded sensors and condition monitoring systems, which can enhance the performance and reliability of hydraulic motors.

2. Digital Twin Technology:

Explore the potential use of digital twin technology, allowing for virtual simulations and predictive analysis of hydraulic motor performance in various scenarios.

3. Energy Efficiency Improvements:

Stay informed about innovations focused on improving the energy efficiency of hydraulic motors, contributing to overall system efficiency and sustainability.

4. Integration with Industry 4.0:

Consider the integration of hydraulic motors with Industry 4.0 principles, enabling connectivity, data exchange, and automation for more efficient and adaptive hydraulic systems.

IX. Conclusion:

The selection and specification of hydraulic motors are crucial steps in designing efficient and reliable hydraulic systems for diverse applications. By thoroughly understanding the application requirements, considering key factors such as torque, speed, efficiency, and environmental conditions, and following a systematic selection process, engineers can ensure the optimal performance and longevity of hydraulic motors in their specific applications. As technology continues to advance, keeping abreast of future trends and innovations will enable engineers to leverage new developments for improved hydraulic system design and performance.

Drive Characteristics

Hydraulic drives are systems that use hydraulic power to transmit force and motion. These systems are prevalent in various industrial applications, providing advantages such as high power density, precise control, and adaptability to different loads. In this comprehensive exploration, we will delve into the characteristics of hydraulic drives, covering aspects such as working principles, types of hydraulic drives, efficiency, controllability, advantages, limitations, and considerations in design.

I. Introduction to Hydraulic Drive Characteristics:

1. Basic Working Principles:

Hydraulic drives operate based on the principle of transmitting power through the pressurized flow of hydraulic fluid. The basic components of a hydraulic drive system include a hydraulic pump, fluid lines, hydraulic motor, and load. The pump generates fluid flow, which is directed to the hydraulic motor, causing it to produce mechanical output, typically in the form of rotary motion.

2. Types of Hydraulic Drives:

There are various types of hydraulic drives, each suitable for specific applications. Common types include:

a. Hydraulic Motors:

Hydraulic motors convert hydraulic energy into mechanical energy, generating rotational motion.

Types include gear motors, vane motors, and piston motors, each with unique characteristics and applications.

b. Hydraulic Cylinders:

Hydraulic cylinders produce linear motion by converting hydraulic pressure into a pushing or pulling force.

They are widely used in applications such as construction equipment, manufacturing machinery, and automotive systems.

c. Hydraulic Actuators:

Hydraulic actuators encompass a broader category of devices that use hydraulic power to perform mechanical work.

They include motors, cylinders, and various other components that enable controlled movement.

II. Characteristics of Hydraulic Drives:

1. Power Density:

One of the key characteristics of hydraulic drives is their high power density. Hydraulic systems can deliver substantial power output relative to their size and weight. This feature is particularly advantageous in applications where space and weight constraints are critical factors.

2. Precision and Controllability:

Hydraulic drives offer precise control over force, speed, and position. This level of controllability is achieved through the variation of fluid flow and pressure, allowing for fine adjustments in the movement of hydraulic actuators. This precision is crucial in applications requiring accurate positioning and control.

3. Adaptability to Variable Loads:

Hydraulic drives exhibit excellent adaptability to variable loads. They can maintain a relatively constant speed and torque output, even in the presence of fluctuating loads. This characteristic makes hydraulic systems well-suited for applications with changing operating conditions.

4. High Torque at Low Speeds:

Hydraulic drives excel in providing high torque at low speeds. This capability is advantageous in applications such as heavy machinery and vehicles, where the initial starting torque is crucial for overcoming inertia.

5. Bi-Directional Operation:

Hydraulic drives can operate in both directions, enabling reversible motion. This bi-directional capability is essential in applications where the load may need to move back and forth, such as in material handling systems or certain types of machinery.

6. Efficiency:

The efficiency of hydraulic drives is a critical characteristic. While hydraulic systems can exhibit high efficiency, factors such as fluid viscosity, friction, and leaks can influence overall efficiency. Design considerations and proper maintenance are essential to optimize efficiency.

7. Dynamic Response:

Hydraulic drives offer rapid and dynamic response times. Changes in input commands result in quick adjustments in the output, allowing for precise control and immediate response to varying operating conditions.

8. Versatility in Speed and Torque:

Hydraulic drives can be designed to provide a wide range of speeds and torques. This versatility is achieved through the use of variable displacement pumps and motors, allowing for flexibility in adapting to different application requirements.

9. Compact Design:

Hydraulic drives often have a compact design compared to other mechanical drive systems. The ability to generate substantial power within a relatively small space is advantageous in applications where size constraints are a consideration.

III. Efficiency and Factors Influencing Efficiency:

1. Overall Efficiency:

The overall efficiency of a hydraulic drive system is the ratio of output power to input power. It takes into account losses in various components such as pumps, valves, hoses, and the hydraulic motor. Achieving high overall efficiency is crucial for minimizing energy consumption and optimizing performance.

2. Factors Influencing Efficiency:

Several factors can influence the efficiency of hydraulic drives:

a. Fluid Viscosity:

Viscosity affects the flow resistance in the hydraulic system. Higher viscosity fluids can result in increased energy losses and reduced overall efficiency.

b. Leakages:

Hydraulic systems are susceptible to fluid leaks, which can occur at connections, seals, and other points. Minimizing and addressing leaks is essential for maintaining efficiency.

c. Friction:

Friction within the hydraulic components, such as pumps and motors, can contribute to energy losses. Proper lubrication and design considerations help reduce friction.

d. Heat Generation:

Excessive heat generation in the hydraulic fluid can indicate energy losses. Efficient cooling systems are necessary to dissipate heat and maintain optimal operating temperatures.

e. System Design:

The overall design of the hydraulic system, including the selection of components, plays a crucial role in determining efficiency. Well-designed systems minimize pressure drops and energy losses.

IV. Advantages of Hydraulic Drives:

1. High Power Density:

Hydraulic drives offer high power density, providing substantial power output relative to their size and weight. This characteristic is advantageous in applications with space constraints.

2. Precise Control:

Hydraulic systems allow for precise control over force, speed, and position. This precision is beneficial in applications where accurate control and positioning are critical.

3. Adaptability to Variable Loads:

Hydraulic drives can adapt to variable loads and maintain a relatively constant speed and torque output. This adaptability is valuable in applications with fluctuating operating conditions.

4. High Torque at Low Speeds:

Hydraulic drives excel in providing high torque at low speeds. This feature is crucial in applications such as heavy machinery and vehicles, where starting torque is essential.

5. Bi-Directional Operation:

Hydraulic drives can operate in both directions, enabling reversible motion. This characteristic is beneficial in applications where the load needs to move back and forth.

6. Versatility in Speed and Torque:

Hydraulic drives can be designed to provide a wide range of speeds and torques, offering versatility in adapting to different application requirements.

7. Compact Design:

Hydraulic drives often have a compact design, making them suitable for applications with limited space. The ability to generate significant power in a small footprint is advantageous.

8. Dynamic Response:

Hydraulic drives offer rapid and dynamic response times, allowing for quick adjustments to changes in input commands. This dynamic response is essential in applications requiring immediate and precise control.

V. Limitations and Considerations:

1. Efficiency Challenges:

Achieving high efficiency in hydraulic drives can be challenging due to factors such as fluid viscosity, leakages, and friction. Careful design, proper maintenance, and the selection of efficient components are essential to address these challenges.

2. Maintenance Requirements:

Hydraulic systems require regular maintenance to address issues such as fluid leaks, component wear, and contamination. Proper maintenance practices are crucial for ensuring the longevity and reliability of hydraulic drives.

3. Noise and Vibration:

Hydraulic drives can produce noise and vibration during operation, which may be a consideration in applications where noise levels are a concern. Noise reduction measures and vibration isolation techniques can be employed to mitigate these effects.

4. Temperature Sensitivity:

Hydraulic systems can be sensitive to temperature changes. Elevated temperatures can affect the viscosity of the hydraulic fluid and impact the overall efficiency and performance of the system. Efficient cooling systems are essential to maintain optimal temperatures.

5. Complexity in Control Systems:

Achieving precise control in hydraulic drives may require sophisticated control systems. The complexity of these control systems can influence the overall system design and implementation.

6. Fluid Compatibility:

The compatibility of hydraulic fluid with system components is crucial. Incompatibility can lead to corrosion, wear, and other issues. Selecting the appropriate hydraulic fluid and ensuring compatibility with system materials are essential considerations.

VI. Considerations in Designing Hydraulic Drives:

1. System Design and Layout:

The overall design and layout of the hydraulic system play a critical role in its performance. Considerations include the arrangement of components, routing of fluid lines, and accessibility for maintenance.

2. Component Selection:

Selecting suitable components, such as pumps, motors, valves, and hoses, is essential for achieving the desired performance and efficiency. Consider factors such as component ratings, compatibility, and reliability.

3. Fluid Selection:

Choosing the right hydraulic fluid is crucial for system performance and longevity. Considerations include fluid viscosity, temperature stability, and compatibility with system components.

4. Control System Design:

The design of the control system influences the precision and responsiveness of the hydraulic drive. Consider incorporating proportional valves, servo valves, and advanced control algorithms to achieve precise control.

5. Noise and Vibration Control:

Implement measures to control noise and vibration, such as the use of dampening materials, isolation mounts, and proper system tuning. This is especially important in applications where noise levels need to be minimized.

6. Efficiency Optimization:

Design the hydraulic system with a focus on optimizing efficiency. Considerations include minimizing pressure drops, addressing leakages, and selecting components with high efficiency ratings.

7. Temperature Management:

Implement effective temperature management strategies to ensure that the hydraulic system operates within the specified temperature range. This may involve the use of cooling systems, heat exchangers, and temperature sensors.

8. Safety Considerations:

Incorporate safety features into the design, such as pressure relief valves, emergency stop systems, and fail-safe mechanisms. Safety is paramount, especially in applications where hydraulic drives interact with human operators or sensitive equipment.

VII. Future Trends and Innovations:

1. Electro-Hydraulic Integration:

Explore advancements in electro-hydraulic integration, where hydraulic systems are combined with electronic control systems for enhanced precision and efficiency.

2. Smart Technologies:

Monitor developments in smart technologies, such as the integration of sensors and IoT (Internet of Things) capabilities, enabling condition monitoring, predictive maintenance, and data-driven insights.

3. Energy Efficiency Improvements:

Stay informed about innovations focused on improving the energy efficiency of hydraulic drives. This includes developments in pump and motor design, as well as energy recovery systems.

4. Digital Twin Technology:

Consider the potential use of digital twin technology for virtual simulations and predictive analysis of hydraulic system performance, allowing for more informed design decisions and optimization.

VIII. Conclusion:

Hydraulic drives are integral components in various industrial applications, offering a combination of high power density, precise control, and adaptability to variable loads. Understanding the characteristics, advantages, and limitations of hydraulic drives is crucial for designing efficient and reliable systems. Careful consideration of factors such as efficiency, controllability, maintenance requirements, and safety considerations is essential in the design and implementation of hydraulic drives. As technology continues to advance, staying informed about future trends and innovations will enable engineers to leverage new developments for improved hydraulic system performance and sustainability.

Linear Actuator

Linear actuators are devices that convert rotary motion into linear motion, providing controlled and precise movement in a straight line. They find widespread use in various applications across industries, ranging from manufacturing and robotics to automotive and healthcare. In this comprehensive exploration, we will delve into the types of linear actuators, mounting details, and the importance of cushioning in linear actuator systems.

I. Introduction to Linear Actuators:

1. Basic Working Principle:

Linear actuators function based on the conversion of rotary motion into linear motion. The primary components of a linear actuator include a motor, a transmission mechanism (such as a lead screw or belt), and a guiding system. As the motor turns, it drives the transmission mechanism, resulting in the linear extension or retraction of the actuator.

2. Types of Linear Actuators:

Linear actuators come in various types, each suited for specific applications based on their characteristics and performance. Common types include:

a. Electromechanical Actuators:

Utilize an electric motor to drive a mechanism (lead screw, belt, or ball screw) for linear motion.

Suitable for applications requiring precise control and moderate force.

b. Hydraulic Actuators:

Operate on the principle of fluid power, using hydraulic pressure to generate linear motion.

Common in heavy-duty applications where high force and robust performance are essential.

c. Pneumatic Actuators:

Rely on compressed air to generate linear motion.

Widely used in applications requiring rapid and repetitive movements.

d. Piezoelectric Actuators:

Use the piezoelectric effect to generate linear motion by applying an electric field to piezoelectric materials.

Ideal for applications requiring precision in micro and nano scales.

e. Mechanical Actuators:

Include mechanisms such as lead screws, belts, or chains to convert rotary motion into linear motion.

Simple and cost-effective, suitable for various applications.

II. Types of Mounting Details:

1. End Mounting:

Linear actuators typically have end mounting options that allow them to be securely attached to other components or structures. Common end mounting configurations include:

a. Clevis Mount:

A clevis mount involves using a clevis, a U-shaped component, to connect the actuator to another part.

Provides a pivot point for the actuator, allowing it to move in one plane.

b. Trunnion Mount:

In a trunnion mount, the actuator is attached using trunnion brackets, allowing rotation around an axis perpendicular to the linear motion.

Useful when the actuator needs to pivot during operation.

c. Flange Mount:

A flange mount involves attaching the actuator using flanges or plates on its ends.

Offers a stable and secure connection, suitable for applications where the actuator needs to be fixed.

2. Body Mounting:

In addition to end mounting, linear actuators may be mounted along their body. The choice of body mounting depends on the specific requirements of the application:

a. Foot Mount:

Foot mounting involves securing the actuator to a surface using mounting feet or brackets.

Provides stability and support, suitable for applications where the actuator needs to be anchored.

b. Side Mount:

Side mounting involves attaching the actuator to the side of a structure or equipment.

Useful in applications where space constraints or specific orientation requirements exist.

3. Guiding Systems:

Linear actuators often incorporate guiding systems to ensure smooth and precise linear motion. The guiding system helps prevent lateral movement and maintains the alignment of the actuator. Common types of guiding systems include:

a. Linear Bearings:

Linear bearings provide support and reduce friction, allowing the actuator to move smoothly along its path.

Common types include ball bearings and roller bearings.

b. Slides and Rails:

Slides and rails guide the actuator along a predefined path, offering stability and accuracy.

Ideal for applications requiring precise linear motion.

III. Importance of Cushioning in Linear Actuators:

1. Overview of Cushioning:

Cushioning in linear actuators refers to the controlled deceleration of the actuator's moving parts at the end of its stroke. This is crucial to avoid abrupt stops, reduce impact forces, and prevent damage to both the actuator and the load it is moving. Cushioning mechanisms are commonly employed in pneumatic and hydraulic actuators to enhance safety, accuracy, and longevity.

2. Types of Cushioning:

Several types of cushioning mechanisms are employed in linear actuators, each designed to provide controlled deceleration at the end of the stroke:

a. Adjustable Cushioning:

Allows users to adjust the level of cushioning to suit specific application requirements.

Commonly used in pneumatic actuators, where adjustable cushioning valves regulate the airflow during the deceleration phase.

b. Fixed Cushioning:

Provides a predetermined level of cushioning without user-adjustable settings.

Often integrated into hydraulic and pneumatic actuators to simplify design and operation.

c. Mechanical Cushioning:

Involves the use of mechanical devices, such as shock absorbers or springs, to dampen the impact forces at the end of the stroke.

Suitable for applications where precise control of deceleration is critical.

d. Deceleration Profiles:

Some advanced linear actuators incorporate electronic control systems that allow for the programming of deceleration profiles.

Enables tailored deceleration characteristics for specific applications.

3. Benefits of Cushioning:

Cushioning in linear actuators offers several benefits that contribute to improved performance and longevity:

a. Reduced Impact Forces:

Cushioning mechanisms reduce the impact forces at the end of the stroke, preventing sudden stops that could lead to damage.

b. Enhanced Accuracy:

Controlled deceleration ensures that the actuator stops precisely at the desired position, contributing to overall accuracy in positioning.

c. Increased Safety:

Cushioning improves safety by minimizing the risk of damage to the actuator, load, and surrounding equipment.

d. Extended Lifespan:

By reducing the stress on components, cushioning mechanisms contribute to the longevity of linear actuators.

4. Considerations in Cushioning Design:

When designing cushioning for linear actuators, certain considerations are essential to ensure optimal performance:

a. Load Characteristics:

The type and weight of the load being moved by the actuator influence the design of the cushioning mechanism. Heavier loads may require more robust cushioning.

b. Speed of Operation:

The speed at which the actuator operates affects the energy that needs to be dissipated during deceleration. Faster operations may require more efficient cushioning.

c. Application Requirements:

Specific applications may have unique requirements for deceleration profiles and cushioning characteristics. Tailoring the cushioning design to meet these requirements is crucial.

5. Integration with Control Systems:

In modern linear actuator systems, cushioning mechanisms can be integrated with electronic control systems. This allows for precise adjustment and control of the deceleration process, enhancing the overall performance of the actuator.

IV. Applications of Linear Actuators:

1. Industrial Automation:

Linear actuators play a vital role in various industrial automation applications, including assembly lines, packaging machinery, and material handling systems.

2. Robotics:

In robotics, linear actuators are used for precise and controlled movement of robot arms, grippers, and other components.

3. Medical Devices:

Linear actuators find applications in medical devices such as hospital beds, patient lifts, and surgical equipment, where precise and reliable linear motion is crucial.

4. Automotive Systems:

Linear actuators are integral components in automotive systems, including power windows, seat adjustments, and convertible top mechanisms.

5. Aerospace:

Linear actuators are used in aerospace applications for functions such as wing adjustments, landing gear deployment, and control surface movements.

6. Home Automation:

In home automation, linear actuators are employed in smart furniture, adjustable beds, and automated window blinds.

7. Construction and Heavy Machinery:

Linear actuators are utilized in construction equipment and heavy machinery for tasks such as extending and retracting hydraulic arms.

V. Future Trends and Innovations:

1. Smart Actuators:

The integration of sensors and IoT capabilities into linear actuators is expected to increase. Smart actuators can provide real-time data, enable condition monitoring, and contribute to predictive maintenance.

2. Advancements in Materials:

Innovations in materials, such as the use of lightweight and high-strength composites, may lead to more efficient and compact linear actuator designs.

3. Energy-Efficient Designs:

Continued focus on energy efficiency may result in the development of linear actuators with reduced power consumption and improved overall efficiency.

4. Enhanced Control Systems:

Advancements in control systems, including the use of artificial intelligence and machine learning algorithms, may contribute to more precise and adaptive control of linear actuators.

VI. Conclusion:

Linear actuators are essential components in a wide range of applications, providing controlled linear motion in diverse industries. The choice of linear actuator type, mounting details, and the incorporation of cushioning mechanisms are critical considerations in designing systems that meet specific performance and safety requirements. As technology continues to advance, innovations in materials, smart technologies, and energy efficiency are expected to shape the future of linear actuator design, enhancing their capabilities and expanding their applications across various domains. Understanding the characteristics and considerations associated with linear actuators is crucial for engineers and designers seeking to optimize the performance and reliability of systems incorporating these versatile devices.

Power Packs and Accumulators

Power packs and accumulators are integral components in hydraulic systems, playing crucial roles in storing and supplying hydraulic energy. In this comprehensive exploration, we will delve into the functions, types, components, applications, and considerations associated with power packs and accumulators in hydraulic systems.

I. Introduction to Power Packs and Accumulators:

1. Power Packs:

A power pack, also known as a hydraulic power unit (HPU), is a self-contained system that generates hydraulic power to drive various hydraulic machinery and equipment. It typically consists of a hydraulic pump, an electric motor or an internal combustion engine, a reservoir for hydraulic fluid, valves, filters, and other components. Power packs are used to provide the necessary pressure and flow of hydraulic fluid to drive actuators, motors, and other hydraulic components in diverse applications.

2. Accumulators:

Accumulators are devices used to store hydraulic energy in the form of pressurized fluid. They play a vital role in hydraulic systems by absorbing and releasing energy to maintain system pressure, dampen shocks, and provide emergency power in case of pump failure. Accumulators store energy during periods of low demand and release it when demand is high. Common types of accumulators include bladder, piston, and diaphragm accumulators.

II. Functions of Power Packs:

1. Generating Hydraulic Power:

The primary function of a power pack is to generate hydraulic power by converting mechanical energy from an electric motor or an internal combustion engine into fluid flow and pressure.

2. Driving Hydraulic Components:

Power packs provide the necessary hydraulic energy to drive hydraulic components such as cylinders, motors, and actuators in various industrial applications.

3. Ensuring System Reliability:

Power packs contribute to the reliability of hydraulic systems by providing a centralized and efficient source of hydraulic power. This centralized design simplifies maintenance and reduces the risk of component failure.

4. Facilitating Remote Operation:

Power packs can be designed for remote operation, allowing for flexibility in system design and installation. This is particularly advantageous in applications where space is limited or accessibility is a challenge.

5. Enabling Control:

Power packs incorporate valves and controls that enable the regulation of hydraulic fluid flow and pressure. This control facilitates precise and efficient operation of hydraulic machinery.

III. Components of Power Packs:

1. Hydraulic Pump:

The hydraulic pump is a key component of the power pack, responsible for generating flow and pressure by converting mechanical energy into hydraulic energy. Common types include gear pumps, vane pumps, and piston pumps.

2. Electric Motor or Internal Combustion Engine:

Power packs are typically powered by an electric motor or an internal combustion engine. The choice depends on factors such as power requirements, application, and environmental considerations.

3. Reservoir:

The reservoir holds hydraulic fluid, providing a storage space and allowing for heat dissipation. It also facilitates the removal of contaminants through filters.

4. Valves:

Various types of valves are used in power packs to control the flow and pressure of hydraulic fluid. These include directional control valves, pressure relief valves, and flow control valves.

5. Filters:

Filters are essential for maintaining the cleanliness of the hydraulic fluid. They remove contaminants and prevent them from entering the hydraulic system, protecting components from damage.

6. Heat Exchangers:

Heat exchangers, such as oil coolers, help regulate the temperature of the hydraulic fluid, preventing overheating and ensuring optimal system performance.

7. Accumulator:

Some power packs incorporate an accumulator to store hydraulic energy and provide additional power during peak demand or in emergency situations.

8. Control Panel:

A control panel contains various controls, indicators, and instruments for monitoring and operating the power pack. It allows operators to regulate the system based on specific requirements.

IV. Types of Power Packs:

1. Standard Power Packs:

Standard power packs are pre-designed and manufactured units with fixed specifications. They are suitable for common applications with standard hydraulic requirements.

2. Custom Power Packs:

Custom power packs are designed and built to meet specific requirements of a particular application. They offer flexibility in terms of features, size, and performance.

3. Mini Power Packs:

Mini power packs are compact units designed for applications with limited space. They are often used in mobile equipment and small hydraulic systems.

4. Compact Power Packs:

Compact power packs are designed to provide high power density in a small footprint. They are suitable for applications where space is a critical factor.

5. Quiet Power Packs:

Quiet power packs are designed with noise reduction features, making them suitable for applications where low noise levels are essential, such as in medical equipment.

V. Functions of Accumulators:

1. Energy Storage:

The primary function of an accumulator is to store hydraulic energy during periods of low demand. This stored energy can be released when demand increases.

2. Damping:

Accumulators help dampen shocks and vibrations in hydraulic systems by absorbing sudden pressure changes. This is especially important in applications where precise control and smooth operation are required.

3. Maintaining System Pressure:

Accumulators help maintain constant system pressure by releasing stored energy during periods of high demand or pump failure. This ensures uninterrupted operation of hydraulic machinery.

4. Emergency Power Source:

In the event of a pump failure, accumulators can act as emergency power sources, providing hydraulic energy to critical components and allowing for controlled shutdown or operation.

5. Compensating for Leakages:

Accumulators compensate for minor leakages in hydraulic systems by supplying additional fluid to maintain pressure. This helps in extending the operational life of the system.

VI. Types of Accumulators:

1. Bladder Accumulators:

Bladder accumulators consist of a flexible bladder inside a pressure vessel. When hydraulic fluid is pumped into the accumulator, the bladder compresses, storing energy.

2. Piston Accumulators:

Piston accumulators use a piston to separate hydraulic fluid and gas. When fluid is pumped into the accumulator, it compresses the gas, storing energy.

3. Diaphragm Accumulators:

Diaphragm accumulators have a flexible diaphragm that separates hydraulic fluid and gas. Similar to bladder accumulators, they store energy by compressing the diaphragm.

VII. Components of Accumulators:

1. Pressure Vessel:

The pressure vessel contains the hydraulic fluid and gas, and it is designed to withstand the pressure generated during compression.

2. Gas Pre-Charge:

The gas pre-charge is a predetermined amount of gas, usually nitrogen, that is initially introduced into the accumulator. It provides the initial compression space for the hydraulic fluid.

3. Piston, Bladder, or Diaphragm:

The piston, bladder, or diaphragm separates the hydraulic fluid from the gas and undergoes compression to store hydraulic energy.

4. Valve:

Accumulators often have a valve to control the flow of hydraulic fluid in and out of the accumulator. This valve helps regulate the pressure and prevents excessive pressure buildup.

5. Mounting Accessories:

Mounting accessories, such as brackets and clamps, secure the accumulator in place within the hydraulic system.

VIII. Applications of Power Packs and Accumulators:

1. Industrial Machinery:

Power packs are widely used in industrial machinery such as presses, injection molding machines, and hydraulic lifts. Accumulators are employed to provide emergency power and dampen shocks.

2. Mobile Equipment:

Mobile equipment, including construction machinery, agricultural vehicles, and forklifts, often use power packs for their compact design and versatility. Accumulators contribute to energy storage and shock absorption.

3. Aerospace:

Hydraulic power packs and accumulators find applications in aerospace for functions such as landing gear extension, flap movement, and thrust reverser actuation.

4. Marine Systems:

Hydraulic systems with power packs are used in marine applications for functions such as steering, winch operation, and stabilizer control. Accumulators assist in maintaining system pressure.

5. Renewable Energy:

Hydraulic systems with power packs are utilized in renewable energy applications, such as in hydraulic power plants and wave energy converters. Accumulators help regulate pressure and provide emergency power.

6. Automotive:

Power packs are used in automotive applications for functions such as power steering and convertible top operation. Accumulators contribute to energy storage and system stability.

7. Oil and Gas:

Hydraulic power packs play a crucial role in oil and gas exploration and production, where they are used in drilling equipment and hydraulic control systems. Accumulators assist in maintaining pressure and absorbing shocks.

IX. Considerations in Design and Selection:

1. Power Pack Design Considerations:

When designing a power pack, considerations include the required flow rate, pressure, and power, as well as factors such as space constraints, environmental conditions, and the type of hydraulic fluid.

2. Accumulator Selection Considerations:

Selecting an accumulator involves considerations such as the required volume of stored energy, pressure ratings, fluid compatibility, and the type of accumulator (bladder, piston, or diaphragm).

3. Integration with Hydraulic Systems:

Both power packs and accumulators must be seamlessly integrated with the overall hydraulic system. Compatibility with existing components, proper sizing, and effective control are essential for optimal performance.

4. Safety Considerations:

Safety is paramount in hydraulic systems. Pressure relief valves, proper venting of accumulators, and fail-safe mechanisms contribute to the safe operation of power packs and accumulators.

5. Maintenance Requirements:

Regular maintenance is crucial for ensuring the reliability and longevity of power packs and accumulators. This includes monitoring fluid cleanliness, inspecting seals, and checking for any signs of wear or leakage.

6. Environmental Considerations:

Considerations such as temperature extremes, exposure to harsh environments, and the use of environmentally friendly hydraulic fluids must be taken into account in both power pack and accumulator designs.

X. Future Trends and Innovations:

1. Smart Hydraulic Systems:

The integration of sensors, IoT capabilities, and advanced control systems is expected to increase in both power packs and accumulators. Smart systems can provide real-time data, optimize performance, and enable predictive maintenance.

2. Energy-Efficient Designs:

Ongoing efforts to enhance the energy efficiency of hydraulic systems may lead to the development of power packs and accumulators with reduced energy consumption and improved overall efficiency.

3. Lightweight Materials:

Innovations in materials, including the use of lightweight and high-strength composites, may contribute to the development of more compact and lightweight power packs and accumulators.

4. Hybrid Power Systems:

The integration of hydraulic systems with other power sources, such as electric or hybrid systems, may become more prevalent, especially in applications where energy efficiency is a priority.

XI. Conclusion:

Power packs and accumulators are indispensable components in hydraulic systems, providing the energy needed to drive machinery, maintain system pressure, and ensure smooth and controlled operation. Understanding the functions, types, components, applications, and considerations associated with power packs and accumulators is crucial for engineers and designers working with hydraulic systems. As technology continues to advance, the integration of smart technologies, energy-efficient designs, and innovative materials is expected to shape the future of power packs and accumulators, contributing to more reliable, efficient, and sustainable hydraulic systems across various industries.

CHAPTER TWO

Control and Regulating Elements

Control and Regulating Elements — Direction, Flow and Pressure Control Valves -Methods of Actuation, Types, Sizing of Ports. Spool Valves - Operating Characteristics -Electro Hydraulic Servo Valves - Types - Characteristics and Performance.

Control and Regulating Elements

Introduction

Hydraulics and pneumatics are branches of fluid power that involve the use of liquids (hydraulics) and gases (pneumatics) to transmit power. These systems are widely used in various industrial applications, including manufacturing, construction, and automation. Control and regulating elements play a crucial role in managing the flow, pressure, and direction of the fluid within these systems.

Basic Principles

Fluid Power

Fluid power systems leverage the incompressibility of liquids (hydraulic systems) or the compressibility of gases (pneumatic systems) to transmit force and energy. These systems are highly efficient and offer precise control over motion and force.

Pascal's Law

Pascal's Law is fundamental to hydraulic systems. It states that any change in pressure applied to an enclosed fluid is transmitted undiminished to all portions of the fluid and to the walls of its container.

Key Components

Hydraulic Systems

Pump: Generates hydraulic pressure by converting mechanical energy into fluid energy.

Actuators: Convert hydraulic energy into mechanical work. Common types include hydraulic cylinders and hydraulic motors.

Valves: Control the direction, flow, and pressure of the hydraulic fluid. Types include directional control valves, pressure control valves, and flow control valves.

Pneumatic Systems

Compressor: Provides compressed air by converting mechanical energy into pneumatic energy.

Actuators: Convert pneumatic energy into mechanical work. Common types include pneumatic cylinders and pneumatic motors.

Valves: Regulate the direction, flow, and pressure of the pneumatic fluid. Types include directional control valves, pressure control valves, and flow control valves.

Control Elements in Hydraulic Systems

Directional Control Valves

Directional control valves determine the path through which hydraulic fluid flows in a system. Common types include:

Spool Valves: These valves use a movable spool to control the flow direction. They are often used in applications where precise control is required.

Poppet Valves: Poppet valves use a disc, ball, or cone to control flow. They are suitable for high-pressure applications and provide quick response times.

Diverter Valves: These valves divert fluid flow from one path to another. They are commonly used in hydraulic systems with multiple actuators.

Pressure Control Valves

Pressure control valves regulate the pressure of the hydraulic fluid. Key types include:

Relief Valves: Protect the system from overpressure by allowing excess fluid to flow back to the reservoir.

Pressure Reducing Valves: Maintain a constant lower pressure in a part of the system, ensuring that components are not subjected to excessive pressure.

Sequence Valves: Control the sequence of operations in a hydraulic system by allowing fluid flow when a preset pressure is reached.

Flow Control Valves

Flow control valves manage the rate of fluid flow in a hydraulic system. Types include:

Throttle Valves: Regulate flow by creating a restriction in the hydraulic circuit.

Priority Flow Control Valves: Prioritize the flow to certain parts of the hydraulic system.

Proportional Control Valves: Provide variable and precise control over the flow rate based on the input signal.

Regulating Elements in Pneumatic Systems

Directional Control Valves

Similar to hydraulic systems, pneumatic directional control valves determine the path of compressed air flow. Common types include:

Solenoid Valves: Controlled by an electric current, these valves are quick-acting and widely used in automation.

Manual Valves: Operated manually to control the direction of airflow.

Pneumatic Pilot Valves: Controlled by air pressure, these valves are suitable for applications where air pressure is readily available.

Pressure Control Valves

Pneumatic pressure control valves manage the pressure of the compressed air. Key types include:

Relief Valves: Release excess air pressure to prevent damage to components.

Pressure Regulators: Maintain a constant pressure level in a specific part of the pneumatic system.

Pressure Sequencers: Control the sequence of operations by allowing compressed air flow when a preset pressure is reached.

Flow Control Valves

Flow control valves in pneumatic systems regulate the rate of compressed air flow. Common types include:

Throttle Valves: Similar to hydraulic systems, throttle valves create a restriction to control airflow.

Quick Exhaust Valves: Allow rapid release of compressed air from pneumatic actuators.

Metering Valves: Gradually control the flow of compressed air to achieve smooth acceleration and deceleration of pneumatic actuators.

Applications and Considerations

Hydraulic Systems

Hydraulic systems find applications in various industries, including:

Manufacturing: Hydraulic systems are used in presses, injection molding machines, and metal forming equipment.

Construction: Hydraulic excavators, bulldozers, and cranes rely on hydraulic systems for precise control and power.

Aerospace: Hydraulic systems are crucial for controlling aircraft landing gear, flaps, and other critical components.

Pneumatic Systems

Pneumatic systems are commonly used in industries such as:

Automation: Pneumatic actuators and control elements are prevalent in automated manufacturing processes.

Packaging: Pneumatic systems are used in packaging machines for tasks such as sealing, labeling, and sorting.

Transportation: Pneumatic systems play a role in braking systems for vehicles and trains.

Considerations for Control and Regulation

Precision and Accuracy: The choice of control and regulating elements depends on the precision and accuracy required in a particular application.

Environment: Environmental factors, such as temperature and humidity, can affect the performance of hydraulic and pneumatic systems. Proper seals and materials must be selected to ensure reliability.

Safety: Safety is paramount in fluid power systems. Pressure relief valves and other safety devices are crucial to prevent overpressure situations.

Maintenance: Regular maintenance is essential to ensure the longevity and reliability of hydraulic and pneumatic systems. This includes checking for leaks, inspecting seals, and replacing worn-out components.

Conclusion

Control and regulating elements are integral to the efficient and precise operation of hydraulic and pneumatic systems. The proper selection and application of directional control valves, pressure control valves, and flow control valves are essential to meet the specific requirements of diverse industrial applications. As technology advances, the integration of smart and proportional control elements further enhances the capabilities and performance of fluid power systems, contributing to increased efficiency and productivity across various industries.

Direction, Flow and Pressure Control Valves

Directional Control Valves

Introduction

Directional control valves are fundamental components in both hydraulic and pneumatic systems, determining the path of fluid or air flow. They play a crucial role in controlling the direction of movement of hydraulic cylinders, motors, or pneumatic actuators. These valves come in various designs, each suitable for specific applications.

Hydraulic Directional Control Valves

Spool Valves

Spool valves are common in hydraulic systems. They consist of a movable spool within a housing. The spool's position determines the flow path, either connecting or blocking ports. When the spool shifts, it directs hydraulic fluid to the desired actuator, controlling the motion of hydraulic machinery.

Poppet Valves

Poppet valves use a disc, ball, or cone to control flow. In hydraulic systems, poppet valves are often employed in high-pressure applications. They offer quick response times and can effectively control flow in demanding conditions.

Diverter Valves

Diverter valves redirect fluid flow from one path to another. These are crucial in hydraulic systems with multiple actuators or functions. By selectively directing the flow, diverter valves enable the hydraulic system to perform various tasks using a single pump.

Pneumatic Directional Control Valves

Solenoid Valves

Solenoid valves are common in pneumatic systems. They use an electromechanical solenoid to control the position of a valve spool. When the solenoid is energized, it shifts the spool, allowing air to flow through specific passages. Solenoid valves are widely used in automation due to their quick response times.

Manual Valves

Manual valves are operated by hand to control the direction of airflow in pneumatic systems. They are simple, cost-effective, and suitable for applications where manual control is sufficient.

Pneumatic Pilot Valves

Pneumatic pilot valves are controlled by air pressure. They use pilot air to shift the valve spool, determining the direction of air flow. These valves are often employed in pneumatic systems where air pressure is readily available.

Flow Control Valves

Introduction

Flow control valves manage the rate of fluid or air flow within a hydraulic or pneumatic system. Proper control of flow is crucial for achieving precise and efficient operation, especially in applications where different actuators require varying flow rates.

Hydraulic Flow Control Valves

Throttle Valves

Throttle valves create a restriction in the hydraulic circuit, regulating the flow rate. These valves are simple and effective for controlling the speed of hydraulic actuators. By adjusting the size of the orifice, the flow of hydraulic fluid can be finely tuned.

Priority Flow Control Valves

Priority flow control valves ensure that a specific part of the hydraulic system receives a prioritized flow. This is crucial in applications where certain actuators or functions require constant and controlled fluid flow.

Proportional Control Valves

Proportional control valves provide variable and precise control over the flow rate based on an input signal. These valves use advanced technology to modulate the flow, allowing for fine adjustments and proportional control of hydraulic machinery.

Pneumatic Flow Control Valves

Quick Exhaust Valves

Quick exhaust valves allow the rapid release of compressed air from pneumatic actuators. By enabling quick depressurization, these valves contribute to faster cylinder retraction and improved overall system efficiency.

Metering Valves

Metering valves gradually control the flow of compressed air, ensuring smooth acceleration and deceleration of pneumatic actuators. These valves are essential in applications where abrupt changes in airflow could impact the performance or safety of the system.

Pressure Control Valves

Introduction

Pressure control valves are crucial for maintaining safe operating conditions within hydraulic and pneumatic systems. They prevent overpressure situations that could lead to equipment failure or safety hazards.

Hydraulic Pressure Control Valves

Relief Valves

Relief valves protect hydraulic systems from overpressure by allowing excess fluid to flow back to the reservoir. They are set to open at a predetermined pressure, preventing damage to components and ensuring system safety.

Pressure Reducing Valves

Pressure reducing valves maintain a constant lower pressure in a specific part of the hydraulic system. These valves are essential when different parts of a hydraulic system require varying pressure levels.

Sequence Valves

Sequence valves control the sequence of operations in a hydraulic system. They allow fluid flow when a preset pressure is reached, ensuring that specific tasks are performed in a predetermined order.

Pneumatic Pressure Control Valves

Relief Valves

Similar to hydraulic systems, relief valves in pneumatic systems protect against overpressure. They release excess compressed air to maintain safe operating conditions.

Pressure Regulators

Pressure regulators maintain a constant pressure level in a specific part of the pneumatic system. They are crucial for applications where consistent pressure is required for optimal performance.

Pressure Sequencers

Pressure sequencers control the sequence of operations by allowing compressed air flow when a preset pressure is reached. These valves are essential for coordinating the timing of different pneumatic functions.

Applications and Considerations

Applications

Hydraulic Systems

Hydraulic directional, flow, and pressure control valves find applications in:

Manufacturing: Hydraulic presses, injection molding machines, and metal forming equipment.

Construction: Hydraulic excavators, bulldozers, and cranes.

Aerospace: Control of aircraft landing gear, flaps, and other critical components.

Pneumatic Systems

Pneumatic control valves are used in various industries, including:

Automation: Pneumatic actuators and control elements in automated manufacturing processes.

Packaging: Pneumatic systems in packaging machines for sealing, labeling, and sorting.

Transportation: Pneumatic braking systems for vehicles and trains.

Considerations for Control Valves

Precision and Accuracy: The choice of control valves depends on the precision and accuracy required for a particular application. Proportional control valves are often preferred for applications demanding fine adjustments.

Environmental Factors: Temperature, humidity, and other environmental factors can impact the performance of control valves. Proper seals and materials must be selected to ensure reliability under specific conditions.

Safety: Safety is paramount in fluid power systems. Pressure relief valves and other safety devices are crucial to prevent overpressure situations that could lead to equipment failure or safety hazards.

Maintenance: Regular maintenance is essential to ensure the longevity and reliability of control valves. This includes checking for leaks, inspecting seals, and replacing worn-out components.

Conclusion

Directional, flow, and pressure control valves are integral components of hydraulic and pneumatic systems, providing the means to precisely control fluid or air flow, direction, and pressure. The proper selection and application of these valves are crucial for achieving optimal performance and safety in a wide range of industrial applications. As technology continues to advance, the integration of smart and proportional control elements enhances the capabilities and efficiency of fluid power systems, contributing to increased precision and productivity across various industries.

Methods of Actuation, Types and Sizing of Ports

Introduction to Fluid Power Systems

Fluid power systems play a crucial role in various industries, providing a reliable and efficient means of transmitting power. Hydraulic and pneumatic systems are two common types of fluid power systems, utilizing liquids and gases, respectively, to transmit force and motion. Actuation, port sizing, and component types are vital aspects in designing and optimizing these systems.

Methods of Actuation

Hydraulic Actuation:

1. Hydraulic Cylinders:

Hydraulic cylinders are one of the most common actuators in hydraulic systems.

They consist of a piston within a cylindrical chamber, and fluid pressure applied to the piston generates linear motion.

Single-acting cylinders use fluid pressure in one direction, while double-acting cylinders use it in both directions.

2. Hydraulic Motors:

Hydraulic motors convert hydraulic energy into rotational motion.

These are often used in applications where continuous rotation is required, such as in heavy machinery and industrial equipment.

3. Hydraulic Pumps:

Hydraulic pumps are responsible for converting mechanical energy into hydraulic energy.

There are various types, including gear pumps, vane pumps, and piston pumps, each with specific advantages depending on the application.

4. Hydraulic Valves:

Hydraulic valves control the flow and pressure of the hydraulic fluid in the system.

Directional control valves determine the direction of fluid flow, while pressure control valves regulate the pressure within the system.

Pneumatic Actuation:

1. Pneumatic Cylinders:

Pneumatic cylinders operate similarly to hydraulic cylinders but use compressed air instead of hydraulic fluid.

They are widely used in applications requiring rapid and repetitive motion due to their quick response times.

2. Pneumatic Motors:

Pneumatic motors, like hydraulic motors, convert pneumatic energy into rotational motion.

These motors find applications in situations where electricity is impractical or unsafe.

3. Pneumatic Pumps:

Pneumatic pumps are less common than hydraulic pumps but are utilized in certain specialized applications.

They use compressed air to create a flow of fluid for specific tasks.

4. Pneumatic Valves:

Pneumatic valves control the flow of compressed air in the system.

Similar to hydraulic valves, they include directional control valves and pressure control valves.

Types of Ports

Ports are openings in a hydraulic or pneumatic system that allow the flow of fluid or air. The size and configuration of these ports are critical for proper system function.

Hydraulic Ports:

1. Inlet and Outlet Ports:

Hydraulic systems typically have designated inlet and outlet ports for fluid entry and exit.

Proper sizing of these ports is essential to maintain the desired flow rate and pressure levels.

2. Pressure and Return Ports:

Pressure ports connect to the hydraulic pump, and return ports allow fluid to return to the reservoir.

Sizes must be carefully selected to prevent pressure drops and ensure efficient operation.

3. Tank Ports:

These ports connect to the hydraulic reservoir, allowing fluid to be replenished.

Adequate sizing prevents cavitation and ensures a steady supply of fluid.

Pneumatic Ports:

1. Inlet and Exhaust Ports:

Inlet ports supply compressed air, while exhaust ports release air from the system.

Proper sizing ensures efficient use of compressed air and prevents pressure imbalances.

2. Pilot Ports:

Pilot ports are used in pneumatic valves to control the larger main ports.

Correct sizing ensures precise control of the valve and the actuator it operates.

3. Muffler Ports:

Muffler ports are used to reduce noise by controlling the release of air from pneumatic components.

Sizing is important for effective noise reduction without impeding system performance.

Sizing of Ports

Hydraulic Port Sizing:

1. Flow Rate Considerations:

The size of hydraulic ports must accommodate the required flow rate for the system.

Calculations involve factors such as fluid viscosity, pressure drop, and system efficiency.

2. Pressure Drop:

Proper sizing prevents excessive pressure drops across the system.

Hydraulic simulations and calculations help determine the optimal port sizes to maintain desired pressure levels.

3. Velocity Constraints:

Hydraulic fluid velocity within the ports must be within acceptable limits to prevent erosion and cavitation.

Correct sizing minimizes fluid velocity-related issues.

Pneumatic Port Sizing:

1. Air Flow Requirements:

Pneumatic port sizing is based on the required air flow for the application.

It involves calculations considering factors such as valve Cv (flow coefficient) and pressure differentials.

2. Pressure Drop and Speed:

Preventing excessive pressure drop is crucial in pneumatic systems.

Port sizing accounts for pressure drop considerations and the speed at which air needs to flow through the system.

3. System Response Time:

Sizing ports appropriately contributes to achieving the desired response time in pneumatic systems.

Rapid actuation requires careful consideration of port sizes to avoid delays.

Conclusion

In conclusion, understanding the methods of actuation, types, and sizing of ports is fundamental to designing efficient and reliable hydraulic and pneumatic systems. Proper actuator selection and port sizing contribute to optimal performance, energy efficiency, and the longevity of the fluid power system. Engineers and designers must carefully consider the specific requirements of each application to ensure the successful implementation of hydraulic and pneumatic technologies.

Spool Valves - Operating Characteristics

Introduction to Spool Valves

Definition and Purpose:

A spool valve, also known as a sliding spool valve, is a type of directional control valve used in fluid power systems. It controls the flow direction of hydraulic fluid or compressed air within a system, thereby directing the movement of actuators such as hydraulic cylinders or pneumatic cylinders.

Basic Components:

1. Spool:

The spool is a cylindrical or tubular component that moves within the valve body.

It often has lands (raised portions) and grooves (recessed portions) that control the flow paths when positioned within the valve.

2. Valve Body:

The valve body houses the spool and contains ports for fluid or air entry and exit.

It provides the structure and support for the spool's movement.

3. Actuation Mechanism:

Spool valves can be actuated manually, mechanically, electrically, or hydraulically, depending on the application.

Operating Characteristics of Spool Valves

Understanding the operating characteristics of spool valves is crucial for proper selection and utilization in hydraulic and pneumatic systems.

1. Flow Paths and Positions:

- Neutral Position:

In the neutral position, the spool blocks or connects ports, preventing fluid or air flow.

This position is often referred to as the center or unactuated position.

- Working Positions:

As the spool shifts, it opens specific flow paths, allowing fluid or air to move in the desired direction.

Working positions determine the movement of actuators and the overall functionality of the system.

2. Actuation Methods:

- Manual Actuation:

Manual spool valves are operated by hand, often through levers or knobs.

Common in applications where human operators need direct control.

- Mechanical Actuation:

Mechanical systems, such as cams or linkages, can actuate spool valves.

Suitable for situations where a specific mechanical motion triggers the valve's operation.

- Solenoid Actuation:

Solenoids use electromagnetic forces to shift the spool.

Solenoid-operated spool valves are common in automated and remotely controlled systems.

- Hydraulic Actuation:

Hydraulic pressure can be employed to shift the spool.

Often used in larger systems where hydraulic power is readily available.

3. Centering Mechanisms:

- Spring-Centered:

Spring-centered spool valves use springs to return the spool to the neutral position when the actuating force is removed.

Common in applications requiring fail-safe functionality.

- Detent-Centered:

Detent-centered valves have a detent mechanism that holds the spool in specific positions until manually or electrically shifted.

Useful in applications where maintaining a specific state is essential.

4. Types of Spool Valves:

- 2-Way Spool Valve:

In a 2-way spool valve, the spool has two working positions.

It either allows or blocks the flow between an inlet and an outlet port.

- 3-Way Spool Valve:

A 3-way spool valve has three working positions.

It can connect one port to either of the other two, allowing control of one actuator.

- 4-Way Spool Valve:

A 4-way spool valve has four working positions.

It can direct fluid or air flow between two pairs of ports, making it suitable for controlling two actuators.

5. Flow Control and Pressure Drop:

- Flow Control:

The design of the spool and the valve body determines the rate of fluid or air flow through the valve.

Careful design consideration is crucial for achieving the desired speed and control.

- Pressure Drop:

The movement of the spool can result in pressure drops across the valve.

Efficient design minimizes pressure losses to maintain system performance.

6. Sealing and Leakage:

- Sealing Mechanisms:

Spool valves employ various sealing methods, including O-rings or lip seals, to prevent leakage.

Proper sealing ensures the integrity of the system.

- Leakage Considerations:

Despite effective seals, some degree of internal leakage can occur.

Understanding and minimizing leakage is crucial for maintaining system efficiency.

7. Response Time and Dynamic Performance:

- Response Time:

The response time of a spool valve refers to the time it takes to shift from one position to another.

Factors like spool mass, actuation method, and system pressure influence response time.

- Dynamic Performance:

Dynamic performance considers the valve's behavior under changing conditions.

Accurate modeling and testing are essential for predicting and optimizing dynamic behavior.

8. Temperature and Fluid Compatibility:

- Temperature Effects:

Spool valves must operate effectively within the temperature range of the fluid or air they control.

Material selection and design considerations address potential temperature-related issues.

- Fluid Compatibility:

Compatibility with the fluid or air is crucial for the longevity of spool valves.

Corrosion resistance and material selection are key considerations.

Conclusion

Spool valves are indispensable components in fluid power systems, providing precise control over the direction of hydraulic fluid or compressed air. Their operating characteristics, including flow paths, actuation methods, centering mechanisms, types, flow control, pressure drop, sealing, response time, and compatibility, significantly influence system performance. Engineers and designers must carefully consider these characteristics during the selection, design, and optimization of spool valves to ensure the efficiency, reliability, and longevity of hydraulic and pneumatic systems.

Electro Hydraulic Servo Valves – Types – Characteristics and Performance

Introduction to Electro-Hydraulic Servo Valves:

Definition and Purpose:

An electro-hydraulic servo valve is a type of valve that combines electrical and hydraulic elements to control the flow of hydraulic fluid. It is a key component in closed-loop control systems, providing accurate and rapid adjustments to maintain desired system parameters. EHSVs are widely used in applications where precise control of hydraulic actuators is essential, such as aerospace, industrial automation, and robotics.

Basic Components:

1. Nozzle-Flapper Assembly:

The core of an electro-hydraulic servo valve is the nozzle-flapper assembly.

It consists of a nozzle that controls the flow of hydraulic fluid and a flapper that responds to electrical input.

2. Torque Motor:

The torque motor is an electromagnetic device that generates a rotational force to position the flapper.

It converts electrical signals into mechanical movement.

3. Feedback Mechanism:

EHSVs often include a feedback mechanism to provide information about the valve's position.

This feedback is crucial for closed-loop control systems to maintain accurate positioning.

Types of Electro-Hydraulic Servo Valves:

1. Flapper-Nozzle Type:

The flapper-nozzle type is the most common design for electro-hydraulic servo valves.

It employs a flapper that moves in response to electrical signals, controlling the flow of hydraulic fluid through a nozzle.

2. Jet Pipe Type:

The jet pipe type utilizes a jet pipe to control the hydraulic flow.

It offers high reliability and is often used in applications with stringent performance requirements.

3. Spool Type:

The spool type electro-hydraulic servo valve uses a spool to regulate fluid flow.

It is suitable for applications where precise control is essential, and it offers good dynamic response.

4. Deflector Type:

The deflector type employs a movable deflector to control the hydraulic fluid's direction.

It is known for its simplicity and reliability.

Characteristics of Electro-Hydraulic Servo Valves:

Understanding the characteristics of electro-hydraulic servo valves is crucial for their proper application in various systems.

1. Linearity:

Linearity refers to the relationship between the electrical input and the resulting hydraulic output.

Achieving linearity is essential for accurate and predictable control.

2. Frequency Response:

Frequency response indicates how quickly the servo valve can respond to changes in the input signal.

High-frequency response is crucial for applications requiring rapid and precise adjustments.

3. Accuracy:

Accuracy is a measure of how closely the valve can achieve the desired position or flow.

Factors such as hysteresis and deadband influence accuracy.

4. Hysteresis:

Hysteresis is the phenomenon where the output of the valve depends on its previous state.

Minimizing hysteresis is vital for precise control and repeatability.

5. Deadband:

Deadband is the range of input signals where there is no output response.

Minimizing deadband is crucial for achieving accurate control around the desired setpoint.

6. Sensitivity:

Sensitivity refers to the responsiveness of the servo valve to small changes in the input signal.

High sensitivity allows for fine control in applications where precision is essential.

7. Temperature Stability:

The performance of electro-hydraulic servo valves can be influenced by temperature variations.

Designs that maintain stability across a range of temperatures are preferred in many applications.

8. Reliability and Maintenance:

Electro-hydraulic servo valves must be reliable for continuous operation.

Regular maintenance practices, such as seal replacements, may be necessary to ensure long-term performance.

Performance Considerations:

1. Dynamic Response:

Dynamic response is crucial for applications requiring rapid changes in hydraulic flow.

It depends on factors such as the valve design, size, and the characteristics of the fluid.

2. Load Sensitivity:

Load sensitivity refers to the valve's ability to maintain consistent performance under varying loads.

Well-designed electro-hydraulic servo valves minimize the impact of external forces on their operation.

3. Pressure and Flow Ratings:

The pressure and flow ratings of electro-hydraulic servo valves determine their suitability for specific applications.

Understanding the system requirements and selecting valves with appropriate ratings is essential.

4. Environmental Considerations:

Electro-hydraulic servo valves may be exposed to harsh environmental conditions.

Designs that account for factors such as humidity, dust, and vibration enhance overall performance and longevity.

5. Integration with Control Systems:

Compatibility with control systems, such as programmable logic controllers (PLCs) or computer-based controllers, is crucial.

Effective integration ensures seamless communication and coordination within the overall system.

Conclusion:

Electro-hydraulic servo valves play a pivotal role in achieving precise control in hydraulic systems. Their intricate design, incorporating electrical and hydraulic elements, enables accurate positioning of hydraulic actuators in various industrial applications. Understanding the types, characteristics, and performance considerations of electro-hydraulic servo valves is essential for engineers and system designers to select, integrate, and optimize these components effectively. As technology advances, ongoing research and development continue to enhance the capabilities and reliability of electro-hydraulic servo valves, contributing to their widespread use in critical applications across different industries.

CHAPTER THREE

Circuit Design for Hydraulic and Pneumatics

Typical Design Methods – Sequencing Circuits Design - Combinational Logic Circuit Design - Cascade Method – KV Mapping - Electrical Control of Pneumatic and Hydraulic Circuits - Use of Relays, Timers, Counters and PLC in pneumatics and hydraulics

Typical Design Methods

Designing circuits for hydraulics and pneumatics involves creating systems that control the flow of fluids (liquid or gas) to achieve specific mechanical tasks. These systems are widely used in various industries, including manufacturing, aerospace, automotive, and more. In this extensive explanation, we'll delve into the typical design methods for circuit design in both hydraulics and pneumatics.

Introduction to Hydraulics and Pneumatics:

Hydraulics and pneumatics are branches of fluid power, utilizing the mechanical properties of liquids (hydraulics) and gases (pneumatics) to transmit power and control motion. These systems offer advantages such as high power density, precise control, and versatility in various applications.

1. System Requirements and Specifications:

Before diving into the design process, it's crucial to understand the system requirements and specifications. This involves determining the intended application, desired performance parameters, environmental conditions, and safety considerations. For instance, a hydraulic system for heavy machinery may require high force and precision, while a pneumatic system for light manufacturing might prioritize speed and simplicity.

2. Fluid Selection:

Selecting the appropriate fluid is a critical step in the design process. In hydraulics, oil-based fluids are common due to their lubricating properties and high power density. Pneumatic systems typically use compressed air, which is readily available and cost-effective. The choice of fluid impacts system efficiency, temperature stability, and overall performance.

3. Component Selection:

Selecting suitable components is fundamental to circuit design. Common hydraulic and pneumatic components include pumps, actuators, valves, filters, and reservoirs. The choice of components depends on factors like system pressure, flow rates, temperature, and the specific requirements of the application.

Pumps: In hydraulic systems, pumps are responsible for generating fluid flow, while compressors serve this purpose in pneumatic systems. Various pump and compressor types are available, each with specific advantages and limitations.

Valves: Valves control fluid flow within the system. Hydraulic and pneumatic valves come in different types such as directional control valves, pressure control valves, and flow control valves. Proper selection and placement of valves are crucial for achieving the desired control and functionality.

Actuators: Actuators convert fluid energy into mechanical motion. In hydraulics, cylinders and motors are common actuators, while pneumatic systems often use cylinders. The choice between hydraulic and pneumatic actuators depends on factors like force requirements, speed, and precision.

4. Circuit Design:

Circuit design involves creating a schematic that represents the flow of fluid within the system. This includes the arrangement of components, connection paths, and control logic. Various circuit designs are employed based on the application requirements:

Hydraulic Circuit Design: Hydraulic circuits are designed to control the flow and pressure of hydraulic fluid. Common hydraulic circuits include open center, closed center, and load-sensing systems. The selection depends on factors like energy efficiency, response time, and system complexity.

Pneumatic Circuit Design: Pneumatic circuits focus on controlling the flow and pressure of compressed air. Sequential control, pressure control, and flow control are key considerations. Pneumatic circuits often emphasize simplicity and quick response times.

5. Safety Considerations:

Safety is paramount in fluid power systems. Hydraulic and pneumatic systems operate under high pressures, and failure can lead to serious consequences. Safety features such as relief valves, pressure sensors, and emergency stop mechanisms must be incorporated into the design to prevent overpressure situations and ensure operator safety.

6. Simulation and Analysis:

Before implementation, it's beneficial to simulate the designed circuit to identify potential issues and optimize performance. Simulation tools can help analyze fluid dynamics, pressure variations, and overall system behavior. This step aids in refining the design, ensuring it meets performance specifications and operates efficiently.

7. Prototyping and Testing:

After simulation and analysis, the next step is prototyping. Building a physical prototype allows for real-world testing and validation of the designed circuit. Testing helps identify any unforeseen issues, validates the performance against specifications, and allows for adjustments and refinements.

8. Integration and Installation:

Once the design is validated, the circuit can be integrated into the larger system. Proper installation is crucial, ensuring that all components are connected correctly, and the system operates within specified parameters. Integration may involve considerations such as mounting, plumbing, and electrical connections.

9. Maintenance and Troubleshooting:

Hydraulic and pneumatic systems require regular maintenance to ensure longevity and optimal performance. Establishing a maintenance schedule that includes fluid checks, filter replacements, and component inspections is essential. Additionally, a well-designed system should facilitate troubleshooting by incorporating diagnostic features and clear documentation.

10. Documentation:

Comprehensive documentation is vital throughout the design process. This includes detailed schematics, component specifications, operating manuals, and maintenance procedures. Clear documentation is invaluable for future reference, system upgrades, and troubleshooting.

Conclusion:

Designing circuits for hydraulics and pneumatics is a complex process that requires a deep understanding of fluid dynamics, control systems, and mechanical engineering principles. The integration of suitable components, adherence to safety standards, and a systematic approach to design and testing are crucial for the successful implementation of fluid power systems. Whether in heavy industry, manufacturing, or other applications, well-designed hydraulic and pneumatic circuits play a vital role in powering and controlling a wide array of mechanical processes.

Sequencing Circuits Design

Designing sequencing circuits for hydraulics and pneumatics involves the integration of fluid power principles with electronic control systems to achieve precise and coordinated control of hydraulic and pneumatic actuators. This intersection of mechanical and electronic engineering is crucial in various industrial applications where controlled motion and force are essential. In this extensive explanation, we will delve into the complexities of sequencing circuit design in the realms of both hydraulics and pneumatics.

1. Introduction to Fluid Power Sequencing:

Fluid power systems, encompassing both hydraulics and pneumatics, rely on the controlled movement of fluids (liquid or gas) to transmit power and perform mechanical work. Sequencing in these systems involves orchestrating the activation and deactivation of hydraulic cylinders or pneumatic actuators in a specific order to achieve a desired motion or force.

2. Components of Fluid Power Sequencing Circuits:

Actuators: In both hydraulics and pneumatics, actuators are the components responsible for converting fluid energy into mechanical motion. Hydraulic systems commonly use cylinders and motors, while pneumatic systems often employ pneumatic cylinders. These actuators execute the physical tasks dictated by the sequencing circuit.

Valves: Valves play a crucial role in fluid power sequencing circuits. They control the flow and pressure of the fluid, directing it to specific actuators at the right time. Directional control valves, pressure control valves, and flow control valves are common in these applications.

Sensors: Sensors detect various parameters in the system, providing feedback to the sequencing circuit. For example, position sensors can signal when an actuator has reached a specific position, enabling the sequencer to proceed to the next step.

Sequencers/Controllers: The heart of the sequencing circuit is the sequencer or controller. In modern applications, programmable logic controllers (PLCs) are often employed. These devices execute custom-coded sequences based on inputs from sensors and other control elements.

Timers and Relays: Timing is critical in fluid power sequencing. Timers and relays ensure that specific actions occur at predetermined intervals. Timers dictate the duration of a particular step, while relays control the activation of specific components.

3. Design Considerations for Hydraulics:

Fluid Selection: Hydraulic systems typically use oil-based fluids due to their lubricating properties and high power density. The choice of fluid impacts the system's efficiency, temperature stability, and overall performance. The fluid should be selected based on the specific requirements of the application.

Pressure and Flow Requirements: Understanding the pressure and flow requirements of the hydraulic system is crucial for proper sequencing. Different actuators may demand varying pressure levels, and the sequencing circuit must be designed to accommodate these variations.

Cylinder Size and Type: The size and type of hydraulic cylinders significantly influence the system's performance. Factors such as load requirements, speed, and precision dictate the selection of cylinder size and type.

4. Design Considerations for Pneumatics:

Compressed Air Quality: Pneumatic systems rely on compressed air, and the quality of this air is essential. Filters and dryers are often integrated into pneumatic sequencing circuits to ensure that the compressed air is clean and dry, preventing damage to components.

Pressure and Flow Requirements: Like in hydraulics, understanding the pressure and flow requirements is crucial in pneumatic sequencing circuit design. The system must be designed to provide the necessary pressure for effective operation.

Pneumatic Actuator Selection: Pneumatic cylinders come in various types, including single-acting and double-acting. The selection depends on the application's requirements, such as the need for both pushing and pulling motions.

5. Sequential Control Strategies:

Sequential Valve Actuation: The most basic form of fluid power sequencing involves the sequential actuation of valves. Each valve corresponds to a specific actuator or action, and the sequence progresses as valves open and close in a predefined order.

Programmable Logic Controllers (PLCs): PLCs are widely used in modern fluid power sequencing circuits. These digital controllers can execute complex sequences with precision. Programming languages like ladder logic are commonly employed to design sequences that involve conditional statements, loops, and timers.

State Machines: Sequencing circuits in fluid power systems often resemble state machines. Different states represent specific steps in the sequence, and transitions between states are triggered by inputs from sensors or timers.

6. Systematic Circuit Design Process:

Define Sequence Requirements: Clearly define the sequence requirements based on the application. Understand the desired order of actions, timing constraints, and any dependencies between different steps.

Select Components: Choose the appropriate actuators, valves, sensors, and controllers based on the system requirements. Ensure compatibility between components and consider factors such as pressure ratings, flow rates, and response times.

Create a Schematic: Develop a schematic diagram that illustrates the flow of fluid, the placement of valves, and the connections between different components. The schematic serves as a visual representation of the sequencing circuit.

Integrate Control Logic: Implement the control logic using a sequencer or PLC. Program the controller to execute the desired sequence, considering inputs from sensors and incorporating timing elements.

Simulate and Test: Utilize simulation tools to test the sequencing circuit in a virtual environment. This step helps identify potential issues, refine the design, and ensure that the sequence operates as intended.

Build and Install: Construct a physical prototype based on the schematic and test the sequencing circuit in real-world conditions. Install the circuit into the larger hydraulic or pneumatic system, considering factors like plumbing, mounting, and electrical connections.

Commission and Optimize: Commission the system, ensuring that the sequencing circuit performs according to specifications. Fine-tune the sequence and optimize parameters based on actual performance.

7. Applications of Fluid Power Sequencing:

Manufacturing Automation: Fluid power sequencing is extensively used in manufacturing automation, where precise control of hydraulic and pneumatic actuators is essential for tasks such as material handling, assembly, and packaging.

Heavy Machinery: Industries involving heavy machinery, such as construction and mining, rely on fluid power sequencing for controlled movement of equipment, ensuring safety and efficiency.

Aerospace: In aerospace applications, fluid power sequencing is employed for tasks like controlling landing gear, deploying flaps, and managing other critical aircraft systems.

Robotics: Robotics often integrate fluid power sequencing for controlling the motion of robotic arms, grippers, and other components.

Material Processing: Fluid power sequencing is vital in material processing industries for tasks like cutting, bending, and forming materials with precision.

8. Safety Considerations:

Pressure Relief Valves: Incorporate pressure relief valves in the system to prevent overpressure situations, which could lead to equipment failure or safety hazards.

Emergency Stop Mechanisms: Implement emergency stop mechanisms that can quickly deactivate the entire system in case of unforeseen issues or emergencies.

Redundancy and Fail-Safe Design: Consider redundancy in critical components and design fail-safe mechanisms to ensure that the system can respond safely to any component failures.

9. Maintenance and Troubleshooting:

Regular Inspection: Schedule regular inspections of the fluid power system, checking for leaks, wear and tear, and proper functioning of valves and actuators.

Fluid Analysis: Periodically analyze the condition of the hydraulic or pneumatic fluid to ensure it meets the required specifications. Contaminated or degraded fluid can adversely affect system performance.

Diagnostic Features: Incorporate diagnostic features into the sequencing circuit, enabling easy identification and troubleshooting of issues. This can include error codes, alarms, and self-diagnostic routines.

10. Documentation:

Comprehensive Manuals: Create comprehensive manuals that document the design, installation, operation, and maintenance procedures for the fluid power sequencing circuit. This documentation is invaluable for future reference and training.

As-Built Drawings: Maintain accurate as-built drawings that reflect any changes or modifications made to the sequencing circuit during its lifecycle.

Conclusion:

Sequencing circuit design in hydraulics and pneumatics is a multidisciplinary endeavor, requiring expertise in fluid power, electronics, and control systems. The integration of precise control mechanisms with hydraulic and pneumatic actuators enables the systematic execution of sequences, facilitating a wide range of industrial applications. Whether in manufacturing, aerospace, robotics, or other industries, well-designed fluid power sequencing circuits play a crucial role in enhancing efficiency, safety, and precision in complex mechanical systems.

Combinational Logic Circuit Design

The application of combinational logic circuit design in hydraulics and pneumatics represents an innovative integration of electronic control with fluid power systems. Combinational logic circuits, commonly used in digital electronics, are employed to control and coordinate the operation of hydraulic and pneumatic components. In this in-depth exploration, we'll delve into the principles, components, design methodologies, and applications of combinational logic circuits in the context of hydraulics and pneumatics.

1. Introduction to Combinational Logic in Fluid Power Systems:

Combinational logic circuits are foundational elements in digital electronics that perform Boolean logic operations based on input signals to produce specific output states. In the context of fluid power systems—hydraulics and pneumatics—combinational logic is leveraged to control valves, actuators, and other components, enabling precise and coordinated operation.

2. Basic Components of Combinational Logic in Fluid Power Systems:

Actuators: Actuators in fluid power systems are responsible for converting fluid energy into mechanical motion. Hydraulic systems typically use cylinders and motors, while pneumatic systems commonly employ pneumatic cylinders. The movement of these actuators is controlled by the combinational logic circuit.

Valves: Valves are integral to fluid power systems, regulating the flow and direction of hydraulic fluid or compressed air. In combinational logic circuits, valves are manipulated based on logical operations, influencing the behavior of the system.

Sensors: Sensors play a critical role in providing feedback to the combinational logic circuit. They detect various parameters such as pressure, position, or temperature, allowing the system to respond intelligently to changes in the environment.

PLCs (Programmable Logic Controllers): PLCs are the brain of the combinational logic circuit. These programmable devices execute custom-coded sequences and logic operations based on input signals from sensors, switches, or other sources.

Input Devices: Input devices, including switches and other manual controls, are essential for user interaction with the fluid power system. These inputs can trigger specific logic operations, influencing the state of the combinational logic circuit.

Output Devices: Output devices represent the tangible results of the combinational logic operations. They include indicators, alarms, and, most importantly, the control of actuators and valves to achieve desired motion or force.

3. Principles of Combinational Logic in Fluid Power Systems:

Boolean Logic Operations: Combinational logic circuits operate based on Boolean logic, which involves logical operations such as AND, OR, and NOT. In the context of fluid power systems, these operations determine the state of valves, the activation of actuators, and the overall behavior of the system.

Truth Tables: Truth tables are used to represent the relationship between input and output states in combinational logic circuits. These tables provide a systematic way to understand how different combinations of inputs result in specific outputs.

Logical Gates: Logical gates, including AND, OR, and NOT gates, are fundamental building blocks of combinational logic circuits. These gates are implemented electronically and determine the logical relationships between input and output signals.

4. Design Methodologies for Combinational Logic in Fluid Power Systems:

Define System Requirements: The first step in designing a combinational logic circuit for fluid power systems is to clearly define the system requirements. This involves understanding the desired sequence of actions, logical conditions for different states, and any safety considerations.

Identify Input Signals: Identify the input signals that will influence the logic operations of the system. These signals can come from sensors, switches, or other sources and may represent parameters such as pressure levels, position feedback, or manual input.

Choose Logical Operations: Based on the system requirements, choose the appropriate logical operations (AND, OR, NOT) to govern the behavior of the combinational logic circuit. For example, an AND operation might be used to ensure that two conditions must be met for a certain action to occur.

Develop Truth Tables: Create truth tables to systematically map the relationship between input signals and desired output states. This step helps in visualizing the logic operations and ensures that the circuit behaves as intended for all possible input combinations.

Select Components: Choose the necessary components, including logical gates, PLCs, and other electronic elements, based on the identified logical operations and system requirements.

Implement Logic Operations: Implement the chosen logic operations using electronic components. This may involve configuring logical gates or programming a PLC to execute the desired logic.

Integration with Fluid Power Components: Integrate the combinational logic circuit with the fluid power components, such as valves and actuators. Ensure that the logic operations directly control the state and behavior of these components.

Testing and Simulation: Test the combinational logic circuit in a controlled environment or using simulation tools. Verify that the logic operations produce the expected results and that the system behaves as intended.

Iterative Refinement: Based on testing results, refine the design iteratively. This may involve adjusting logical operations, modifying input conditions, or fine-tuning the response of the fluid power system.

5. Applications of Combinational Logic in Fluid Power Systems:

Automated Manufacturing: Combinational logic circuits find extensive use in automated manufacturing processes where precise control of hydraulic and pneumatic components is crucial. This includes tasks such as material handling, assembly, and quality control.

Motion Control Systems: In systems requiring controlled motion, such as robotics and conveyor systems, combinational logic circuits are employed to coordinate the movement of actuators and valves.

Hydraulic Presses: Combinational logic is often used in hydraulic presses for tasks like stamping, molding, or forming materials. The logic circuit ensures the proper sequencing of actions to achieve the desired result.

Pneumatic Clamping Systems: In applications where pneumatic clamping is required, combinational logic circuits control the activation and deactivation of clamping mechanisms based on specific conditions.

Aerospace Systems: Fluid power systems in aerospace applications utilize combinational logic for tasks such as controlling landing gear, deploying flaps, and managing other critical systems in aircraft.

6. Safety Considerations:

Emergency Shutdown Logic: Integrate emergency shutdown logic into the combinational circuit to rapidly deactivate the system in case of safety hazards or unforeseen issues.

Redundancy and Fault Tolerance: Consider incorporating redundancy in critical components and implementing fault-tolerant designs to ensure the reliability and safety of the fluid power system.

Safety Interlocks: Implement safety interlocks that prevent certain actions or movements unless specific safety conditions are met. This can include the use of sensors to detect potential hazards.

7. Maintenance and Troubleshooting:

Diagnostic Features: Include diagnostic features in the combinational logic circuit to facilitate troubleshooting. These features may include error codes, status indicators, and self-diagnostic routines.

Regular Inspection: Schedule regular inspections of the fluid power system, checking for wear and tear, loose connections, and the proper functioning of sensors and actuators.

Documentation: Maintain comprehensive documentation that includes circuit diagrams, truth tables, and logic descriptions. This documentation is invaluable for troubleshooting and future maintenance.

8. Integration with Human-Machine Interface (HMI):

User Interaction: Integrate the combinational logic circuit with a Human-Machine Interface (HMI) to allow users to interact with the system. This can include touchscreens, buttons, or other input devices that influence the logic operations.

Visual Feedback: Provide visual feedback on the HMI to inform users about the current state of the system, any ongoing sequences, or potential issues. This enhances the user's understanding and control over the fluid power system.

9. Future Trends and Innovations:

Smart Fluid Power Systems: The integration of artificial intelligence and machine learning into fluid power systems is an emerging trend. Smart systems can adapt their behavior based on real-time data, improving efficiency and responsiveness.

Industry 4.0 Integration: The concept of Industry 4.0, which emphasizes the interconnectedness of industrial processes, is influencing fluid power systems. Integration with data networks allows for remote monitoring, predictive maintenance, and enhanced control.

Advanced Sensor Technologies: Advancements in sensor technologies, including the use of IoT (Internet of Things) devices, contribute to more accurate and real-time feedback. This, in turn, enhances the capabilities of combinational logic circuits in fluid power systems.

10. Conclusion:

The application of combinational logic circuit design in hydraulics and pneumatics represents a synergistic fusion of digital electronics with fluid power principles. This integration enables precise control, coordination, and automation of hydraulic and pneumatic systems in various industrial applications. From manufacturing and robotics to aerospace and beyond, combinational logic circuits play a pivotal role in enhancing efficiency, safety, and adaptability in complex fluid power systems. As technology continues to evolve, the future holds exciting possibilities for further innovations in the intersection of electronics and fluid power engineering.

Cascade Method

The cascade method in hydraulics and pneumatics refers to a control strategy that involves connecting multiple actuators in a sequential manner, where the output from one actuator becomes the input for the next. This approach allows for the creation of complex motion sequences or tasks by breaking them down into a series of simpler, interconnected steps. In this comprehensive explanation, we will delve into the principles, components, design considerations, and applications of the cascade method in both hydraulics and pneumatics.

1. Introduction to Cascade Method:

The cascade method is a systematic approach to fluid power control, specifically designed for achieving coordinated and sequential motion in hydraulic and pneumatic systems. This method is based on the principle of connecting multiple actuators in a cascade or series, where the output of one actuator becomes the input for the next actuator in the sequence. This enables the execution of complex tasks through the controlled movement of interconnected actuators.

2. Basic Components of Cascade Systems:

Actuators: Actuators, such as hydraulic cylinders or pneumatic cylinders, are essential components in cascade systems. These devices are responsible for converting fluid energy into mechanical motion. The output motion of one actuator becomes the input for the next actuator in the cascade.

Valves: Directional control valves play a crucial role in managing the flow of fluid within cascade systems. These valves are responsible for directing the fluid to the appropriate actuator in the sequence, enabling controlled and sequential movement.

Sensors: Sensors provide feedback to the control system, allowing it to monitor the position, speed, or other relevant parameters of the actuators. This feedback is essential for precise control and coordination within the cascade system.

PLCs (Programmable Logic Controllers): PLCs are the brains behind cascade systems. They execute custom-coded sequences and logic operations based on input signals from sensors, switches, or other sources. PLCs are programmable, allowing for flexibility in designing complex motion sequences.

Input Devices: Input devices, such as switches or HMI (Human-Machine Interface) elements, allow users to initiate or modify the cascade sequence. These inputs can trigger the start of a sequence or introduce changes in the ongoing motion.

Output Devices: Output devices represent the physical results of the cascade sequence. These devices can include indicators, alarms, or other elements that signify the completion of a particular motion step.

3. Principles of Cascade Systems:

Sequential Actuation: The fundamental principle of cascade systems is sequential actuation, where one actuator is activated in a specific order, and its motion becomes the input for the next actuator in the sequence. This sequential activation allows for the controlled progression of a task.

Feedback Control: Cascade systems rely on feedback control mechanisms to ensure that each actuator's position or status is monitored. Sensors provide real-time feedback to the control system, allowing for adjustments and corrections during the cascade sequence.

Directional Control: Directional control valves play a pivotal role in managing the flow of fluid between actuators. These valves ensure that the fluid is directed to the correct actuator based on the current position and status of the cascade system.

4. Design Considerations for Cascade Systems:

Task Decomposition: Break down the overall task or motion sequence into individual steps. Identify the sequence of actions required to achieve the desired result. Each step corresponds to the activation of a specific actuator in the cascade.

Actuator Selection: Choose appropriate actuators based on the requirements of each step in the sequence. Consider factors such as load capacity, speed, precision, and any environmental conditions that may impact actuator performance.

Valve Selection: Select directional control valves that can manage the flow of fluid between actuators. Valve types, such as 2/2-way or 3/2-way valves, depend on the specific needs of the cascade system.

Sensor Placement: Determine the optimal placement of sensors to provide accurate feedback on actuator positions. Sensors should be strategically located to capture relevant data for effective control.

PLC Programming: Program the PLC to execute the cascade sequence based on input signals from sensors and other sources. Implement logic operations, timers, and conditional statements to control the timing and conditions for actuator activation.

Safety Considerations: Incorporate safety features into the cascade system design. Emergency stop mechanisms, pressure relief valves, and safety interlocks ensure the safe operation of the system and prevent potential hazards.

Testing and Simulation: Test the cascade system in a controlled environment or using simulation tools before implementation. Simulation helps identify potential issues, refine the design, and ensure that the cascade sequence operates as intended.

5. Applications of Cascade Systems:

Material Handling: Cascade systems are widely used in material handling applications, such as conveyor systems or sorting machines. The sequential activation of actuators enables the precise movement and positioning of materials.

Assembly Lines: In manufacturing assembly lines, cascade systems are employed to control the movement of robotic arms or other automated systems. This ensures the accurate assembly of components in a predefined sequence.

Packaging Systems: Cascade systems play a crucial role in packaging machinery, where controlled motion is required for tasks like filling, sealing, and labeling. The sequential activation of actuators ensures the efficient packaging of products.

Automated Warehousing: In automated warehouses, cascade systems are utilized for tasks like retrieving and storing goods. The controlled movement of actuators enables efficient and organized warehouse operations.

Machine Tools: Cascade systems are integrated into machine tools for tasks such as cutting, shaping, or milling. The sequential activation of actuators contributes to the precision and efficiency of machining processes.

6. Advanced Cascade System Concepts:

Position Synchronization: Advanced cascade systems may incorporate position synchronization mechanisms to ensure that multiple actuators reach their target positions simultaneously. This is crucial for applications requiring precise alignment or coordination.

Load Balancing: In some applications, load balancing features may be introduced to distribute loads evenly among multiple actuators. This enhances the overall efficiency and lifespan of the cascade system.

Adaptive Control: Adaptive control concepts, such as fuzzy logic or machine learning algorithms, can be applied to cascade systems for adaptive and self-optimizing behavior. These systems can adapt to changes in operating conditions or task requirements.

7. Maintenance and Troubleshooting:

Regular Inspection: Schedule regular inspections of the cascade system to check for wear and tear, leaks, and the proper functioning of valves and actuators. This proactive approach helps identify potential issues before they escalate.

Sensor Calibration: Calibrate sensors regularly to ensure accurate feedback. Misaligned or faulty sensors can lead to errors in the cascade sequence, impacting the overall performance of the system.

Diagnostic Features: Incorporate diagnostic features into the PLC programming to facilitate troubleshooting. This can include error codes, status indicators, and self-diagnostic routines that provide insights into the health of the cascade system.

8. Future Trends in Cascade Systems:

Industry 4.0 Integration: The integration of cascade systems with Industry 4.0 concepts involves connectivity, data exchange, and automation. Cascade systems may become part of interconnected smart factories, allowing for remote monitoring, predictive maintenance, and real-time optimization.

IoT Integration: The Internet of Things (IoT) can be leveraged to enhance the capabilities of cascade systems. IoT-enabled sensors and actuators can provide data for analysis, contributing to improved efficiency and decision-making.

Advanced Human-Machine Interface (HMI): Advanced HMIs with intuitive visualization and control capabilities may become more prevalent in cascade systems. Touchscreens, augmented reality interfaces, and voice commands could enhance user interaction and control.

9. Conclusion:

The cascade method in hydraulics and pneumatics represents a sophisticated approach to fluid power control, enabling the precise and coordinated movement of multiple actuators. By breaking down complex tasks into a series of interconnected steps, cascade systems contribute to the efficiency and versatility of various industrial applications. From material handling and assembly lines to packaging systems and beyond, cascade systems play a pivotal role in achieving controlled motion and automation. As technology continues to advance, the integration of cascade systems with emerging concepts such as Industry 4.0 and IoT promises to further enhance their capabilities, paving the way for more intelligent and adaptive fluid power control systems.

KV Mapping

The cascade method in hydraulics and pneumatics refers to a control strategy that involves connecting multiple actuators in a sequential manner, where the output from one actuator becomes the input for the next. This approach allows for the creation of complex motion sequences or tasks by breaking them down into a series of simpler, interconnected steps. In this comprehensive explanation, we will delve into the principles, components, design considerations, and applications of the cascade method in both hydraulics and pneumatics.

1. Introduction to Cascade Method:

The cascade method is a systematic approach to fluid power control, specifically designed for achieving coordinated and sequential motion in hydraulic and pneumatic systems. This method is based on the principle of connecting multiple actuators in a cascade or series, where the output of one actuator becomes the input for the next actuator in the sequence. This enables the execution of complex tasks through the controlled movement of interconnected actuators.

2. Basic Components of Cascade Systems:

Actuators: Actuators, such as hydraulic cylinders or pneumatic cylinders, are essential components in cascade systems. These devices are responsible for converting fluid energy into mechanical motion. The output motion of one actuator becomes the input for the next actuator in the cascade.

Valves: Directional control valves play a crucial role in managing the flow of fluid within cascade systems. These valves are responsible for directing the fluid to the appropriate actuator in the sequence, enabling controlled and sequential movement.

Sensors: Sensors provide feedback to the control system, allowing it to monitor the position, speed, or other relevant parameters of the actuators. This feedback is essential for precise control and coordination within the cascade system.

PLCs (Programmable Logic Controllers): PLCs are the brains behind cascade systems. They execute custom-coded sequences and logic operations based on input signals from sensors, switches, or other sources. PLCs are programmable, allowing for flexibility in designing complex motion sequences.

Input Devices: Input devices, such as switches or HMI (Human-Machine Interface) elements, allow users to initiate or modify the cascade sequence. These inputs can trigger the start of a sequence or introduce changes in the ongoing motion.

Output Devices: Output devices represent the physical results of the cascade sequence. These devices can include indicators, alarms, or other elements that signify the completion of a particular motion step.

3. Principles of Cascade Systems:

Sequential Actuation: The fundamental principle of cascade systems is sequential actuation, where one actuator is activated in a specific order, and its motion becomes the input for the next actuator in the sequence. This sequential activation allows for the controlled progression of a task.

Feedback Control: Cascade systems rely on feedback control mechanisms to ensure that each actuator's position or status is monitored. Sensors provide real-time feedback to the control system, allowing for adjustments and corrections during the cascade sequence.

Directional Control: Directional control valves play a pivotal role in managing the flow of fluid between actuators. These valves ensure that the fluid is directed to the correct actuator based on the current position and status of the cascade system.

4. Design Considerations for Cascade Systems:

Task Decomposition: Break down the overall task or motion sequence into individual steps. Identify the sequence of actions required to achieve the desired result. Each step corresponds to the activation of a specific actuator in the cascade.

Actuator Selection: Choose appropriate actuators based on the requirements of each step in the sequence. Consider factors such as load capacity, speed, precision, and any environmental conditions that may impact actuator performance.

Valve Selection: Select directional control valves that can manage the flow of fluid between actuators. Valve types, such as 2/2-way or 3/2-way valves, depend on the specific needs of the cascade system.

Sensor Placement: Determine the optimal placement of sensors to provide accurate feedback on actuator positions. Sensors should be strategically located to capture relevant data for effective control.

PLC Programming: Program the PLC to execute the cascade sequence based on input signals from sensors and other sources. Implement logic operations, timers, and conditional statements to control the timing and conditions for actuator activation.

Safety Considerations: Incorporate safety features into the cascade system design. Emergency stop mechanisms, pressure relief valves, and safety interlocks ensure the safe operation of the system and prevent potential hazards.

Testing and Simulation: Test the cascade system in a controlled environment or using simulation tools before implementation. Simulation helps identify potential issues, refine the design, and ensure that the cascade sequence operates as intended.

5. Applications of Cascade Systems:

Material Handling: Cascade systems are widely used in material handling applications, such as conveyor systems or sorting machines. The sequential activation of actuators enables the precise movement and positioning of materials.

Assembly Lines: In manufacturing assembly lines, cascade systems are employed to control the movement of robotic arms or other automated systems. This ensures the accurate assembly of components in a predefined sequence.

Packaging Systems: Cascade systems play a crucial role in packaging machinery, where controlled motion is required for tasks like filling, sealing, and labeling. The sequential activation of actuators ensures the efficient packaging of products.

Automated Warehousing: In automated warehouses, cascade systems are utilized for tasks like retrieving and storing goods. The controlled movement of actuators enables efficient and organized warehouse operations.

Machine Tools: Cascade systems are integrated into machine tools for tasks such as cutting, shaping, or milling. The sequential activation of actuators contributes to the precision and efficiency of machining processes.

6. Advanced Cascade System Concepts:

Position Synchronization: Advanced cascade systems may incorporate position synchronization mechanisms to ensure that multiple actuators reach their target positions simultaneously. This is crucial for applications requiring precise alignment or coordination.

Load Balancing: In some applications, load balancing features may be introduced to distribute loads evenly among multiple actuators. This enhances the overall efficiency and lifespan of the cascade system.

Adaptive Control: Adaptive control concepts, such as fuzzy logic or machine learning algorithms, can be applied to cascade systems for adaptive and self-optimizing behavior. These systems can adapt to changes in operating conditions or task requirements.

7. Maintenance and Troubleshooting:

Regular Inspection: Schedule regular inspections of the cascade system to check for wear and tear, leaks, and the proper functioning of valves and actuators. This proactive approach helps identify potential issues before they escalate.

Sensor Calibration: Calibrate sensors regularly to ensure accurate feedback. Misaligned or faulty sensors can lead to errors in the cascade sequence, impacting the overall performance of the system.

Diagnostic Features: Incorporate diagnostic features into the PLC programming to facilitate troubleshooting. This can include error codes, status indicators, and self-diagnostic routines that provide insights into the health of the cascade system.

8. Future Trends in Cascade Systems:

Industry 4.0 Integration: The integration of cascade systems with Industry 4.0 concepts involves connectivity, data exchange, and automation. Cascade systems may become part of interconnected smart factories, allowing for remote monitoring, predictive maintenance, and real-time optimization.

IoT Integration: The Internet of Things (IoT) can be leveraged to enhance the capabilities of cascade systems. IoT-enabled sensors and actuators can provide data for analysis, contributing to improved efficiency and decision-making.

Advanced Human-Machine Interface (HMI): Advanced HMIs with intuitive visualization and control capabilities may become more prevalent in cascade systems. Touchscreens, augmented reality interfaces, and voice commands could enhance user interaction and control.

9. Conclusion:

The cascade method in hydraulics and pneumatics represents a sophisticated approach to fluid power control, enabling the precise and coordinated movement of multiple actuators. By breaking down complex tasks into a series of interconnected steps, cascade systems contribute to the efficiency and versatility of various industrial applications. From material handling and assembly lines to packaging systems and beyond, cascade systems play a pivotal role in achieving controlled motion and automation. As technology continues to advance, the integration of cascade systems with emerging concepts such as Industry 4.0 and IoT promises to further enhance their capabilities, paving the way for more intelligent and adaptive fluid power control systems.

Electrical Control of Pneumatic and Hydraulic Circuits

The electrical control of pneumatic and hydraulic circuits plays a crucial role in modern industrial automation. These control systems integrate electrical components with pneumatic and hydraulic technologies to achieve precise and efficient control of various processes and machinery. In this comprehensive explanation, we'll delve into the principles, components, design methodologies, and applications of electrical control in pneumatic and hydraulic circuits.

1. Introduction to Electrical Control in Fluid Power Systems:

Electrical control in fluid power systems, specifically pneumatic and hydraulic systems, involves the use of electrical signals to regulate and command the operation of components such as valves, actuators, and pumps. This integration of electrical and fluid power technologies enables automation, improved precision, and enhanced safety in diverse industrial applications.

2. Basic Components of Electrical Control Systems:

Sensors: Sensors are crucial components that provide feedback on various parameters such as pressure, flow rate, temperature, and position within the fluid power system. This information is essential for the control system to make informed decisions.

Actuators: Actuators, including hydraulic cylinders and pneumatic cylinders, are responsible for converting fluid power into mechanical motion. Electrical signals control the activation and deactivation of these actuators to achieve specific movements.

Valves: Directional control valves, proportional valves, and servo valves are common in fluid power systems. Electrical signals manipulate these valves to regulate the flow and direction of hydraulic fluid or compressed air, influencing the movement of actuators.

PLCs (Programmable Logic Controllers): PLCs serve as the brain of the electrical control system. These programmable devices receive input signals from sensors, process information based on pre-programmed logic, and generate output signals to control actuators and valves.

Relays and Contactors: Relays and contactors are used to switch high-power electrical circuits, allowing low-power control signals from PLCs to manage larger electrical loads, such as motors and solenoids.

HMI (Human-Machine Interface): HMIs provide a means for human interaction with the control system. Touchscreens, buttons, and indicators on HMIs allow operators to monitor and control the fluid power system.

Cabling and Wiring: Reliable cabling and wiring are essential to ensure proper communication between electrical components. Robust wiring practices are crucial to prevent electrical interference and maintain system integrity.

3. Principles of Electrical Control in Fluid Power Systems:

Closed-Loop Control: Many fluid power systems utilize closed-loop control, where feedback from sensors is continuously compared to a desired state. The control system adjusts the output based on this feedback to maintain or achieve the desired conditions.

Proportional Control: Proportional control involves adjusting the output proportionally to the difference between the actual and desired states. This enables fine-tuned control and precise positioning of hydraulic or pneumatic actuators.

On/Off Control: On/off control is a basic form of control where the system operates in discrete states. For example, a solenoid valve may be fully open or fully closed based on the control signal.

Feedback Systems: Feedback systems use sensors to provide real-time information about the state of the system. This feedback is crucial for the control system to make dynamic adjustments and ensure accurate performance.

4. Design Methodologies for Electrical Control in Fluid Power Systems:

System Requirements Analysis: Begin by analyzing the requirements of the fluid power system. Understand the desired functionalities, performance criteria, and safety considerations.

Sensor Selection: Choose sensors that are appropriate for the parameters you need to monitor. Common sensors include pressure transducers, flow sensors, temperature sensors, and position sensors.

Actuator Selection: Select actuators based on the application requirements, considering factors such as load capacity, speed, precision, and environmental conditions.

Valve Selection: Choose valves that suit the specific needs of the system. Directional control valves are essential for managing fluid flow, and proportional valves offer finer control in certain applications.

PLC Programming: Develop the logic for the PLC based on the system requirements. Program the PLC to interpret sensor feedback, make decisions, and generate control signals for actuators and valves.

Safety Considerations: Integrate safety features into the control system design. Emergency stop functions, safety interlocks, and fail-safe mechanisms contribute to the overall safety of the fluid power system.

Communication Protocols: Select appropriate communication protocols for the system. Common protocols include Modbus, Profibus, and CAN (Controller Area Network). Ensure reliable communication between PLCs and other components.

Testing and Simulation: Test the control system in a controlled environment or using simulation tools before full implementation. This step helps identify potential issues, validate the design, and fine-tune the control logic.

5. Applications of Electrical Control in Fluid Power Systems:

Industrial Automation: Electrical control in fluid power systems is extensively used in industrial automation for tasks such as material handling, assembly lines, and packaging. Automated processes benefit from precise control of actuators and valves.

Motion Control Systems: In applications requiring controlled motion, such as robotics and conveyor systems, electrical control plays a key role in coordinating the movement of hydraulic or pneumatic actuators.

Hydraulic Presses: Hydraulic presses in manufacturing operations utilize electrical control for precise control of force and speed during tasks like stamping, molding, or forming materials.

Aerospace Systems: Fluid power systems in aerospace applications use electrical control to manage critical functions such as landing gear operation, flaps deployment, and control surface movements.

Injection Molding Machines: Injection molding machines use electrical control to regulate hydraulic systems responsible for injecting molten material into molds with high precision.

6. Integration of Electrical Control with Pneumatics:

Solenoid Valves: Solenoid valves are commonly used in pneumatic systems and are controlled by electrical signals. The opening and closing of these valves regulate the flow of compressed air to pneumatic actuators.

Pneumatic Actuators: Pneumatic cylinders, controlled by solenoid valves, convert the energy from compressed air into mechanical motion. Electrical control determines when and how these actuators operate.

Proportional Pressure Control: Proportional pressure control in pneumatic systems involves adjusting the pressure of the compressed air based on electrical signals. This allows for precise control of force and speed in pneumatic actuators.

Pneumatic Sequencing: Electrical control is employed to sequence the operation of multiple pneumatic actuators, ensuring coordinated and timed movements in applications such as material handling.

7. Integration of Electrical Control with Hydraulics:

Servo Valves: Servo valves in hydraulic systems are controlled by electrical signals, allowing for precise control of hydraulic fluid flow and pressure. These valves are often used in applications requiring high accuracy.

Hydraulic Actuators: Hydraulic cylinders, controlled by servo valves or other directional control valves, convert the energy from pressurized hydraulic fluid into mechanical motion. Electrical control determines the activation and deactivation of these actuators.

Closed-Loop Hydraulic Systems: Closed-loop hydraulic systems utilize electrical feedback from sensors to continuously adjust the flow and pressure of hydraulic fluid. This results in accurate and dynamic control of hydraulic actuators.

Hydraulic Proportional Control: Similar to pneumatic systems, hydraulic systems can employ proportional control, adjusting the flow and pressure of hydraulic fluid proportionally to electrical input signals.

Hydraulic Press Brakes: In manufacturing, hydraulic press brakes use electrical control to precisely adjust the position and force of the hydraulic ram during bending operations.

8. Challenges in Electrical Control of Fluid Power Systems:

Integration Complexity: Integrating electrical control with fluid power systems can be complex, especially in applications with multiple actuators, sensors, and valves. Proper integration requires careful consideration of system requirements and thorough testing.

Maintenance and Reliability: Electrical components in fluid power systems are susceptible to wear and environmental factors. Regular maintenance is crucial to ensure the reliability and longevity of the control system.

Environmental Considerations: Fluid power systems often operate in challenging environments, including high temperatures, humidity, and exposure to contaminants. Electrical components must be selected and protected to withstand these conditions.

Safety Concerns: The integration of electrical control introduces safety considerations, especially in applications with large forces or high speeds. Implementing safety features and fail-safe mechanisms is essential to mitigate risks.

9. Future Trends and Innovations:

Smart Fluid Power Systems: The integration of smart technologies, including IoT (Internet of Things) and Industry 4.0 concepts, is a growing trend. Smart fluid power systems leverage data analytics and connectivity for remote monitoring, predictive maintenance, and real-time optimization.

Machine Learning in Control: Machine learning algorithms are being explored for advanced control strategies in fluid power systems. These algorithms can adapt and optimize control parameters based on historical data and real-time conditions.

Energy Efficiency: The emphasis on energy efficiency in industrial processes is driving innovations in the electrical control of fluid power systems. Variable frequency drives and energy recovery systems are being integrated to minimize energy consumption.

Advanced Sensor Technologies: Advancements in sensor technologies, including the use of non-contact sensors and advanced feedback systems, contribute to more accurate and reliable control in fluid power systems.

10. Conclusion:

The electrical control of pneumatic and hydraulic circuits represents a pivotal aspect of modern industrial automation. By integrating electrical components with fluid power systems, industries can achieve precise, efficient, and automated control of various processes. From manufacturing and robotics to aerospace and beyond, the synergy between electrical control and fluid power technologies enables sophisticated applications with improved safety, accuracy, and productivity. As technology continues to advance, the future holds exciting possibilities for smart and adaptive fluid power systems that contribute to the evolution of industrial processes.

Use of Relays, Timers, Counters and PLC in Pneumatics and Hydraulics

The use of relays, timers, counters, and programmable logic controllers (PLCs) in pneumatics and hydraulics plays a crucial role in achieving precise control, automation, and sequencing of fluid power systems. In this comprehensive explanation, we will explore the principles, applications, and integration of these components in both pneumatic and hydraulic systems.

1. Introduction to Relays, Timers, Counters, and PLCs:

Fluid power systems, including pneumatics and hydraulics, often require sophisticated control mechanisms to achieve specific tasks in industrial applications. Relays, timers, counters, and PLCs are essential components that contribute to the automation and optimization of these systems.

Relays: Relays are electromechanical devices that act as switches, allowing low-power control signals to manage higher-power circuits. They play a crucial role in controlling the activation and deactivation of various components in fluid power systems.

Timers: Timers are devices that provide a time delay before initiating or terminating a specific action. In fluid power systems, timers are used to control the duration of certain processes, ensuring precise timing in tasks such as actuator movement or valve switching.

Counters: Counters, as the name suggests, are used to count events or pulses. In fluid power systems, counters can track the number of cycles, rotations, or other events, providing valuable information for control and monitoring purposes.

PLCs: Programmable Logic Controllers (PLCs) are advanced digital devices that serve as the central control unit in many industrial applications. PLCs are programmable, allowing users to define logic operations, sequences, and control parameters for various components within the fluid power system.

2. Relays in Pneumatics and Hydraulics:

Relays are widely used in fluid power systems to interface low-power control circuits with high-power actuators, valves, and other components. In both pneumatic and hydraulic systems, relays serve several key functions:

Switching Control Signals: Relays act as switches to control the flow of control signals, allowing the activation or deactivation of components such as solenoid valves or contactors.

Safety Interlocks: Relays are often used in safety circuits to implement interlocks, ensuring that certain conditions are met before specific actions are allowed in the fluid power system.

Amplification of Control Signals: Control signals from sensors or PLCs may not have sufficient power to directly control large actuators or valves. Relays amplify these signals, enabling the control of high-power components.

Time-Delayed Switching: Some relays feature time-delay functions, allowing for time-delayed switching of components in the fluid power system. This is particularly useful in applications where precise timing is critical.

3. Timers in Pneumatics and Hydraulics:

Timers are essential components in fluid power systems, providing control over the duration of certain actions. In both pneumatic and hydraulic systems, timers find applications in various scenarios:

Actuator Control: Timers are used to control the duration of actuator movements. For example, in a pneumatic system, a timer may regulate how long a cylinder remains extended or retracted.

Valve Timing: Timers play a role in regulating the timing of valve operations. This is crucial for controlling the flow of compressed air or hydraulic fluid to different sections of the system.

Dwell Time Control: In applications where a specific dwell time is required, timers ensure that a certain state is maintained for a precise duration before transitioning to the next state.

Sequencing Control: Timers are integral to sequencing control in fluid power systems, allowing for the coordinated and timed activation of different components in a specific order.

4. Counters in Pneumatics and Hydraulics:

Counters are used in fluid power systems to keep track of events or cycles, providing valuable feedback for monitoring and control purposes. In both pneumatic and hydraulic systems, counters play essential roles:

Cycle Counting: Counters are employed to keep track of the number of cycles in applications such as reciprocating motion of cylinders or rotations of hydraulic motors.

Maintenance Monitoring: Counters are used to monitor the usage of components and machinery, providing data for predictive maintenance. By tracking the number of cycles, maintenance intervals can be scheduled more efficiently.

Position Monitoring: In hydraulic and pneumatic systems where positioning is critical, counters can be used to monitor and control the position of actuators or other moving components.

Production Monitoring: Counters contribute to production monitoring by tracking the number of completed cycles or operations in a manufacturing process. This data is valuable for efficiency analysis and quality control.

5. PLCs in Pneumatics and Hydraulics:

PLCs are central to the automation and control of fluid power systems. They offer programmability, flexibility, and the capability to integrate various control components seamlessly. In both pneumatic and hydraulic systems, PLCs serve diverse functions:

Logic Control: PLCs provide logic control for the entire fluid power system. The programming within the PLC dictates the sequences, conditions, and responses of different components.

Sensor Integration: PLCs interface with sensors to receive real-time data about pressure, temperature, position, and other parameters. This data is used to make informed decisions and adjustments in the system.

Actuator Control: PLCs send signals to control actuators, regulating their movements based on the programmed logic and sensor feedback. This allows for precise and coordinated control of mechanical components.

Valve Control: PLCs control directional and proportional valves in fluid power systems. This control over valves enables the regulation of fluid flow and pressure to different sections of the system.

Sequence Control: PLCs excel in sequence control, orchestrating the timed and sequential activation of various components in the fluid power system. This is vital for applications requiring specific sequences of movements or operations.

Communication with HMIs: PLCs often communicate with Human-Machine Interfaces (HMIs) to provide operators with a user-friendly interface for monitoring and controlling the fluid power system.

Fault Diagnostics: PLCs can be programmed to monitor system parameters and detect faults or abnormalities. Diagnostic information can be relayed to operators or maintenance personnel for timely intervention.

6. Integration of Components for Control:

In a well-designed fluid power system, relays, timers, counters, and PLCs often work in harmony to achieve efficient control and automation. The integration of these components follows a systematic approach:

Sensor Input to PLC: Sensors in the fluid power system provide input signals to the PLC, conveying information about pressure, temperature, position, or other relevant parameters.

PLC Processing: The PLC processes the sensor inputs based on pre-programmed logic. This involves decision-making, sequence control, and adjustments to achieve the desired system behavior.

PLC Output to Relays, Timers, and Counters: The PLC generates output signals to control relays, timers, and counters. These components, in turn, manage the activation and timing of actuators, valves, and other system elements.

Actuator and Valve Control: Relays and timers are commonly used for direct control of actuators and valves, while counters may be employed for cycle monitoring. The coordinated action of these components achieves the desired fluid power system behavior.

Feedback to PLC: Sensors and feedback devices provide real-time information on the state of the system, including the position of actuators, pressure levels, and cycle counts. This feedback loop allows the PLC to continuously adapt and optimize system performance.

Human-Machine Interface (HMI) Interaction: In many applications, an HMI allows operators to interact with the fluid power system. The HMI may display system status, enable manual control, or provide access to diagnostic information.

7. Applications of Control Components in Pneumatics and Hydraulics:

Automated Manufacturing: In manufacturing processes, fluid power systems controlled by relays, timers, counters, and PLCs are used for tasks such as material handling, assembly, and packaging. Precise control and sequencing are essential for efficient production.

Robotics: Robotic systems often rely on fluid power for motion control. Control components are integral in regulating the movement of robotic arms and grippers in applications ranging from automotive assembly lines to warehouse automation.

Injection Molding: Injection molding machines, commonly used in the plastics industry, utilize hydraulic systems controlled by PLCs for precise control of the injection process, including the timing and pressure applied to the mold.

Presses and Stamping Machines: Hydraulic and pneumatic presses, as well as stamping machines, use control components to regulate force, speed, and timing during the compression or stamping processes.

Conveyor Systems: Material handling systems, including conveyor belts and sorting mechanisms, use fluid power systems with integrated control components to achieve smooth and controlled movement of goods.

Aerospace Systems: Aircraft and aerospace applications leverage fluid power systems for landing gear deployment, wing flap control, and other critical functions. Control components ensure precise and reliable operation in these demanding environments.

8. Challenges and Considerations:

Compatibility and Interfacing: Ensuring compatibility between different components, especially when sourced from different manufacturers, can be a challenge. Proper interfacing is crucial to avoid communication issues.

Reliability and Maintenance: Reliability is paramount in industrial applications. Regular maintenance and monitoring are essential to prevent failures in control components and ensure the continued performance of fluid power systems.

Programming Complexity: The programming of PLCs for complex systems can be intricate. Skilled personnel are required to develop and maintain the logic control programs effectively.

Environmental Conditions: Fluid power systems may operate in harsh environments, including extremes of temperature, humidity, and exposure to contaminants. Control components must be selected and protected to withstand these conditions.

Safety Concerns: Safety is a critical consideration in industrial applications. Proper safety features, emergency stop mechanisms, and fail-safe designs must be implemented to mitigate risks associated with the control of high-power components.

9. Future Trends and Innovations:

IoT Integration: The integration of the Internet of Things (IoT) in fluid power systems allows for remote monitoring, predictive maintenance, and real-time data analysis. Smart sensors and connectivity enable more informed decision-making.

Edge Computing: Edge computing technologies bring processing power closer to the devices in the fluid power system. This can enhance real-time control, reduce latency, and improve the overall responsiveness of the system.

Advanced Diagnostics: Future control components may incorporate advanced diagnostic capabilities, leveraging artificial intelligence (AI) for predictive analysis and identification of potential issues before they lead to system failures.

Energy Efficiency: Ongoing efforts in energy efficiency are likely to impact the design of control systems. Variable frequency drives, energy recovery systems, and optimized control algorithms will contribute to more sustainable and energy-efficient fluid power systems.

10. Conclusion:

Relays, timers, counters, and PLCs are integral components in the control of pneumatic and hydraulic systems, providing the means to achieve precision, automation, and reliability in diverse industrial applications. The integration of these components allows for sophisticated control strategies, sequencing, and monitoring, contributing to the efficiency and safety of fluid power systems. As technology continues to advance, the future holds exciting possibilities for smart and adaptive control systems that further enhance the performance and capabilities of pneumatic and hydraulic applications in various industries.

CHAPTER FOUR

Programmable Logic Controller

Industrial Automation - Programmable Logic Controller - Functions of PLCs - Features of PLC - Selection of PLC - Architecture – IEC61131-3 programming standard and types - Basics of PLC Programming – Ladder Logic Diagrams – Communication in PLC – Programming Timers and Counters – Data Handling - PLC modules – Advanced motion controlled Multi Axis PLC

Industrial Automation

Introduction

Industrial automation represents a technological leap that has transformed the landscape of manufacturing and production. It involves the use of control systems such as computers or robots for handling different processes and machinery in an industry to replace human intervention. The primary goal is to increase efficiency, reliability, and productivity while minimizing human intervention and errors.

Historical Perspective

The roots of industrial automation can be traced back to the early 20th century with the advent of the assembly line, pioneered by automobile manufacturer Henry Ford. This marked the beginning of a gradual shift from manual labor to mechanized processes. However, true automation, as we understand it today, started to emerge in the mid-20th century with the development of programmable logic controllers (PLCs) and computer numerical control (CNC) systems.

Key Components of Industrial Automation

1. Sensors and Actuators:

Sensors: These devices are used to measure physical quantities such as temperature, pressure, or position. In industrial automation, sensors provide the necessary input data for the control system to make decisions.

Actuators: They are responsible for executing the commands issued by the control system. Examples include motors, valves, and pumps.

2. Control Systems:

PLCs: Programmable Logic Controllers are the workhorses of industrial automation. These rugged computers are designed to withstand harsh industrial environments and are programmed to control specific processes.

DCS: Distributed Control Systems manage complex processes across multiple locations. They are commonly used in industries where the manufacturing process is spread out, such as in oil refineries.

3. Human Machine Interface (HMI):

HMI allows operators to interact with the industrial automation system. It provides a graphical representation of the manufacturing process and allows for monitoring and control.

4. Communication Networks:

Industrial automation systems rely on robust communication networks to transmit data between different components. Ethernet, fieldbus systems, and wireless communication play crucial roles in establishing connectivity.

5. Robotics:

Industrial robots are programmable machines capable of performing tasks in manufacturing. They can be used for tasks such as welding, painting, assembling, and packaging, thereby increasing efficiency and precision.

Advantages of Industrial Automation

1. Increased Productivity:

Automation allows for continuous operation without breaks, leading to increased productivity compared to human-operated systems.

2. Improved Quality:

Consistency is a hallmark of automation. Machines perform tasks with precision and repeatability, leading to higher quality products.

3. Enhanced Safety:

Dangerous tasks can be assigned to automated systems, reducing the risk of workplace accidents and improving overall safety.

4. Cost Savings:

While the initial investment in automation can be significant, the long-term cost savings, especially in terms of labor and operational efficiency, often outweigh the initial expenses.

5. Flexibility:

Automation systems can be easily reprogrammed or reconfigured to adapt to changes in production requirements, providing a high degree of flexibility.

Applications of Industrial Automation

Industrial automation finds applications across various industries, including:

1. Manufacturing:

From automotive assembly lines to electronics manufacturing, industrial automation has revolutionized the way products are made.

2. Chemical Processing:

Automation plays a crucial role in chemical plants, ensuring precise control over reactions and improving safety.

3. Oil and Gas:

In the oil and gas industry, automation is used for drilling, refining, and distribution processes.

4. Food and Beverage:

Automation is employed in food processing and packaging, ensuring hygiene, consistency, and efficiency.

5. Pharmaceuticals:

The pharmaceutical industry benefits from automation in manufacturing drugs with precision and meeting stringent quality standards.

Challenges and Considerations

1. Initial Costs:

The implementation of industrial automation systems often requires a substantial upfront investment in technology and infrastructure.

2. Skill Gaps:

The transition to automated systems necessitates a skilled workforce capable of designing, implementing, and maintaining these complex systems.

3. Integration Issues:

Integrating automation into existing systems can be challenging. Compatibility issues and the need for seamless integration are critical considerations.

4. Cybersecurity Concerns:

With increased connectivity, the risk of cyber threats to industrial automation systems has risen. Robust cybersecurity measures are essential to safeguard against potential attacks.

Future Trends in Industrial Automation

1. Internet of Things (IoT):

The integration of IoT devices allows for even greater connectivity and data exchange between different components of an industrial automation system.

2. Artificial Intelligence (AI) and Machine Learning:

AI and machine learning algorithms enable systems to learn and adapt, enhancing decision-making capabilities in real-time.

3. Edge Computing:

Edge computing involves processing data closer to the source, reducing latency and improving the efficiency of industrial automation systems.

4. Digital Twins:

Digital twins are virtual replicas of physical systems. They enable real-time monitoring, analysis, and optimization of processes, leading to improved performance.

Conclusion

In conclusion, industrial automation has come a long way from the early days of assembly lines. It has become an integral part of modern manufacturing, bringing about improvements in efficiency, quality, and safety. As technology continues to advance, the future holds exciting possibilities for further integration of smart technologies, ultimately reshaping the industrial landscape. However, it's essential to navigate challenges such as cybersecurity and workforce readiness to fully realize the potential benefits of industrial automation.

Programmable Logic Controller

Introduction

Programmable Logic Controllers, or PLCs, are critical components in the realm of industrial automation. These robust electronic devices play a pivotal role in controlling and automating various manufacturing processes across a wide range of industries. Developed to replace traditional relay control systems, PLCs have evolved into sophisticated controllers capable of handling complex automation tasks.

Historical Context

The roots of PLCs can be traced back to the late 1960s and early 1970s. The advent of digital computing and the need for more flexible and efficient control systems in manufacturing spurred the development of the first PLCs. Companies like Modicon (now part of Schneider Electric) were pioneers in introducing these programmable controllers to the market.

Key Components of a PLC

1. Central Processing Unit (CPU):

At the heart of every PLC is its CPU. This component executes the control program stored in the PLC's memory and is responsible for making decisions based on input conditions.

2. Input Modules:

Input modules are responsible for interfacing with the external environment. They receive signals from sensors and other input devices, converting physical phenomena (like temperature or pressure) into electrical signals that the PLC can process.

3. Output Modules:

Output modules are responsible for taking the control decisions made by the PLC and translating them into actions. These actions could include activating motors, solenoids, or other output devices.

4. Memory:

PLCs have two main types of memory:

RAM (Random Access Memory): Used for storing the program currently being executed.

ROM (Read-Only Memory): Contains the firmware and the user program, ensuring that the program persists even after power is lost.

5. Programming Device:

To program a PLC, engineers use specialized software and programming devices. These programs are typically written in ladder logic, a graphical programming language that resembles electrical relay logic diagrams.

Programming Languages in PLCs

1. Ladder Logic:

Ladder Logic is the most common programming language for PLCs. It uses graphical representation similar to electrical relay diagrams, making it intuitive for engineers with a background in electrical control systems.

2. Structured Text:

This text-based programming language is more akin to traditional programming languages. It allows for more complex algorithms and is often used for tasks that are challenging to express in ladder logic.

3. Function Block Diagram (FBD):

FBD is another graphical programming language that represents a control system as a network of functions blocks, each describing a specific function or operation.

4. Sequential Function Chart (SFC):

SFC is used for systems with sequential and parallel operations. It breaks down the control process into steps, making it particularly useful for complex processes with multiple stages.

Operating Cycle of a PLC

Understanding the operating cycle of a PLC provides insights into how it processes information and controls a system:

Input Scan:

The PLC continuously scans its input devices to read their current states. This process is known as the input scan.

Program Execution:

The CPU executes the control program stored in its memory based on the input conditions. This involves processing the logic defined in the user program.

Output Scan:

Once the program has been executed, the PLC updates the states of its output devices during the output scan. This, in turn, affects the controlled system.

Housekeeping:

The PLC performs housekeeping tasks, such as updating timers and counters, before starting the next scan cycle.

Advantages of PLCs

1. Flexibility:

PLCs offer a high degree of flexibility. The control program can be easily modified to accommodate changes in the manufacturing process.

2. Reliability:

PLCs are designed to operate in harsh industrial environments. Their reliability is crucial for maintaining continuous and stable operation.

3. Modularity:

The modular nature of PLCs allows for easy expansion or modification. Additional input and output modules can be added without significant changes to the overall system.

4. Ease of Troubleshooting:

The graphical representation of the control logic in ladder logic makes it easier for engineers to understand and troubleshoot the system.

5. Integration Capabilities:

PLCs can be seamlessly integrated with other automation components, such as Human Machine Interfaces (HMIs) and Supervisory Control and Data Acquisition (SCADA) systems.

Applications of PLCs

PLCs find applications in various industries, including:

1. Manufacturing:

PLCs control assembly lines, robotic systems, and material handling processes in manufacturing plants.

2. Automotive:

In the automotive industry, PLCs are used for tasks ranging from controlling conveyor belts to managing robotic welding systems.

3. Oil and Gas:

PLCs play a crucial role in controlling processes in oil refineries, pipeline systems, and drilling operations.

4. Utilities:

PLCs are employed in utilities for tasks like controlling water treatment plants, managing power distribution, and regulating HVAC systems.

5. Food and Beverage:

In the food industry, PLCs control various processes, including mixing, baking, and packaging, ensuring precision and efficiency.

Advanced Features and Considerations in PLCs

1. High-Speed Counting and Timing:

PLCs are equipped with high-speed counters and timers, allowing them to precisely control processes that require accurate timing, such as motion control and fast counting applications.

2. Analog I/O:

In addition to handling discrete signals (on/off), many modern PLCs support analog input and output. This capability is crucial in processes where variables such as temperature, pressure, or flow rate need to be controlled with precision.

3. Communication Protocols:

PLCs communicate with other devices in the automation system through various communication protocols. Common protocols include Modbus, Profibus, and Ethernet/IP. The choice of protocol depends on the specific requirements of the application.

4. Redundancy:

Redundancy is a critical feature in industrial applications where downtime can be costly. Some PLC systems offer redundancy, ensuring that if one PLC fails, another can take over seamlessly.

5. Safety PLCs:

In safety-critical applications, such as those involving heavy machinery or potentially hazardous processes, safety PLCs are employed. These specialized PLCs are designed to meet stringent safety standards and include features like self-checking and redundancy.

PLC Programming Best Practices

1. Documentation:

Thorough documentation of the PLC program is essential for troubleshooting and future modifications. This includes detailed comments, descriptions of functions, and a clear structure.

2. Testing and Simulation:

Before deploying a PLC program to control a physical process, it's common practice to test and simulate the program using virtual environments. This helps identify and rectify potential issues without affecting the actual production process.

3. Modularity and Structured Programming:

Structuring the PLC program in a modular and organized way improves readability and maintainability. Functions should be logically grouped, and code should follow best practices of structured programming.

4. Version Control:

Implementing version control for PLC programs is crucial for tracking changes over time. This ensures that previous versions can be restored if issues arise after an update.

5. Security Considerations:

As industrial systems become more interconnected, security becomes a paramount concern. Implementing cybersecurity measures, such as firewalls and secure communication protocols, helps protect PLCs from unauthorized access and cyber threats.

Future Trends in PLC Technology

1. Edge Computing Integration:

With the rise of edge computing, PLCs are increasingly being equipped with edge capabilities. This allows them to process data closer to the source, reducing latency and improving overall system efficiency.

2. Machine Learning and AI:

Integrating machine learning algorithms into PLCs enables them to adapt and optimize control strategies based on historical data and real-time feedback, enhancing efficiency and predictive maintenance.

3. Cloud Connectivity:

PLCs are embracing cloud connectivity for data storage, analysis, and remote monitoring. This facilitates centralized management and the ability to access real-time data from anywhere in the world.

4. Cybersecurity Advancements:

As the threat landscape evolves, PLC manufacturers are continually improving cybersecurity features to safeguard industrial systems against sophisticated cyber attacks.

5. Augmented Reality (AR) Integration:

AR technologies are being integrated into PLC maintenance and troubleshooting processes. Technicians can use AR devices to visualize PLC data, making diagnostics and repairs more efficient.

Challenges and Considerations

1. Interoperability:

Ensuring seamless communication between PLCs from different manufacturers and with other automation components can be challenging due to differences in communication protocols and standards.

2. Skill Shortages:

As PLC technology advances, there is a growing need for skilled professionals who can design, program, and maintain these complex systems. Bridging the skills gap is crucial for successful implementation.

3. Legacy Systems:

Many industrial facilities still rely on legacy PLC systems, which may lack the advanced features of modern PLCs. Upgrading these systems requires careful planning to avoid disruption to ongoing operations.

4. Cybersecurity Risks:

The increasing connectivity of industrial systems exposes PLCs to cybersecurity threats. Robust cybersecurity measures are essential to protect against unauthorized access and potential disruptions.

5. Cost Considerations:

While PLCs offer numerous advantages, the initial costs of implementation and maintenance can be significant. Organizations must weigh these costs against the expected benefits over the lifespan of the system.

Functions of PLCs

Programmable Logic Controllers (PLCs) are versatile and integral components in industrial automation, designed to control and automate a wide array of manufacturing processes. These robust devices execute specific functions to ensure efficient and precise operation. Let's explore the fundamental functions of PLCs in detail.

1. Input Signal Processing:

At the core of a PLC's functionality is its ability to process input signals from various sensors and devices. PLCs are equipped with input modules that interface with the external environment, collecting data on variables such as temperature, pressure, position, and other relevant parameters. These signals are then processed to determine the state of the system and inform the control program.

2. Control Program Execution:

The control program, typically written in languages such as ladder logic, structured text, function block diagram, or sequential function chart, dictates the decision-making process of the PLC. The Central Processing Unit (CPU) within the PLC executes this program based on the input conditions. The program contains logic and instructions that determine the desired outcome based on the current state of the system.

3. Output Signal Generation:

Once the control program has been executed, the PLC generates output signals to control various actuators and devices. Output modules in the PLC interface with motors, solenoids, valves, and other output devices, translating the control decisions into physical actions. This function is critical for manipulating the manufacturing process according to the programmed logic.

4. Timing and Counting Operations:

PLCs are equipped with timers and counters to facilitate precise control over time-dependent and counting operations. Timers allow the PLC to introduce delays or trigger events at specific intervals, ensuring accurate timing in processes. Counters keep track of events or occurrences, enabling the PLC to execute actions after a predefined number of cycles.

5. Arithmetic and Logic Operations:

PLCs perform arithmetic and logic operations as part of their decision-making process. These operations include mathematical calculations, comparisons, and logical evaluations. Arithmetic functions are used for tasks like scaling input values, while logical operations determine the flow of the control program based on specified conditions.

6. Data Handling and Storage:

PLCs have memory components, including both Random Access Memory (RAM) and Read-Only Memory (ROM). RAM is used for temporarily storing data during program execution, while ROM stores the firmware and the user program. Efficient data handling is crucial for maintaining the integrity of the control program and ensuring accurate processing of information.

7. Communication with External Devices:

Communication capabilities enable PLCs to interact with other components in the automation system. PLCs use various communication protocols such as Modbus, Profibus, and Ethernet/IP to exchange data with Human Machine Interfaces (HMIs), Supervisory Control and Data Acquisition (SCADA) systems, and other PLCs. This function enhances the overall connectivity and coordination of the industrial automation system.

8. Error Handling and Fault Diagnosis:

PLCs are equipped with features to handle errors and diagnose faults in the system. Diagnostic routines within the control program can identify issues such as sensor malfunctions or communication errors. Error handling mechanisms help the PLC respond appropriately to faults, minimizing downtime and contributing to the overall reliability of the industrial process.

9. Security and Access Control:

As industrial systems become more interconnected, security features are increasingly integrated into PLCs. Access control mechanisms ensure that only authorized personnel can modify or access the control program. Encryption and secure communication protocols are employed to protect PLCs from potential cyber threats, contributing to the overall cybersecurity of the automation system.

10. Integration with Safety Systems:

In safety-critical applications, PLCs often integrate with safety systems to ensure the well-being of personnel and the protection of equipment. Safety PLCs, designed to meet stringent safety standards, include features such as self-checking, redundancy, and fail-safe mechanisms. This function enhances the overall safety and reliability of industrial processes.

11. Scalability and Modularity:

PLCs are designed to be scalable and modular, allowing for easy expansion and modification of the control system. Additional input and output modules can be added to accommodate changes in the manufacturing process without requiring significant alterations to the existing setup. This scalability contributes to the flexibility of PLC-based control systems.

12. Monitoring and Data Logging:

PLCs provide real-time monitoring capabilities, allowing operators to visualize the status of the industrial process through HMIs or SCADA systems. Data logging features enable the PLC to record important process variables over time. This data can be analyzed for performance optimization, troubleshooting, and adherence to quality standards.

13. Remote Access and Control:

With advancements in connectivity, many PLCs support remote access and control. This function enables authorized personnel to monitor and modify PLC programs from remote locations, facilitating efficient maintenance and troubleshooting without the need for physical presence at the industrial site.

14. Energy Management:

Some PLCs incorporate energy management features to optimize the use of resources and reduce energy consumption. By controlling the activation and deactivation of equipment based on demand and operational requirements, PLCs contribute to energy efficiency in industrial processes.

15. Advanced Control Strategies:

Modern PLCs are capable of implementing advanced control strategies, including Proportional-Integral-Derivative (PID) control. PID control algorithms allow the PLC to regulate processes with precision, maintaining desired setpoints and responding dynamically to changes in operating conditions.

Features of PLC

Programmable Logic Controllers (PLCs) are sophisticated control devices with a rich set of features designed to meet the diverse needs of industrial automation. These features contribute to the reliability, flexibility, and efficiency of PLC-based control systems. Let's explore these features in detail.

1. Input and Output (I/O) Modules:

One of the fundamental features of PLCs is the capability to interface with the external environment through Input and Output (I/O) modules. Input modules receive signals from sensors and other devices, converting physical phenomena into electrical signals. Output modules, on the other hand, control actuators and devices based on the decisions made by the PLC's control program. The modular nature of I/O modules allows for easy expansion and modification of the control system.

2. Central Processing Unit (CPU):

At the heart of every PLC is the Central Processing Unit (CPU), responsible for executing the control program. The CPU processes input signals, makes control decisions based on the programmed logic, and generates output signals to control the industrial process. The processing power and capabilities of the CPU influence the overall performance and responsiveness of the PLC.

3. Memory:

PLCs have two main types of memory: Random Access Memory (RAM) and Read-Only Memory (ROM). RAM is used for temporary data storage during program execution, while ROM stores the firmware and the user program. Memory management is a crucial feature, ensuring the stability and integrity of the control program even in the event of power loss.

4. Programming Languages:

PLCs support various programming languages, each suited for different applications and user preferences. The most common language is Ladder Logic, a graphical representation of control logic resembling electrical relay diagrams. Additionally, PLCs may support languages like Structured Text, Function Block Diagram, and Sequential Function Chart, providing flexibility in expressing control strategies.

5. Modularity and Expandability:

PLCs are designed with modularity in mind, allowing for easy expansion and modification of the control system. Additional I/O modules can be added to accommodate changes in the manufacturing process without disrupting the existing setup. This modularity contributes to the scalability and adaptability of PLC-based control systems.

6. Communication Ports and Protocols:

Communication capabilities are essential for PLCs to interact with other components in the automation system. PLCs feature communication ports that support various protocols such as Modbus, Profibus, Ethernet/IP, and more. These protocols enable data exchange between PLCs, Human Machine Interfaces (HMIs), Supervisory Control and Data Acquisition (SCADA) systems, and other devices, fostering seamless integration in complex industrial environments.

7. Real-Time Clock:

Many PLCs are equipped with a real-time clock to provide accurate timekeeping within the system. The real-time clock is crucial for time-dependent operations and for timestamping data in applications such as data logging. This feature enhances the precision and synchronization of processes in the industrial environment.

8. High-Speed Counters and Timers:

PLCs include high-speed counters and timers for applications that demand precise timing and counting operations. High-speed counters accurately track events, while timers introduce delays or control time-dependent processes. These features are crucial for applications such as motion control, where precise timing is essential.

9. Analog Input and Output:

In addition to handling discrete signals (on/off), many modern PLCs support analog input and output. Analog signals, representing continuous variables like temperature or pressure, can be accurately processed by PLCs. This capability is vital for applications where fine control and monitoring of analog variables are required.

10. Redundancy:

Redundancy is a feature that enhances the reliability of PLC-based control systems. Some PLC systems offer redundancy, where two or more PLCs operate in parallel. In the event of a failure in one PLC, the redundant unit seamlessly takes over, minimizing downtime and ensuring continuous operation in critical applications.

11. Safety Features:

Safety is paramount in industrial automation, and PLCs incorporate features to enhance safety in manufacturing processes. Safety PLCs, designed for safety-critical applications, include self-checking mechanisms, redundancy, and fail-safe functions. These features ensure that the PLC can respond to emergency situations and protect personnel and equipment.

12. HMI Integration:

PLCs can be seamlessly integrated with Human Machine Interfaces (HMIs) to provide a user-friendly interface for monitoring and controlling the industrial process. HMIs display real-time data, alarms, and allow operators to interact with the PLC system. This integration enhances the overall visibility and control of the automation system.

13. Remote Access and Monitoring:

With advancements in connectivity, many PLCs support remote access and monitoring. This feature allows authorized personnel to access and modify PLC programs from remote locations. Remote access facilitates efficient troubleshooting, maintenance, and monitoring without the need for physical presence at the industrial site.

14. Data Logging and Trending:

PLCs often include data logging capabilities to record and store important process variables over time. This historical data can be analyzed for performance optimization, troubleshooting, and adherence to quality standards. Trending features visually represent the historical data, aiding in the identification of patterns and anomalies.

15. Diagnostic and Error Handling:

PLCs are equipped with diagnostic features to identify and handle errors in the system. Diagnostic routines within the control program can detect issues such as sensor malfunctions or communication errors. Error handling mechanisms ensure that the PLC responds appropriately to faults, contributing to the overall reliability of the industrial process.

16. Security Measures:

As industrial systems become more interconnected, PLCs incorporate security features to protect against unauthorized access and potential cyber threats. Access control mechanisms ensure that only authorized personnel can modify or access the control program. Encryption and secure communication protocols are employed to safeguard PLCs from cybersecurity risks.

17. Energy Management:

Some PLCs feature energy management capabilities to optimize the use of resources and reduce energy consumption. By controlling the activation and deactivation of equipment based on demand and operational requirements, PLCs contribute to energy efficiency in industrial processes.

18. Advanced Control Strategies:

Modern PLCs are capable of implementing advanced control strategies, including Proportional-Integral-Derivative (PID) control. PID control algorithms allow the PLC to regulate processes with precision, maintaining desired setpoints and responding dynamically to changes in operating conditions.

19. Augmented Reality (AR) Integration:

Innovative PLCs are incorporating Augmented Reality (AR) technologies into maintenance and troubleshooting processes. Technicians can use AR devices to visualize PLC data in real-time, making diagnostics and repairs more efficient. This integration enhances the overall maintenance capabilities of the PLC system.

20. Edge Computing Capabilities:

With the rise of edge computing, PLCs are increasingly being equipped with edge capabilities. Edge computing involves processing data closer to the source, reducing latency and improving the efficiency of industrial automation systems. PLCs with edge computing capabilities enhance real-time decision-making and responsiveness.

21. Cloud Connectivity:

PLCs are embracing cloud connectivity for data storage, analysis, and remote monitoring. This feature facilitates centralized management and allows access to real-time data from anywhere in the world. Cloud connectivity enhances collaboration and decision-making in distributed industrial environments.

22. Condition Monitoring:

Some PLCs incorporate condition monitoring features, enabling the continuous monitoring of equipment and processes. This includes the use of sensors and algorithms to detect changes in the condition of machinery, allowing for predictive maintenance and minimizing unplanned downtime.

23. Machine Learning and AI Integration:

Integrating machine learning and artificial intelligence (AI) capabilities into PLCs enables adaptive control strategies. These advanced algorithms can learn from historical data and adjust control parameters in real-time, optimizing processes and improving overall efficiency.

24. Digital Twins:

The concept of digital twins involves creating virtual replicas of physical systems. Some PLCs support digital twin integration, allowing real-time monitoring, analysis, and optimization of processes. Digital twins enhance the understanding and control of complex industrial systems.

Selection of PLC

Introduction

Programmable Logic Controllers (PLCs) serve as the brains of industrial automation systems, providing the intelligence to control and monitor various processes. The selection of a PLC is a crucial step in the design and implementation of an automation solution. The chosen PLC must align with the unique requirements of the application, ensuring efficiency, reliability, and long-term performance. This guide delves into the essential considerations for selecting the right PLC, covering aspects from technical specifications to environmental factors.

1. Understanding Application Requirements:

a. Process Complexity:

Evaluate the complexity of the industrial process that the PLC will control. Simple processes with minimal inputs and outputs may require basic PLCs, while complex systems with intricate control logic and numerous I/O points may demand advanced PLCs with higher processing capabilities.

b. Number and Type of I/O Points:

Determine the number and types of Input and Output (I/O) points required for the application. Consider both digital and analog signals. Ensure that the selected PLC has sufficient I/O capacity to accommodate current needs and potential future expansion.

c. Communication Requirements:

Assess the communication needs of the automation system. Consider protocols required for communication with other devices such as Human Machine Interfaces (HMIs), sensors, actuators, and other PLCs. Compatibility with industry-standard protocols like Modbus, Profibus, or Ethernet/IP is crucial for seamless integration.

d. Control System Architecture:

Determine the control system architecture. Decide whether a centralized or distributed control system is more suitable for the application. Some PLCs are designed for decentralized control in distributed systems, offering flexibility and scalability.

2. Technical Specifications:

a. Processing Speed and Memory:

Evaluate the processing speed and memory capacity of the PLC. The processing speed influences the PLC's ability to execute complex control algorithms in real-time, while sufficient memory is crucial for storing the control program and handling data.

b. Programming Languages:

Consider the programming languages supported by the PLC. Common languages include ladder logic, structured text, function block diagram, and sequential function chart. Choose a PLC that supports the programming language best suited to the expertise of the programming team and the complexity of the control logic.

c. Analog I/O and Specialized Modules:

If the application involves analog signals or requires specialized modules (e.g., high-speed counters, motion control), ensure that the selected PLC supports these features. Analog I/O capability is essential for applications where precise control over variables such as temperature or pressure is required.

d. Redundancy and Reliability Features:

Assess the need for redundancy and reliability features. Some PLCs offer redundancy options, ensuring continuous operation in the event of a PLC failure. Consider features like fault diagnostics, self-checking, and fail-safe functions for enhanced reliability.

3. Environmental Considerations:

a. Operating Conditions:

Consider the operating conditions of the industrial environment. PLCs are often exposed to harsh conditions, including temperature extremes, humidity, and vibration. Choose a PLC with a suitable environmental rating to ensure reliable operation in challenging conditions.

b. Enclosure Type and Ingress Protection (IP) Rating:

Select the appropriate enclosure type and Ingress Protection (IP) rating based on the environmental conditions. The enclosure protects the PLC from dust, moisture, and other contaminants. The IP rating indicates the level of protection against these environmental factors.

c. Hazardous Area Certification:

In industries where explosive or hazardous atmospheres are present, ensure that the selected PLC has the necessary certifications, such as ATEX or UL Class I, Div. 2. Compliance with safety standards is crucial for the safety of personnel and equipment.

4. Scalability and Expandability:

a. Future Expansion:

Consider the scalability and expandability of the selected PLC. Choose a PLC that allows for easy expansion of I/O points and additional features as the automation system grows. Modularity in PLC design facilitates seamless integration of new components.

b. Compatibility with Existing Systems:

If the automation system is part of an existing infrastructure, ensure that the selected PLC is compatible with the existing control hardware and software. Compatibility reduces integration challenges and facilitates a smooth transition.

5. Budgetary Constraints:

a. Initial Investment:

Evaluate the initial investment required for the PLC system, including hardware, software, and installation costs. Consider both the short-term and long-term costs, factoring in potential expansion and maintenance expenses.

b. Total Cost of Ownership (TCO):

Assess the Total Cost of Ownership (TCO) over the lifecycle of the PLC system. Consider factors such as maintenance costs, software licensing fees, and potential downtime. A PLC with a higher initial cost but lower TCO may be a more cost-effective choice.

6. Vendor Support and Service:

a. Vendor Reputation:

Choose a reputable PLC vendor with a track record of providing reliable and durable products. Research customer reviews, testimonials, and case studies to gauge the vendor's reputation in the industry.

b. Technical Support and Training:

Evaluate the technical support and training provided by the vendor. A vendor with responsive technical support and comprehensive training programs can contribute to the successful implementation and maintenance of the PLC system.

c. Software Updates and Compatibility:

Check the vendor's policy on software updates and compatibility. Regular software updates ensure that the PLC system remains secure and up-to-date with the latest features and enhancements.

7. Regulatory Compliance:

a. Industry Standards:

Ensure that the selected PLC complies with relevant industry standards and regulations. Compliance with standards such as IEC 61131-3 ensures interoperability and adherence to best practices in industrial automation.

b. Safety Standards:

If the application involves safety-critical processes, verify that the PLC complies with safety standards such as ISO 13849 or IEC 61508. Safety-rated PLCs often have additional features and certifications to enhance safety in automation systems.

8. Cybersecurity Considerations:

a. Security Features:

Evaluate the cybersecurity features of the PLC. Look for features such as secure communication protocols, access control mechanisms, and encryption to protect the PLC system from unauthorized access and cyber threats.

b. Update Mechanisms:

Assess the PLC's capability for receiving and implementing firmware updates. Regular updates are crucial for addressing security vulnerabilities and ensuring the ongoing security of the automation system.

Conclusion

The selection of a Programmable Logic Controller is a multifaceted process that involves careful consideration of technical specifications, environmental factors, scalability, budget constraints, vendor support, and regulatory compliance. By thoroughly assessing the specific requirements of the application and aligning them with the features offered by different PLCs, engineers and decision-makers can make informed choices that result in reliable and efficient automation systems. Keep in mind that the optimal PLC selection is not a one-size-fits-all approach; rather, it involves tailoring the choice to the unique needs and constraints of each industrial scenario.

PLC Architecture

The use of Programmable Logic Controllers (PLCs) has revolutionized the automation industry by providing a reliable and cost-effective platform for a wide range of industrial processes. They are in huge demand, making the value of the PLC industry stand close to $36 billion. PLC architectures help maximize performance while reducing maintenance costs associated with automated systems, making them an attractive option for many businesses.

What is a PLC Architecture?

Programmable Logic Controllers (PLCs) are industrial computers designed to control and monitor processes in automated systems. PLC architectures refer to the different types of hardware components used in a PLC system, such as controllers, input/output modules, communication modules, and power supplies.

Each type of component has its own specific function in the automation process. Choosing the right architecture for your application maximizes performance while reducing maintenance costs associated with automation systems. To learn more about PLC architecture, you can pursue a PLC programming course.

Types of PLC Architecture

There are three distinct types of architecture of PLC. They are as follows:

1. Fixed Architecture

Fixed PLC architecture is the most basic type of architecture. This arrangement has a single central processor that controls all inputs and outputs. It can be used in applications with only a few input signals and output commands to control.

The main advantage of this setup is its simplicity; however, it limits the scalability of the overall system as additional I/O points must be added with an external module or expansion board. In addition, these systems are usually more expensive than modular architectures due to their fixed nature.

2. Modular Architecture

Modular PLC architectures consist of multiple individual modules connected through a common bus or network connection like Ethernet or Modbus TCP/IP. This allows each module to act independently while still being able to communicate with other modules within the system.

It provides enhanced flexibility when constructing an automation system from scratch or attempting to adapt an existing one for different purposes. Modules can range from simple digital I/O cards to complex motion controllers capable of easily controlling sophisticated robotic arms and other robotic devices.

3. Distributed Architecture

Distributed PLC architecture involves several separate components distributed around a facility that work together as part of an overall automation solution without having one centralized location for all elements involved in the process control scheme.

Examples include wireless communications between various sensors located throughout a production line that feed information about machine performance, such as temperature readings, pressure levels, etc. This allows operators at remote locations (such as offices) access real-time data without needing physical access to them on-site at any given time, which helps promote efficiency.

How Does Architecture of Programmable Logic Controller (PLC) Work?

The CPU (Central Processing Unit) is the brain of the PLC system. It consists of a control module and a processor. While the CPU processor does all of the number crunching and program execution, the CPU control unit controls how the various PLC hardware components interact with one another.

The CPU processor receives data from the input devices, processes it, and sends it to the output devices. It also communicates with the data and program memory to exchange data. Once all the data has been collected, the program is cycled through for processing. The output interface processes the generated data and sends it to the output devices for execution.

The diagram given below shows the PLC architecture.

Benefits of PLC Architecture

Some of the benefits of the architecture of PLC are:

1. Increased Performance

By choosing the right architecture for your particular application, you can ensure optimal operation and reduce downtime associated with troubleshooting issues or dealing with malfunctions in the system.

Modular architectures allow users to easily expand their systems as needed, allowing companies to quickly adapt to changing market conditions.

2. Less Maintenance Cost

PLC architectures also offer reduced maintenance costs when compared to traditional control systems such as hardwired relays or contactors. Modular designs are easier to troubleshoot than their hardwired counterparts since each component can be replaced individually if necessary instead of replacing an entire system.

This helps reduce both repair time and money spent on repairs, which ultimately leads to improved operational efficiency and higher profits for businesses utilizing these types of automation solutions.

3. Compatibility

Another great advantage that comes with using PLC architecture is its wide range of compatibility across different vendors' products, due to its adherence to open standards like CANopen or Ethernet/IP protocols.

Therefore, most of the third-party components can be added to existing installations easily, saving time during initial setup stages as well as future expansions.

Challenges of PLC Architecture

Some of the challenges of the architecture of PLC are:

1. High Cost

One of the biggest challenges associated with PLC architectures is their relatively high cost compared to other industrial automation systems. As these are often used in highly specific applications, such as those found in manufacturing and industrial processes, they require specialized components that can be expensive to purchase and maintain.

Additionally, most PLCs use proprietary software for programming, which are not compatible with existing hardware or other systems, more costly upgrades and modifications are necessary when expanding or changing a system's capabilities.

2. Security Concerns

Since these systems are responsible for controlling critical processes within factories and production lines, they must have secure access controls to prevent unauthorized users from accessing them remotely or altering any of their settings without permission.

This requires additional resources that need to be allocated towards implementing reliable security measures, such as firewalls, encryption protocols, etc. This increases costs further while also posing technical issues due to the complexity of integrating different elements properly.

3. Inflexibility

One major challenge concerning PLC architecture is its inflexibility when it comes to modifying programs once they have been written and uploaded into the system's memory banks.

This means any changes must involve writing new code from scratch rather than simply adapting existing code, which can lead to significant delays during development cycles

IEC61131-3 Programming Standard and Types

Introduction

The IEC 61131-3 standard, established by the International Electrotechnical Commission (IEC), is a fundamental framework for the development of software in industrial control systems. It was created to standardize the programming of PLCs, ensuring interoperability, consistency, and efficiency in the design and maintenance of industrial automation software. The standard defines several programming languages, each serving specific purposes and catering to different aspects of control system development.

IEC 61131-3 Programming Languages

The IEC 61131-3 standard consists of several programming languages, providing a range of options for engineers and programmers developing control software for industrial applications. Let's explore the key programming languages defined by this standard.

1. Ladder Diagram (LD):

Ladder Diagram is one of the most widely used programming languages in industrial automation. It derives its name from the graphical representation that resembles an electrical ladder diagram. LD is particularly intuitive for individuals with a background in electrical engineering. It uses graphical symbols to represent relay logic and control sequences, making it easy to understand and implement.

Features:

Graphical representation of control logic.

Sequential execution of instructions.

Intuitive for engineers familiar with electrical relay diagrams.

2. Structured Text (ST):

Structured Text is a high-level text-based programming language that resembles programming languages such as Pascal or C. It provides a flexible and powerful way to describe control algorithms and complex logic. ST is suitable for engineers with a background in software development, offering the capability to implement sophisticated algorithms.

Features:

Text-based, high-level language.

Allows complex algorithm development.

Well-suited for mathematical computations and data manipulation.

3. Function Block Diagram (FBD):

Function Block Diagram is a graphical programming language that represents a control system as a network of interconnected function blocks. Each function block encapsulates a specific function or operation, and connections between blocks define the flow of data and control. FBD is useful for visualizing and organizing complex control processes.

Features:

Graphical representation using interconnected function blocks.

Encapsulation of specific functions into modular blocks.

Suitable for complex control processes.

4. Instruction List (IL):

Instruction List is a low-level, text-based programming language that uses mnemonic codes to represent control instructions. It is similar to assembly language and provides a concise representation of control logic. IL is often used for applications that require fine control over specific hardware components.

Features:

Low-level, text-based language.

Mnemonic codes represent control instructions.

Allows fine control over hardware components.

5. Sequential Function Chart (SFC):

Sequential Function Chart is a graphical language that represents the behavior of a system using a series of steps and transitions. SFC is particularly useful for modeling sequential and parallel processes. It breaks down the control process into states and transitions, providing a visual representation of the system's behavior.

Features:

Graphical representation of sequential and parallel processes.

States and transitions model the system's behavior.

Suitable for complex control systems with multiple stages.

Types of IEC 61131-3 Programming Languages

In addition to the individual programming languages, the IEC 61131-3 standard defines two types of languages: continuous and event-driven. These types describe how the control program is executed and how it responds to inputs and events.

1. Continuous (Continuous Flow) Languages:

Continuous languages execute their control logic in a continuous and cyclic manner. The program runs in a loop, continuously scanning inputs, executing control logic, and updating outputs. The most common continuous language in the IEC 61131-3 standard is Ladder Diagram (LD).

Continuous Languages include:

Ladder Diagram (LD): Executes control logic continuously in a loop, updating outputs based on input conditions.

2. Event-Driven (Event-Driven Flow) Languages:

Event-driven languages respond to specific events or triggers, executing control logic when a predefined event occurs. These languages do not necessarily operate in a continuous loop but rather respond to changes in the system's state. Event-driven languages are suitable for applications where the control logic needs to be executed based on specific conditions or events.

Event-Driven Languages include:

Structured Text (ST): Executes control logic based on specific conditions or events, providing flexibility for complex algorithms.

Function Block Diagram (FBD): Represents control logic as interconnected function blocks that respond to events or triggers.

Sequential Function Chart (SFC): Models sequential and parallel processes with states and transitions, responding to events or conditions.

Considerations for Choosing IEC 61131-3 Programming Languages

1. Application Complexity:

Choose a programming language based on the complexity of the control logic required for the application. For simple sequential processes, Ladder Diagram (LD) or Sequential Function Chart (SFC) may be suitable. For complex algorithms, consider using Structured Text (ST) or Function Block Diagram (FBD).

2. Programming Team Expertise:

Consider the expertise of the programming team. If the team is more familiar with graphical representation, Ladder Diagram (LD) or Function Block Diagram (FBD) may be preferable. If the team has a background in software development, Structured Text (ST) may be a more natural choice.

3. System Modeling and Visualization:

If the control system requires clear visualization and modeling of sequential and parallel processes, Sequential Function Chart (SFC) may be advantageous. This language provides a visual representation of states and transitions.

4. Flexibility and Extensibility:

Consider the flexibility and extensibility required for the control system. Structured Text (ST) offers high-level programming capabilities, making it suitable for applications that demand flexibility and complex algorithms. Function Block Diagram (FBD) provides modularity and encapsulation of functions.

5. Execution Mode:

Determine whether the control logic needs to execute continuously in a loop (continuous flow) or respond to specific events or triggers (event-driven flow). Choose the programming languages accordingly.

6. Standardization and Interoperability:

IEC 61131-3 standardization promotes interoperability among different PLCs and automation systems. Choosing programming languages defined by this standard ensures that the control software is portable and can be implemented on various platforms.

7. Maintenance and Debugging:

Consider the ease of maintenance and debugging when selecting a programming language. Graphical languages like Ladder Diagram (LD) and Function Block Diagram (FBD) provide a visual representation that aids in debugging, while text-based languages like Structured Text (ST) offer powerful debugging tools.

8. Compliance with Industry Standards:

Ensure that the chosen programming languages comply with relevant industry standards. IEC 61131-3 standardization ensures adherence to best practices in industrial automation programming.

Conclusion

The IEC 61131-3 programming standard provides a comprehensive framework for developing control software in industrial automation. By offering a variety of programming languages and specifying their types, the standard caters to diverse application requirements and programming team preferences. When selecting programming languages, it is crucial to consider factors such as application complexity, programming team expertise, system modeling needs, flexibility, execution mode, standardization, and compliance with industry standards. This holistic approach ensures that the chosen programming languages align with the unique characteristics and goals of the industrial control system.

Basics of PLC Programming

Introduction to PLC Programming

1. What is a PLC?

A Programmable Logic Controller (PLC) is a specialized computing device designed for industrial control applications. It operates by continuously monitoring inputs, executing a control program, and producing outputs to control machines and processes. PLCs play a crucial role in automating tasks that would be impractical or unsafe for humans to perform manually.

2. Components of a PLC:

A typical PLC comprises the following components:

Central Processing Unit (CPU): Executes the control program and processes input/output data.

Input Modules: Interface with sensors and other input devices to collect data.

Output Modules: Interface with actuators and other output devices to control the process.

Memory: Stores the control program, data, and system parameters.

Communication Ports: Enable communication with other devices, such as Human Machine Interfaces (HMIs) or other PLCs.

3. PLC Programming Basics:

PLC programming involves creating a set of instructions that dictate how the PLC should respond to different input conditions. The programming process includes defining the logic, configuring inputs and outputs, and specifying the control actions to achieve the desired automation.

PLC Programming Languages

PLC programming languages are standardized methods used to create control programs. The IEC 61131-3 standard defines several programming languages commonly used in the industry.

1. Ladder Diagram (LD):

Description: LD is a graphical programming language that uses ladder-like symbols to represent control logic. It is intuitive for individuals with a background in electrical engineering.

Use Cases: LD is often used for simple to moderately complex control logic, especially in applications where the control process resembles electrical relay logic.

2. Structured Text (ST):

Description: ST is a high-level, text-based programming language resembling languages like Pascal or C. It allows for the development of complex algorithms and mathematical computations.

Use Cases: ST is suitable for applications requiring sophisticated control algorithms, mathematical computations, and data manipulation.

3. Function Block Diagram (FBD):

Description: FBD is a graphical language representing control logic as interconnected function blocks. Each block encapsulates a specific function or operation.

Use Cases: FBD is ideal for visualizing and organizing complex control processes, providing modularity through encapsulation of functions.

4. Instruction List (IL):

Description: IL is a low-level, text-based language using mnemonic codes to represent control instructions. It is similar to assembly language and offers fine control over specific hardware components.

Use Cases: IL is used in applications where low-level control is required, providing a concise representation of control logic.

5. Sequential Function Chart (SFC):

Description: SFC is a graphical language representing the behavior of a system using a series of steps and transitions. It models sequential and parallel processes.

Use Cases: SFC is suitable for applications with multiple stages or phases, where the control process can be represented visually as states and transitions.

PLC Programming Workflow

1. Define Control Objectives:

Before starting the PLC programming process, clearly define the control objectives. Understand the behavior of the system, the desired outcomes, and the conditions under which the PLC should respond.

2. Identify Inputs and Outputs:

Identify the sensors and devices that provide inputs to the PLC and the actuators or devices that receive outputs from the PLC. This involves understanding the physical components of the system.

3. Develop Control Logic:

Choose the appropriate programming language (LD, ST, FBD, IL, or SFC) based on the application requirements. Develop the control logic by creating a set of instructions that define how the PLC should respond to different input conditions.

4. Configure Inputs and Outputs:

In the PLC programming environment, configure the input and output modules to correspond to the identified sensors and actuators. Define the addressing and scaling for analog inputs and outputs.

5. Write the Control Program:

Using the chosen programming language, write the control program. Implement the control logic by arranging graphical elements (for LD, FBD, and SFC) or writing text-based code (for ST and IL).

6. Download the Program to the PLC:

Once the control program is written, download it to the PLC's memory. This step transfers the program from the programming environment to the PLC, allowing it to execute the control logic.

7. Test and Debug:

Test the PLC program in a controlled environment to ensure that it behaves as expected. Use simulation tools or test the program on the actual hardware. Debug any issues and refine the control logic if necessary.

8. Commission the System:

Commissioning involves deploying the PLC program in the actual industrial environment. Verify the system's behavior, responsiveness, and accuracy. Fine-tune the control logic as needed to optimize performance.

9. Monitor and Maintain:

Regularly monitor the PLC system to ensure proper functioning. Implement preventive maintenance strategies to address potential issues before they impact the system's performance.

Best Practices in PLC Programming

1. Modularity and Reusability:

Design the control program with modularity in mind. Use functions or function blocks to encapsulate specific operations, promoting reusability across different parts of the program.

2. Documentation:

Thoroughly document the PLC program, including comments within the code, a comprehensive program description, and a clear outline of the control logic. This documentation aids in understanding, troubleshooting, and future modifications.

3. Error Handling:

Implement robust error-handling mechanisms within the PLC program. Use diagnostic routines to identify issues, and incorporate fail-safe features to ensure safe operation in the event of a failure.

4. Security Measures:

Incorporate security measures to protect the PLC program from unauthorized access and potential cyber threats. Restrict access to the programming environment, use secure communication protocols, and follow cybersecurity best practices.

5. Testing Procedures:

Establish thorough testing procedures during the development and commissioning phases. Use simulation tools to test the program in a controlled environment before deploying it on the actual hardware. Conduct comprehensive testing to identify and address potential issues.

6. Version Control:

Implement version control for the PLC program to track changes, manage updates, and maintain a history of modifications. This practice ensures traceability and facilitates rollback to previous versions if necessary.

7. Backup and Recovery:

Regularly back up the PLC program and configuration settings. This practice safeguards against data loss in case of hardware failures or unexpected issues. Establish recovery procedures to restore the system quickly.

8. Training and Knowledge Transfer:

Provide training for personnel involved in PLC programming and maintenance. Foster knowledge transfer to ensure that multiple team members are proficient in understanding and modifying the control program.

Challenges and Considerations

1. Real-Time Processing:

PLCs operate in real-time environments, and the control program must respond to inputs and generate outputs within specific time constraints. Consider the processing speed and efficiency of the control logic to meet real-time requirements.

2. I/O Addressing and Scaling:

Accurate configuration of input and output addressing is crucial. Ensure proper scaling for analog inputs and outputs to interpret and represent physical values accurately in the control program.

3. Environmental Conditions:

Consider the environmental conditions in which the PLC operates. Harsh conditions, such as temperature extremes, humidity, or vibration, may require additional protective measures or specialized PLC hardware.

4. Cybersecurity:

With increasing connectivity, PLCs are susceptible to cyber threats. Implement cybersecurity measures, including secure communication protocols, access controls, and regular updates, to protect the PLC system from unauthorized access and potential attacks.

5. Scalability and Future Expansion:

Design the control program with scalability in mind to accommodate future expansions or modifications. Choose a PLC system that supports additional I/O modules and features to facilitate scalability.

6. Interoperability:

Ensure that the PLC programming adheres to industry standards, promoting interoperability with other devices and systems. Compliance with standards such as IEC 61131-3 enhances the portability of the control program.

Conclusion

PLC programming is a foundational aspect of industrial automation, enabling the efficient and reliable control of machinery and processes. Understanding the basics of PLC programming involves familiarity with PLC components, programming languages, and the workflow from design to commissioning. By adhering to best practices and considering challenges and considerations, engineers can develop robust PLC programs that meet the control objectives of diverse industrial applications.

Ladder Logic Diagrams

Introduction to Ladder Logic

Ladder Logic is a graphical programming language used in industrial control systems for designing and documenting control systems. It's particularly prevalent in programmable logic controllers (PLCs) and plays a crucial role in automation processes. Ladder Logic Diagrams (LLDs) are the visual representation of the logical and sequential control operations within a system.

Components of Ladder Logic Diagrams

1. Contacts and Coils:

Contacts: Represent input devices or conditions that can be either open or closed. They include symbols for switches, sensors, and other input devices.

Coils: Indicate the output devices or actions to be performed based on the conditions set by the contacts. Motors, valves, and other output devices are represented by coil symbols.

2. Power Rails:

Power Rails: Ladder Logic typically consists of two vertical lines called power rails. These represent the power supply of the system, usually denoted as L (for Line) and N (for Neutral) in electrical terms.

3. Rungs:

Rungs: Each horizontal line in a ladder diagram is called a rung. A rung represents a specific control operation or a logical step in the program. Contacts and coils are placed on rungs to create the desired control sequence.

4. Symbols:

Symbols: Ladder Logic symbols are standardized and universally recognized. Common symbols include normally open (NO) and normally closed (NC) contacts, relay coils, timers, counters, and more.

Working Principles of Ladder Logic Diagrams

1. Scan Cycle:

Scan Cycle: The PLC continuously scans the ladder diagram from top to bottom. During each scan cycle, the controller evaluates the state of each contact and updates the state of the corresponding coil.

2. Logic Continuity:

Logic Continuity: For a coil to be energized (turn on), there must be a continuous path of closed contacts leading to it. If any contact in the path is open, the logic continuity is broken, and the coil remains de-energized.

3. Logic Execution:

Logic Execution: The ladder diagram's logic is executed based on the state of the contacts and the defined control sequence. This sequence determines the behavior of the output devices and the overall control of the system.

Common Ladder Logic Elements

1. Timers and Counters:

Timers: Used to introduce time delays into the control system. Timers can be on-delay (TON), off-delay (TOF), or retentive (RTO).

Counters: Keep track of the number of input events or pulses. They can be up counters (CTU) or down counters (CTD).

2. Comparison and Mathematical Operations:

Comparison Operations: Ladder Logic supports comparison operations such as equal, not equal, greater than, and less than, allowing for conditional branching in the control sequence.

Mathematical Operations: Basic mathematical functions like addition, subtraction, multiplication, and division can be implemented in ladder logic.

3. Branching and Jumping:

Branching: Conditional branching is achieved through the use of contacts and coils in parallel or series, enabling the creation of decision-making structures.

Jumping: Some PLCs support jump instructions, allowing the program to skip rungs or sections based on specific conditions.

Advantages of Ladder Logic Diagrams

1. Graphical Representation:

Graphical Representation: Ladder Logic provides a visual representation of control logic, making it easy for engineers and technicians to understand and troubleshoot the system.

2. Ease of Programming:

Ease of Programming: The graphical nature of ladder diagrams simplifies the programming process, especially for those with a background in electrical engineering.

3. Modularity and Reusability:

Modularity: Ladder Logic encourages modular programming, allowing designers to break down complex systems into smaller, manageable units.

Reusability: Once a ladder diagram is created, it can be reused in similar applications, saving time and effort in programming.

4. Debugging and Troubleshooting:

Debugging: Troubleshooting ladder logic is relatively straightforward, as engineers can visually trace the logic flow and identify issues quickly.

Applications of Ladder Logic

1. Industrial Automation:

Industrial Automation: Ladder Logic is extensively used in manufacturing and industrial processes for controlling machinery, production lines, and other automated systems.

2. Building Automation:

Building Automation: Ladder Logic finds applications in building management systems, controlling HVAC (heating, ventilation, and air conditioning) systems, lighting, and security systems.

3. Traffic Control Systems:

Traffic Control: PLCs with ladder logic are employed in traffic light control systems to manage the flow of traffic at intersections efficiently.

4. Water Treatment and Utilities:

Water Treatment: Ladder Logic is used in water treatment plants for controlling pumps, valves, and other equipment in the purification process.

Challenges and Considerations

1. Learning Curve:

Learning Curve: While ladder logic is user-friendly, newcomers may face a learning curve, especially if they are not familiar with electrical symbols and control systems.

2. Limited Complexity:

Complexity: For highly complex control systems, ladder logic may become less intuitive, and other programming languages like structured text or function block diagrams might be more suitable.

3. Maintenance and Documentation:

Maintenance: Proper documentation of ladder logic diagrams is essential for system maintenance. Changes in the control logic should be well-documented to ensure the reliability of the system.

Conclusion

Ladder Logic Diagrams are a fundamental aspect of industrial automation and control systems. Their graphical nature facilitates the design, analysis, and maintenance of control logic in a wide range of applications. As technology evolves, so does the landscape of programmable logic controllers and their associated programming languages. However, ladder logic remains a cornerstone in the world of industrial automation, providing a reliable and visual means of controlling complex systems. Understanding and mastering ladder logic is a valuable skill for engineers and technicians involved in the design and maintenance of automated processes.

Communication in PLC

Introduction

Communication in Programmable Logic Controllers (PLCs) plays a pivotal role in the realm of industrial automation. PLCs are widely used for controlling and monitoring complex processes in manufacturing, utilities, and various industries. Communication enables PLCs to exchange information with other devices, controllers, and systems, creating a cohesive and interconnected automation environment.

Basics of PLC Communication

1. PLC Communication Protocols:

Protocols: PLC communication relies on established protocols that define the rules and conventions for data exchange. Common protocols include Modbus, Profibus, Ethernet/IP, DeviceNet, and more. These protocols determine how PLCs communicate with each other and with other devices on the network.

2. PLC Networks:

Networks: PLCs are often interconnected through networks, allowing them to share data and coordinate tasks. Networks can be local, such as within a factory, or extend over larger areas, connecting multiple facilities.

3. I/O Communication:

I/O Communication: Input and output (I/O) modules are crucial components of PLCs. Communication between the PLC and I/O devices, such as sensors and actuators, occurs through digital or analog signals. Digital I/O communication is typically faster and more common in industrial applications.

Types of PLC Communication

1. Point-to-Point Communication:

Point-to-Point: In a point-to-point communication setup, a PLC communicates directly with another PLC or device. This method is suitable for simple systems where direct communication suffices.

2. Multidrop Communication:

Multidrop: Multidrop communication involves connecting multiple devices to a single communication line. The PLC communicates with each device sequentially. Modbus is an example of a multidrop communication protocol.

3. Network Communication:

Networks: PLCs often communicate over industrial networks. Ethernet and fieldbus networks, such as Profibus and DeviceNet, enable PLCs to share data efficiently in larger and more complex automation systems.

4. Serial Communication:

Serial Communication: Serial communication, such as RS-232 or RS-485, is used for connecting PLCs to devices like human-machine interfaces (HMIs) or printers. It's a common choice for short-distance communication.

5. Wireless Communication:

Wireless Communication: With advancements in technology, some PLCs support wireless communication protocols. This is beneficial in situations where running physical cables is impractical.

Communication Interfaces in PLCs

1. Serial Interfaces:

RS-232 and RS-485: Serial interfaces like RS-232 and RS-485 are common in PLC communication for connecting to devices like computers, HMI panels, and other controllers.

2. Ethernet Interfaces:

Ethernet: PLCs equipped with Ethernet interfaces facilitate high-speed communication and are integral in connecting PLCs to industrial networks and the internet. Ethernet/IP is a widely used industrial Ethernet protocol.

3. Fieldbus Interfaces:

Profibus, DeviceNet, CANopen: Fieldbus interfaces, such as Profibus, DeviceNet, and CANopen, provide a standardized way for PLCs to communicate with various devices on the factory floor, including sensors, actuators, and other controllers.

4. Wireless Interfaces:

Wi-Fi and Bluetooth: Some PLCs come with built-in Wi-Fi or Bluetooth interfaces, allowing for wireless communication with other devices or systems.

PLC-to-PLC Communication

1. Data Exchange:

Data Exchange: PLCs communicate with each other to share information such as process data, control signals, and diagnostic data. This exchange is crucial for coordinating tasks in complex automation systems.

2. Master-Slave Configuration:

Master-Slave: In a master-slave configuration, one PLC (the master) controls and coordinates communication with other PLCs (slaves). This hierarchical structure is common in distributed control systems.

3. Peer-to-Peer Communication:

Peer-to-Peer: In peer-to-peer communication, PLCs communicate with each other on an equal footing, sharing data and making joint decisions. This approach is often used in collaborative and redundant control systems.

PLC-to-Device Communication

1. HMI Communication:

HMI (Human-Machine Interface): PLCs communicate with HMIs to provide a graphical interface for operators to monitor and control industrial processes. This communication enables real-time data visualization and system interaction.

2. Sensor and Actuator Communication:

Sensor and Actuator Interfaces: PLCs communicate with sensors and actuators to gather input data and send control signals. This interaction is fundamental to the automation of industrial processes.

3. Variable Frequency Drives (VFDs) Communication:

VFDs: PLCs often communicate with VFDs to control the speed and operation of motors. This communication ensures precise control over motor-driven processes.

4. SCADA Systems Communication:

SCADA (Supervisory Control and Data Acquisition): PLCs communicate with SCADA systems for centralized monitoring, control, and data acquisition. This enables operators to oversee and manage entire industrial processes.

Communication Protocols in PLCs

1. Modbus:

Modbus Protocol: Modbus is a widely used open-source protocol for serial communication between PLCs and other devices. It supports point-to-point and multidrop configurations and is known for its simplicity and reliability.

2. Profibus:

Profibus Protocol: Profibus is a fieldbus communication protocol used in industrial automation. It supports high-speed data exchange and is often used for connecting PLCs to various devices on the factory floor.

3. Ethernet/IP:

Ethernet/IP Protocol: Ethernet/IP is an industrial Ethernet protocol used for communication between PLCs and other devices. It allows for high-speed data transfer and is widely adopted in modern industrial automation.

4. DeviceNet:

DeviceNet Protocol: DeviceNet is a network protocol used for communication between industrial devices. It is often used in PLCs to connect to sensors, actuators, and other devices in the field.

5. CANopen:

CANopen Protocol: CANopen is a communication protocol based on the Controller Area Network (CAN) bus. It is used for communication in distributed control systems, often in automotive and manufacturing applications.

Challenges in PLC Communication

1. Interoperability:

Interoperability: Integrating PLCs from different manufacturers can be challenging due to differences in communication protocols and standards. This can lead to the need for gateway devices or protocol converters.

2. Network Security:

Security: As PLCs become more connected, ensuring the security of communication networks is crucial. Implementing measures such as firewalls and secure communication protocols helps protect against cyber threats.

3. Data Integrity and Reliability:

Data Integrity: Maintaining data integrity is vital for the reliability of PLC communication. Issues such as data corruption or loss can lead to incorrect control decisions and affect the overall performance of the automation system.

4. Scalability:

Scalability: Designing communication systems that can scale with the growing complexity of industrial processes is a challenge. Ensuring that communication architectures can accommodate additional devices and controllers is essential.

Future Trends in PLC Communication

1. IIoT Integration:

IIoT (Industrial Internet of Things): The integration of PLCs with IIoT technologies is a growing trend. This involves leveraging sensors, connectivity, and data analytics to enhance the efficiency and intelligence of industrial processes.

2. Edge Computing:

Edge Computing: Edge computing in PLCs involves processing data closer to the source, reducing latency and improving real-time decision-making. This trend is particularly relevant in applications where low latency is critical.

3. 5G Connectivity:

5G Technology: The adoption of 5G technology in industrial settings is expected to revolutionize communication in PLCs. High-speed, low-latency communication will enable more responsive and connected automation systems.

4. Cybersecurity Enhancements:

Cybersecurity: With the increasing connectivity of PLCs, there's a growing emphasis on enhancing cybersecurity measures. This includes implementing robust encryption, authentication, and intrusion detection systems.

Conclusion

Communication in Programmable Logic Controllers is a dynamic and integral aspect of industrial automation. PLCs play a crucial role in controlling and monitoring processes, and their ability to communicate with other devices and controllers is fundamental to the efficiency and effectiveness of automation systems. As technology continues to advance, the landscape of PLC communication evolves, incorporating trends such as IIoT integration, edge computing, and enhanced cybersecurity measures. Engineers and professionals in the field of industrial automation must stay abreast of these developments to design, implement, and maintain robust communication systems that meet the demands of modern industrial processes. Understanding the principles of PLC communication, the various protocols and interfaces involved, and the challenges and future trends in this field is essential for building reliable and interconnected automation solutions.

Programming Timers and Counters

Introduction

Timers and counters are essential components of PLC programming, serving as crucial tools for managing time-related and counting operations in industrial automation. Timers enable the introduction of time delays, while counters keep track of events or occurrences. Understanding how to program timers and counters efficiently is fundamental for designing effective and precise control logic in PLCs.

Basics of Timers and Counters

1. Timers:

Purpose: Timers are used to introduce time delays into a control system. They are essential for coordinating actions, sequencing processes, and controlling the timing of specific events.

Types of Timers:

On-Delay Timers (TON): These timers initiate a delay when the input condition turns on and only allow the output to turn on after the preset time has elapsed.

Off-Delay Timers (TOF): These timers initiate a delay when the input condition turns off and only allow the output to turn off after the preset time has elapsed.

Retentive Timers (RTO): Retentive timers maintain the accumulated time value even when the input condition turns off, ensuring continuity when the input condition is reactivated.

2. Counters:

Purpose: Counters keep track of the number of events or pulses received. They are employed to monitor and control processes that require a specific count of occurrences.

Types of Counters:

Up Counters (CTU): These counters increment the count value each time the input condition transitions from off to on.

Down Counters (CTD): These counters decrement the count value each time the input condition transitions from off to on.

Programming Timers

1. On-Delay Timers (TON):

Ladder Logic Representation:

plaintext

Copy code

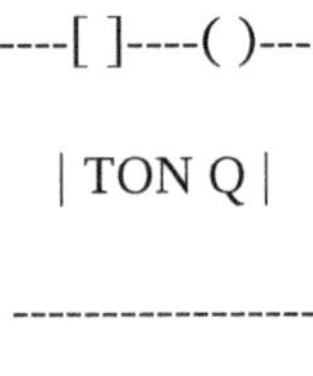

```
----[ ]----( )----
   | TON Q |

   -----------------
```

Explanation:

The timer (TON) is represented by the symbol [ ].

The input condition is connected to the timer's coil.

The output (Q) becomes true only after the preset time has elapsed following the activation of the input condition.

Example:

If TON is set for 5 seconds and the input condition becomes true, the output (Q) will turn on 5 seconds later and remain on until the input condition turns off.

2. Off-Delay Timers (TOF):

Ladder Logic Representation:

plaintext

Copy code

```
----[ ]----( )----
   | TOF Q |

   -----------------
```

Explanation:

The off-delay timer (TOF) operates similarly to the on-delay timer but introduces a delay after the input condition turns off.

The output (Q) remains true for the preset time after the input condition turns off.

Example:

If TOF is set for 3 seconds and the input condition turns off, the output (Q) will remain on for an additional 3 seconds before turning off.

3. Retentive Timers (RTO):

Ladder Logic Representation:

plaintext

plaintext

Copy code

```
----[ ]----( )----
   | RTO Q |

   ------------------
```

Explanation:

The retentive timer (RTO) maintains its accumulated time value even if the input condition turns off.

The accumulated time value is retained until reset.

Example:

If RTO is set for 10 seconds and the input condition turns on, the output (Q) will turn on after 10 seconds. If the input condition turns off after 5 seconds, the accumulated time will still be 5 seconds. If the input condition turns on again, the timer resumes counting from 5 seconds.

Programming Counters

1. Up Counters (CTU):

Ladder Logic Representation:

plaintext

Copy code

```
----[ ]----( )----
   | CTU CU |

   ------------------
```

Explanation:

The up counter (CTU) increments the count value each time the input condition transitions from off to on.

The count value is displayed by the counter (CU) output.

Example:

If CTU is set for a count of 5 and the input condition turns on five times, the output CU will be true, indicating that the count value has reached 5.

2. Down Counters (CTD):

Ladder Logic Representation:

plaintext

Copy code

----[ ]----( )----

| CTD CD |

Explanation:

The down counter (CTD) decrements the count value each time the input condition transitions from off to on.

The count value is displayed by the counter (CD) output.

Example:

If CTD is set for a count of 3 and the input condition turns on three times, the output CD will be true, indicating that the count value has reached 0.

Timing and Counting Applications

1. Conveyor Belt Control:

Timers can be used to control the duration of motor operation, ensuring that a conveyor belt runs for a specific period before stopping.

2. Batch Processing:

Counters are employed to monitor the quantity of materials or products in a batch process, ensuring that the correct number of items is processed.

3. Traffic Light Sequencing:

Timers are utilized to create time delays in traffic light control systems, ensuring a smooth transition between signal states.

4. Pump Control:

Timers can be programmed to control the operation of pumps, introducing delays to avoid rapid cycling and extend equipment lifespan.

5. Temperature Control:

Timers can be used in conjunction with sensors to implement temperature control, adjusting the operation of heating or cooling devices based on time intervals.

Advanced Timer and Counter Programming

1. Cascade Control:

Cascade control involves using multiple timers or counters in a sequential manner, creating more complex and sophisticated control logic.

2. Interrupts and Priorities:

In some PLC programming languages, interrupts can be used to temporarily pause the execution of a routine and handle higher-priority tasks.

3. Feedback and Control Loops:

Integrating feedback from sensors and other devices allows for closed-loop control, where the system adjusts its behavior based on real-time information.

Challenges and Considerations

1. Accuracy and Precision:

Achieving precise timing and counting requires careful consideration of the PLC scan time and the resolution of timers and counters.

2. Synchronization:

When multiple timers or counters are used, ensuring synchronization and avoiding conflicts is crucial to maintaining accurate control.

3. System Response Time:

The responsiveness of the overall control system depends on how well timers and counters are programmed and configured.

4. Debugging and Troubleshooting:

Identifying issues in timing and counting logic requires thorough testing and debugging, often involving the use of simulation tools.

Conclusion

Programming timers and counters in PLCs is a fundamental aspect of industrial automation, allowing engineers to control and sequence processes with precision. Timers enable the introduction of time delays, while counters keep track of events, both essential for achieving accurate and efficient control. Whether used in simple applications like conveyor belt control or in more complex scenarios such as cascade control, timers and counters are versatile tools that form the backbone of PLC programming. Understanding the principles of programming timers and counters, considering their applications, and addressing challenges in accuracy and synchronization are crucial for designing robust and reliable control systems in industrial automation. As technology advances, the integration of timers and counters with other advanced control strategies, such as closed-loop feedback and prioritized interrupts, will continue to enhance the capabilities of PLCs in meeting the evolving demands of industrial processes.

Data Handling

Introduction

In the realm of industrial automation, Programmable Logic Controllers (PLCs) play a central role in controlling and monitoring complex processes. PLC data handling is a critical aspect of programming, encompassing the management, storage, retrieval, and manipulation of data within a control system. Understanding how PLCs handle data is essential for designing efficient and reliable automation solutions.

Basics of PLC Data Handling

1. Memory Types in PLCs:

RAM (Random Access Memory): Volatile memory used for storing temporary data during program execution. Data in RAM is lost when power is turned off.

ROM (Read-Only Memory): Non-volatile memory that stores the PLC operating system and the user program. Data in ROM is retained even when power is off.

2. Data Types:

Boolean: Represents binary states (true or false).

Integer: Represents whole numbers.

Real: Represents decimal numbers.

String: Represents sequences of characters.

Timers and Counters: Specialized data types for handling time and counting operations.

3. Data Storage:

Registers: Memory locations where data is stored. Different types of registers (input, output, internal) serve various purposes in the PLC program.

Bits and Bytes: Fundamental units of data storage. Bits represent binary values (0 or 1), and bytes are groups of eight bits.

PLC Data Addressing

1. Bit-Level Addressing:

Syntax: Address:Bit

Example: I:1/0 refers to the first input (I) and its first bit.

2. Byte-Level Addressing:

Syntax: Address:Byte

Example: O:2 refers to the second output (O) and its entire byte.

3. Word-Level Addressing:

Syntax: Address:Word

Example: B3:1 refers to the second word in the B3 data table.

4. Double-Word Addressing:

Syntax: Address:DoubleWord

Example: N7:1 refers to the second double-word in the N7 data table.

5. Structural Data Types:

Arrays and Structures: PLCs support arrays and structures for organizing and manipulating complex data sets.

Data Handling Instructions

1. Load and Store Instructions:

LD (Load): Loads data into a register.

ST (Store): Stores data from a register to memory.

2. Comparison Instructions:

Equal (EQ), Not Equal (NE), Greater Than (GT), Less Than (LT): Used for comparing data values.

3. Mathematical Instructions:

Add (ADD), Subtract (SUB), Multiply (MUL), Divide (DIV): Perform arithmetic operations on data.

4. Move Instructions:

MOV (Move): Transfers data from one register to another.

5. Conversion Instructions:

CONV (Convert): Converts data from one type to another.

6. Bit-Level Instructions:

AND, OR, XOR, NOT: Perform logical operations on individual bits.

7. Shift and Rotate Instructions:

SHL (Shift Left), SHR (Shift Right), ROL (Rotate Left), ROR (Rotate Right): Manipulate bit positions.

8. Data Handling for Timers and Counters:

Timer On (TON), Timer Off (TOF): Control the timing functions of timers.

Counter Up (CTU), Counter Down (CTD): Control the counting functions of counters.

Data Handling in PLC Programming Languages

1. Ladder Logic:

Contacts and Coils: Representing input conditions and outputs, ladder logic symbols simplify the visual representation of data handling operations.

Branching and Logic Continuity: Ensures proper flow of data handling instructions.

2. Structured Text (ST):

High-Level Language: Allows for more complex and structured programming.

Data Types and Structures: Supports a wide range of data types and complex data structures.

3. Function Block Diagram (FBD):

Graphical Representation: Uses blocks to represent functions, facilitating the organization of data handling instructions.

Connectivity: Defines the flow of data between blocks.

4. Sequential Function Chart (SFC):

Sequential Programming: Represents a sequential control structure, organizing data handling instructions into steps.

Parallel Branches: Allows for parallel execution of data handling operations.

Advanced Data Handling Techniques

1. Data Logging:

Recording Data: PLCs can log data for analysis, troubleshooting, and historical record-keeping.

2. PID Control (Proportional-Integral-Derivative):

Closed-Loop Control: Uses feedback to adjust the control process based on the error between the desired and actual values.

3. Recipe Handling:

Recipe Management: PLCs can handle and store recipes for different production processes.

4. Communication Protocols:

Industrial Networks: PLCs use various communication protocols (Modbus, Profibus, Ethernet/IP) to exchange data with other PLCs and devices.

5. Security Measures:

Access Control: Implementing user privileges and password protection to secure sensitive data.

Challenges and Considerations

1. Data Integrity:

Ensuring Accuracy: Maintaining data integrity is crucial for the reliability and accuracy of the control system.

2. Memory Management:

Optimizing Memory Usage: Effectively managing memory resources to prevent overloading the PLC.

3. Real-Time Constraints:

Deterministic Timing: Ensuring that data handling operations meet real-time requirements in applications with time-sensitive processes.

4. Data Conversion:

Handling Different Data Types: Addressing challenges related to converting data between different types to ensure compatibility.

Future Trends in PLC Data Handling

1. Edge Computing Integration:

Decentralized Data Processing: Integrating edge computing for faster and more efficient data processing at the source.

2. Machine Learning and AI:

Data Analytics: Utilizing machine learning and artificial intelligence for predictive maintenance, anomaly detection, and process optimization.

3. IIoT (Industrial Internet of Things) Connectivity:

Enhanced Communication: Leveraging IIoT for increased connectivity and data exchange between PLCs and other smart devices.

4. Cybersecurity Enhancements:

Secure Data Handling: Implementing advanced cybersecurity measures to protect sensitive data from potential threats.

Conclusion

PLC data handling is a multifaceted aspect of industrial automation, encompassing a wide range of techniques and considerations. From basic data types and addressing methods to advanced programming instructions and future trends, a comprehensive understanding of data handling is essential for PLC programmers and automation engineers. As technology continues to advance, the integration of PLCs with emerging trends such as edge computing, machine learning, and IIoT connectivity will shape the future landscape of data handling in industrial automation. The challenges and considerations associated with data integrity, memory management, and real-time constraints highlight the importance of careful planning and implementation to ensure the robustness and reliability of PLC-based control systems. In conclusion, PLC data handling is a dynamic and evolving field that continues to play a pivotal role in the efficiency and intelligence of industrial processes.

PLC Modules

Introduction

Programmable Logic Controllers (PLCs) are at the heart of industrial automation, providing a robust and flexible platform for controlling and monitoring processes. PLC modules are integral components that enhance the functionality of PLC systems. These modules encompass a diverse range of input and output devices, communication interfaces, and specialized units that allow PLCs to interface with various sensors, actuators, and other automation components. Understanding the types, functions, and applications of PLC modules is essential for designing and implementing effective control systems in industrial settings.

Basic Components of PLC Modules

1. Central Processing Unit (CPU):

Role: The CPU is the brain of the PLC, responsible for executing the control program, handling data processing, and coordinating communication between modules.

Varieties: PLCs come with different CPU types, ranging from basic models for simple control tasks to advanced processors for complex automation processes.

2. Input Modules:

Role: Input modules are responsible for interfacing with external sensors and devices, converting physical signals into digital data that the PLC can process.

Types: Digital input modules handle on/off signals, while analog input modules process continuous signals with varying voltage or current levels.

3. Output Modules:

Role: Output modules are responsible for controlling external devices, such as motors, valves, and indicators, by converting digital signals from the PLC into physical actions.

Types: Digital output modules control on/off devices, while analog output modules manage devices requiring variable control, like regulating motor speed.

4. Power Supply Modules:

Role: Power supply modules ensure a stable and reliable power source for the PLC and its connected modules.

Redundancy: Some PLC systems may include redundant power supplies for enhanced reliability.

Specialized PLC Modules

1. Communication Modules:

Role: Communication modules enable PLCs to exchange data with other PLCs, computers, or external devices. They support various communication protocols such as Modbus, Profibus, and Ethernet/IP.

Applications: Used in distributed control systems and networked automation environments.

2. Analog Modules:

Role: Analog modules handle analog signals, allowing PLCs to interact with devices that provide continuous feedback, such as temperature sensors or pressure transmitters.

Conversion: Analog-to-digital converters and digital-to-analog converters are commonly integrated into these modules.

3. High-Speed Counter Modules:

Role: High-speed counter modules allow PLCs to monitor and count high-frequency input signals, enabling precise control of fast-moving processes.

Applications: Used in applications like conveyor belt speed control or high-speed production lines.

4. Temperature Control Modules:

Role: These modules are designed to interface with temperature sensors and control devices such as heaters or coolers to maintain specific temperature conditions.

Applications: Commonly used in industrial processes where temperature control is critical.

5. Motion Control Modules:

Role: Motion control modules interface with servo drives and motors, enabling PLCs to execute complex motion control tasks such as positioning, speed control, and trajectory planning.

Applications: Found in robotics, CNC machines, and other applications requiring precise motion control.

6. Safety Modules:

Role: Safety modules ensure compliance with safety standards by monitoring and managing safety-related aspects of the control system, such as emergency stops and safety interlocks.

Applications: Critical in industries where human safety is a top priority, such as manufacturing and processing plants.

PLC Module Installation and Configuration

1. Physical Installation:

Rack-Based Systems: PLC modules are often installed in modular racks. Input, output, and specialized modules are inserted into slots in the rack.

Remote I/O Systems: In remote I/O configurations, modules are distributed across the plant, connected to the PLC through communication networks.

2. Module Configuration:

Addressing: Each module is assigned a unique address, allowing the PLC to identify and communicate with it.

Configuration Software: PLC programming software is used to configure module parameters, such as input types, output statuses, and communication settings.

3. I/O Mapping:

Input Mapping: Associates physical input signals with specific input modules and addresses.

Output Mapping: Maps PLC output data to the corresponding output modules and addresses.

4. Network Configuration:

Communication Modules: Network configuration involves setting up communication modules with appropriate network addresses and parameters.

Network Topology: Configuring the network topology to ensure efficient data exchange between PLCs and other devices.

PLC Module Communication

1. PLC-to-PLC Communication:

Data Exchange: Communication modules facilitate data exchange between PLCs in distributed control systems.

Protocols: Communication protocols such as Ethernet/IP or Profibus are used for seamless integration.

2. Human-Machine Interface (HMI) Integration:

HMI Modules: Some PLC systems include HMI modules that allow for the integration of graphical interfaces for operators to monitor and control processes.

Data Exchange: Communication between the PLC and HMI modules enables real-time data visualization.

3. SCADA Integration:

SCADA Systems: PLCs communicate with SCADA systems for centralized monitoring, control, and data acquisition.

Data Transfer: Communication modules play a crucial role in transferring data between the PLC and the SCADA system.

Challenges and Considerations

1. Compatibility Issues:

Vendor-Specific Modules: Different PLC manufacturers may have proprietary module designs, potentially leading to compatibility issues when integrating modules from different vendors.

2. Scalability:

System Expansion: Designing PLC systems that can easily accommodate additional modules as the automation requirements evolve.

3. Reliability and Redundancy:

Redundant Systems: Implementing redundant modules and power supplies to ensure system reliability and minimize downtime in the event of a module failure.

4. Maintenance and Troubleshooting:

Diagnostic Tools: Utilizing built-in diagnostic features and software tools to troubleshoot and maintain PLC modules effectively.

Future Trends in PLC Modules

1. Edge Computing Integration:

Local Processing: Integrating edge computing capabilities into modules for local data processing and decision-making.

2. Wireless Communication:

Wi-Fi and 5G: Increasing the use of wireless communication modules for flexibility in module placement and reduced wiring complexity.

3. Modular and Scalable Architectures:

Plug-and-Play Modules: Designing PLC systems with modular architectures that allow for easy integration of new modules without extensive reconfiguration.

4. Cybersecurity Enhancements:

Secure Communication: Implementing advanced security features in communication modules to protect against cyber threats in the era of Industry 4.0.

Conclusion

PLC modules represent the building blocks of industrial automation, providing the means to interface with a wide array of sensors, actuators, and devices. From basic input and output modules to specialized units for motion control, safety, and communication, PLC modules contribute to the flexibility and versatility of control systems. The installation, configuration, and communication aspects of PLC modules are crucial considerations in designing efficient and reliable automation solutions. As technology continues to advance, trends such as edge computing, wireless communication, and enhanced cybersecurity are shaping the future of PLC modules, making them more intelligent, interconnected, and adaptable to the evolving demands of industrial processes. In conclusion, a comprehensive understanding of PLC modules is essential for automation engineers and PLC programmers to harness the full potential of these components in creating robust and sophisticated control systems.

Advanced Motion Controlled Multi Axis PLC

Introduction

Motion control in industrial automation involves the precise regulation of the movement of machinery and equipment. Advanced Motion Control Multi-Axis Programmable Logic Controllers (PLCs) represent a sophisticated and integral component in modern automation systems. These systems allow for precise coordination and synchronization of multiple axes of motion, facilitating complex operations in various industries. This comprehensive overview will delve into the key aspects of advanced motion control multi-axis PLC systems, covering the underlying principles, components, applications, programming techniques, and future trends.

Key Components of Advanced Motion Control Multi-Axis PLC Systems

1. Multi-Axis Servo Drives and Motors:

Role: Multi-axis servo drives and motors are the actuators responsible for executing precise motion control commands. They convert electrical signals from the PLC into mechanical motion.

Features: These components often include features such as high torque, high precision, and the ability to provide feedback to the control system.

2. Motion Controller:

Role: The motion controller is a dedicated component that processes motion control algorithms and generates control signals for the servo drives and motors.

Capabilities: Advanced motion controllers support complex motion profiles, trajectory planning, and synchronization of multiple axes.

3. PLC with Motion Control Capabilities:

Role: The PLC serves as the brain of the automation system, providing a platform for motion control programming and integration with other control processes.

Capabilities: PLCs with advanced motion control capabilities offer specialized instructions and functions for coordinating the motion of multiple axes.

4. Feedback Devices (Encoders/Resolvers):

Role: Feedback devices, such as encoders and resolvers, provide real-time feedback on the position, speed, and direction of motion. This information is crucial for closed-loop control and ensuring accuracy.

Types: Incremental encoders, absolute encoders, and resolvers are commonly used feedback devices in motion control systems.

5. Human-Machine Interface (HMI):

Role: The HMI allows operators and engineers to monitor and control the motion control system. It provides a user-friendly interface for setting parameters, initiating motion, and troubleshooting.

Features: Touchscreens, graphical displays, and interactive controls enhance the user experience.

Principles of Motion Control in Multi-Axis Systems

1. Trajectory Planning:

Definition: Trajectory planning involves determining the desired path that each axis should follow to achieve a specific motion profile.

Considerations: Factors such as acceleration, deceleration, and jerk (rate of change of acceleration) are considered to ensure smooth and controlled motion.

2. Synchronization:

Definition: Synchronization ensures that multiple axes move in harmony to achieve coordinated motion. It is crucial for applications requiring precise interaction between different elements.

Methods: Time-based synchronization and event-triggered synchronization are common methods employed in multi-axis systems.

3. Interpolation:

Definition: Interpolation involves calculating intermediate points between two specified positions. This is particularly important in multi-axis systems where coordinated motion may involve complex paths.

Types: Linear interpolation, circular interpolation, and spline interpolation are techniques used to determine intermediate points.

4. Velocity and Acceleration Control:

Velocity Control: Ensures that each axis moves at the desired speed during various segments of the motion profile.

Acceleration Control: Regulates the rate at which the velocity changes, preventing sudden jerks or rapid changes that could affect system stability.

Applications of Advanced Motion Control Multi-Axis PLC Systems

1. Robotics and Automated Manufacturing:

Pick-and-Place Operations: Multi-axis systems are used in robotic arms for pick-and-place tasks, providing precise positioning and orientation control.

Assembly Lines: Automated manufacturing processes leverage multi-axis motion control for assembling complex products.

2. CNC Machining:

Milling and Turning Operations: CNC machines use multi-axis motion control for cutting, shaping, and forming materials with high precision.

Complex Geometry: Multi-axis systems enable the creation of intricate shapes and contours in manufacturing.

3. Packaging and Material Handling:

Conveyor Systems: Multi-axis control ensures smooth and coordinated movement of products on conveyor systems.

Packaging Machines: Precise control is essential in packaging machines for accurate filling, sealing, and labeling.

4. Printing and Labeling:

Digital Printing: Multi-axis systems are utilized in digital printing machines to position print heads accurately.

Labeling Machines: Achieving precise label placement on products is facilitated by multi-axis motion control.

5. Medical Device Manufacturing:

Surgical Robots: Multi-axis motion control is integral to surgical robotic systems for performing minimally invasive procedures with high precision.

Diagnostic Equipment: Precision in positioning is crucial in medical devices such as scanning and imaging machines.

Programming Techniques for Advanced Motion Control

1. PLC Programming Languages:

Structured Text (ST): High-level programming language suitable for expressing complex motion control algorithms.

Function Block Diagram (FBD): Graphical representation of motion control functions and interconnections.

Ladder Logic: Commonly used for expressing sequential and parallel motion control operations.

2. Use of Motion Control Libraries:

Pre-Defined Functions: PLC manufacturers often provide motion control libraries that include pre-defined functions for trajectory planning, synchronization, and interpolation.

Simplified Programming: Engineers can leverage these libraries to simplify programming and reduce development time.

3. Coordinated Motion Programming:

Axis Grouping: Coordinated motion programming involves grouping multiple axes and defining their relationships to achieve synchronous motion.

Master-Slave Configurations: One axis may act as the master, dictating the motion profile, while others follow as slaves.

4. Advanced Algorithms:

PID Control (Proportional-Integral-Derivative): Used for closed-loop control, PID algorithms enhance the system's ability to maintain accurate positioning.

Feedforward Control: Predictive algorithms that anticipate system behavior and adjust control inputs in advance.

Challenges and Considerations in Advanced Motion Control Multi-Axis PLC Systems

1. Mechanical Coupling:

Precision Mechanisms: Mechanical components must be carefully designed and maintained to ensure minimal backlash, compliance, and hysteresis.

Mechanical Wear: Over time, wear in mechanical components can affect the overall accuracy of the motion control system.

2. System Integration:

Compatibility: Ensuring seamless integration of various components from different manufacturers, such as servo drives, motors, and controllers.

Communication Protocols: Standardized communication protocols are essential for effective communication between motion control components.

3. Real-Time Requirements:

Deterministic Timing: Achieving real-time motion control requires the system to respond with high precision within specified time intervals.

PLC Scan Time: Optimizing PLC scan time is crucial to meet real-time requirements.

4. Error Compensation:

Feedback Systems: Utilizing advanced feedback devices and algorithms to compensate for errors, drift, and disturbances in the motion control system.

Calibration: Regular calibration of feedback devices to maintain accuracy over time.

Future Trends in Advanced Motion Control Multi-Axis PLC Systems

1. Integration with Machine Learning:

Adaptive Control: Incorporating machine learning algorithms for adaptive control, allowing the system to learn and optimize its performance over time.

Predictive Maintenance: Using machine learning to predict and prevent potential issues, reducing downtime and maintenance costs.

2. Connectivity in Industry 4.0:

IoT Integration: Integrating motion control systems with the Internet of Things (IoT) for enhanced connectivity, remote monitoring, and data analytics.

Cloud-Based Solutions: Utilizing cloud-based platforms for centralized control and data storage in distributed multi-axis systems.

3. Advanced Simulation and Digital Twins:

Virtual Prototyping: Employing advanced simulation techniques and digital twins to simulate and optimize multi-axis motion control systems before physical implementation.

Augmented Reality (AR): Using AR for real-time visualization and monitoring of complex motion control processes.

4. Energy Efficiency:

Regenerative Systems: Implementing regenerative braking and energy recovery systems to enhance the energy efficiency of motion control systems.

Smart Power Management: Integrating intelligent power management features for optimizing energy consumption.

Conclusion

Advanced Motion Control Multi-Axis PLC Systems represent the pinnacle of precision and sophistication in industrial automation. These systems play a crucial role in diverse applications, ranging from manufacturing and robotics to medical devices and beyond. Understanding the principles, components, programming techniques, and challenges associated with advanced motion control is essential for engineers and automation professionals seeking to design, implement, and optimize highly efficient and accurate automation solutions. As technology continues to evolve, the integration of machine learning, Industry 4.0 principles, and advanced simulation techniques will likely shape the future landscape of advanced motion control systems, offering new levels of adaptability, connectivity, and efficiency in industrial automation. In conclusion, the world of advanced motion control multi-axis PLC systems is dynamic, continuously pushing the boundaries of what is achievable in precision motion control and automation.

CHAPTER FIVE

Data Communication and Supervisory Control Systems

Industrial Data Communications -– Modbus – HART – DeviceNet – Profibus – Fieldbus – RS232-RS485- Modbus/ Modbus TCP/IP - mechatrolink – CAN – EtherCAT - Introduction to Supervisory Control Systems – SCADA - Distributed Control System (DCS) – Safety Systems – human machine interfaces - Total Integrated Automation (TIA) – Industry 4.0.

Modbus

Modbus is a widely used communication protocol in industrial automation and control systems. It was developed in the late 1970s and has since become a de facto standard for connecting various devices in industrial settings, allowing them to exchange data and control information. In this article, we will provide a comprehensive overview of Modbus, covering its history, architecture, communication modes, and applications.

1. History and Evolution of Modbus

The Modbus protocol was originally developed by Modicon, now a part of Schneider Electric, in 1979. It was created to facilitate communication between programmable logic controllers (PLCs) and other automation devices, such as sensors, actuators, and human-machine interface (HMI) systems. Since its inception, Modbus has undergone several revisions and adaptations to meet the evolving needs of the industrial automation sector.

2. Modbus Architecture

Modbus is based on a client-server architecture, where one device (the client) initiates a request for data or control functions from another device (the server). The client can be a PLC, a computer, or any device capable of initiating communication, while the server is typically a device or sensor that responds to requests.

There are two primary variants of the Modbus protocol:

Modbus RTU (Remote Terminal Unit): This is a binary-based protocol and is widely used over serial communication, such as RS-232 or RS-485. It is known for its efficiency in terms of data transmission, making it suitable for applications with limited bandwidth.

Modbus TCP: This variant uses the Transmission Control Protocol (TCP) for communication over Ethernet networks. It has become increasingly popular due to its compatibility with standard Ethernet hardware and its ability to transmit data over long distances.

3. Communication Modes

Modbus supports multiple communication modes, each with its own characteristics and use cases:

Request-Response: This is the most common communication mode in Modbus. The client sends a request to the server, which then responds with the requested data or executes the requested action. It's a straightforward and reliable way to exchange data and control information.

Broadcast: In this mode, a client sends a message to all devices on the network without specifying a target server. Only servers that recognize the message content will respond. Broadcast mode is useful for sending commands or data updates to multiple devices simultaneously.

Function Codes: Modbus defines various function codes that correspond to specific operations, such as reading or writing registers, performing diagnostics, or controlling devices. The client specifies the appropriate function code in its request to instruct the server on what action to take.

4. Data Representation

Modbus uses a well-defined data representation format, which includes various data types:

Coils: Coils are binary values, representing discrete inputs or outputs. A coil can be in an "on" or "off" state, making it suitable for representing simple binary data, like the state of a switch.

Discrete Inputs: Discrete inputs are read-only binary values, typically representing the status of sensors or other external devices. These values cannot be manipulated through Modbus communication.

Holding Registers: Holding registers store 16-bit data values and are used for various purposes, such as storing setpoints, control parameters, and configuration data. They can be read from and written to by the client.

Input Registers: Similar to holding registers, input registers store 16-bit data values but are typically read-only. They provide a way for a server to share data with a client without allowing the client to modify it.

5. Addressing in Modbus

In Modbus, each data point is identified by a unique address. The addressing format depends on the data type:

Coils and Discrete Inputs: These use 1-based addresses, meaning they are addressed from 1 to 65536. For example, a request to read coil 1000 would address the 1000th coil.

Holding Registers and Input Registers: These also use 1-based addresses, but they have a separate address space from coils and discrete inputs. The address range is from 1 to 65536, like the other data types.

6. Modbus Function Codes

Modbus defines a range of function codes that enable different types of operations. Some of the most commonly used function codes include:

Read Coils (Function Code 01): This function code is used to read the status of coils. The client can request a range of coil values within the address space.

Read Discrete Inputs (Function Code 02): Similar to Function Code 01, but used for reading discrete input values.

Read Holding Registers (Function Code 03): This function code is used to read the content of holding registers.

Read Input Registers (Function Code 04): Similar to Function Code 03, but used for reading input register values.

Write Single Coil (Function Code 05): This function code allows the client to write a single coil, changing its state.

Write Single Register (Function Code 06): Similar to Function Code 05, but used for writing a single holding register.

Write Multiple Coils (Function Code 15): This function code allows the client to write multiple coils in a single request.

Write Multiple Registers (Function Code 16): Similar to Function Code 15, but used for writing multiple holding registers.

7. Error Handling

Modbus includes mechanisms for error detection and reporting. When a client sends a request to a server, the server can respond with an exception response if it encounters an error. The exception response includes an error code, which helps the client understand the nature of the problem. Common error codes include "Illegal Function," "Illegal Data Address," and "Server Device Failure."

8. Modbus in Industrial Applications

Modbus is widely used in various industrial applications, such as manufacturing, process control, and building automation. Some common use cases include:

PLC Communication: Modbus is often used to connect PLCs with other devices in an industrial system. PLCs can collect data from sensors, control actuators, and communicate with higher-level systems using Modbus.

Remote Monitoring and Control: Modbus enables remote monitoring and control of industrial processes. This is especially important for applications where it's necessary to manage operations from a central location.

SCADA Systems: Supervisory Control and Data Acquisition (SCADA) systems use Modbus to gather data from various field devices and display it on a centralized HMI. Operators can monitor processes and issue control commands through Modbus communication.

Building Automation: Modbus is employed in building automation systems to control HVAC systems, lighting, and other building services. It allows for efficient energy management and increased comfort.

Energy Management: In energy management systems, Modbus helps collect data from energy meters, monitor consumption, and optimize energy usage.

9. Modbus Variants and Extensions

While Modbus RTU and Modbus TCP are the most common variants, there are other versions and extensions of the protocol. These include:

Modbus ASCII: This variant uses ASCII characters for communication, making it human-readable. It is less common but still used in some applications.

Modbus Plus: Developed by Schneider Electric, Modbus Plus is an extended version of Modbus that operates on a token-passing network. It offers higher performance and additional features.

Modbus/IEC 61850 Gateway: This gateway allows Modbus devices to communicate with IEC 61850-based systems commonly used in the utility and energy sectors.

Modbus Security: With the increasing importance of cybersecurity in industrial systems, there are efforts to add security features to Modbus. These enhancements aim to protect communication from unauthorized access and data tampering.

10. Modbus Limitations and Considerations

While Modbus is a versatile and widely used protocol, it has some limitations and considerations to keep in mind:

Lack of Security: Traditional Modbus protocols, such as Modbus RTU and Modbus TCP, lack built-in security features. Implementing additional security measures is crucial to protect against unauthorized access and data breaches.

Limited Bandwidth: Modbus RTU, being a binary protocol, is efficient in terms of bandwidth usage. However, in large and complex systems, it may encounter limitations in data throughput.

No Auto-Discovery: Modbus devices need to be configured manually with their addresses and function codes. This can be time-consuming in large networks.

Deterministic Timing: Modbus communication doesn't guarantee real-time communication or deterministic timing. In applications requiring precise timing, additional measures may be needed.

11. Future of Modbus

As industrial automation and communication technologies continue to evolve, the future of Modbus may involve the integration of more advanced features, such as enhanced security, support for new data types, and compatibility with emerging IoT standards. However, Modbus is likely to remain a vital protocol in the industrial sector due to its widespread adoption and extensive legacy infrastructure.

In conclusion, Modbus is a versatile and widely adopted communication protocol that plays a crucial role in industrial automation and control systems. Its various variants, addressing modes, and data representations make it suitable for a wide range of applications, from PLC communication to building automation. While it has its limitations, it continues to be a fundamental technology in the world of industrial automation, and its future development will likely address emerging industry needs while preserving its legacy compatibility.

HART

HART (Highway Addressable Remote Transducer) is a widely used communication protocol in industrial automation and process control. Developed in the 1980s, HART is known for its ability to transmit digital and analog signals simultaneously over a 4-20 mA analog current loop, making it highly versatile and suitable for various applications. In this comprehensive explanation, we will delve into the history, architecture, communication modes, applications, and advantages of HART.

1. History of HART

HART was developed in the early 1980s as a collaborative effort between several major process automation companies, including Fisher Controls, Honeywell, and Rosemount. The primary goal was to enhance the capabilities of traditional 4-20 mA analog current loops by enabling two-way communication over the same wires used for analog signals. This innovation was driven by the need for more sophisticated process control and monitoring in industrial environments.

HART was designed to be backward-compatible with existing 4-20 mA systems, ensuring a smooth transition for industries already relying on analog current loops. This backward compatibility allowed companies to integrate HART-enabled devices into their existing infrastructure without significant changes.

2. HART Architecture

The HART communication protocol is built on a master-slave architecture, with a host or master device (such as a process control system or handheld communicator) communicating with one or more field devices (sensors, transmitters, or control valves) that act as slaves. The communication takes place over a 4-20 mA analog current loop, providing both analog and digital information simultaneously.

The key components of HART communication include:

Host or Master Device: This is the central controller responsible for sending commands, configuring, and collecting data from HART-enabled field devices. It can be a distributed control system (DCS), a programmable logic controller (PLC), a human-machine interface (HMI), or a handheld communicator.

Field Device: Field devices are the HART-enabled devices located in the field, such as pressure transmitters, flow meters, temperature sensors, and control valves. They are equipped with HART communication capabilities and can respond to commands from the master device.

4-20 mA Analog Current Loop: HART communication operates on the same 4-20 mA analog current loop used in traditional process control systems. The 4 mA signal typically represents the lower range value, while 20 mA represents the upper range value. The HART digital communication is superimposed on this analog signal.

3. Communication Modes

HART communication supports multiple modes of operation, allowing for different types of interactions between the host and field devices:

Point-to-Point Mode: In this mode, the host communicates with a single field device. It's a simple, one-to-one communication, typically used when a single device needs to be configured or monitored.

Multi-Drop Mode: Multi-drop mode enables a single host to communicate with multiple field devices connected in a daisy-chain configuration. Each field device is assigned a unique device address, and the host can address and communicate with each device separately. Multi-drop mode is commonly used in scenarios where several field devices need to be monitored or controlled from a central location.

Burst Mode: Burst mode is a feature of HART that allows the host to request data from multiple field devices simultaneously. This mode is particularly useful for collecting data from several devices in a brief period, optimizing the efficiency of data retrieval.

4. Digital and Analog Data in HART

One of the significant advantages of HART communication is its ability to transmit both digital and analog data simultaneously. This dual-mode operation offers several benefits:

Analog Signal: The 4-20 mA analog signal provides real-time process measurement data. This signal is ideal for applications where high accuracy and reliability are crucial, as it's immune to electrical interference and can travel long distances without significant signal degradation.

Digital Signal: The digital portion of HART communication carries additional information beyond the analog measurement. This digital data includes device diagnostics, configuration parameters, calibration data, and status information. It allows for remote configuration, monitoring, and troubleshooting of field devices without the need for physical access.

5. HART Commands and Messages

HART communication involves the exchange of commands and messages between the host and field devices. The most common types of HART commands and messages include:

Universal Commands: These commands are standardized and supported by all HART devices. They include functions like device reset, device identification, measurement value request, and device status query.

Common Practice Commands: These commands are specific to certain types of field devices or manufacturers and are used for device-specific functions and features. They can include specialized calibration procedures, sensor-specific configurations, or advanced diagnostic commands.

Device Descriptions (DDs): Device Descriptions are electronic files that provide a standardized representation of a field device's capabilities, parameters, and functions. Host systems can use DDs to display device-specific information and options to the user, simplifying device configuration and monitoring.

6. Benefits and Advantages of HART

HART communication offers numerous advantages that have contributed to its widespread adoption in process automation and industrial control:

Compatibility: HART is designed to work alongside existing 4-20 mA analog systems, allowing for easy integration into legacy infrastructures. This backward compatibility minimizes the cost and disruption of transitioning to digital communication.

Two-Way Communication: The ability to communicate both digitally and via analog signals provides a wealth of information beyond simple process measurements. It allows for remote device configuration, diagnostics, and troubleshooting, reducing maintenance costs and downtime.

Diagnostics and Condition Monitoring: HART-enabled devices can provide real-time diagnostic information, alerting operators to potential issues or failures. This proactive approach to maintenance improves process reliability and reduces unplanned downtime.

Device Configuration: HART allows for remote configuration of field devices, eliminating the need for manual adjustments in the field. This saves time and ensures consistency in device settings.

Calibration and Verification: Field devices can be remotely calibrated and verified using HART communication, reducing the need for expensive and time-consuming manual calibration procedures.

Improved Asset Management: HART data can be used for asset management, enabling companies to track device performance, history, and maintenance requirements. This data is valuable for asset optimization and predictive maintenance.

Enhanced Safety: HART enables safer working conditions by reducing the need for personnel to access hazardous or hard-to-reach areas for device configuration and diagnostics.

Energy Efficiency: HART communication can aid in optimizing energy usage by providing data on device efficiency and process performance. This is particularly valuable in energy-intensive industries.

7. HART in Industrial Applications

HART finds applications in various industries, including:

Process Industries: HART is widely used in process industries like oil and gas, petrochemical, chemical, and pharmaceutical manufacturing. It helps in monitoring and controlling critical process parameters.

Utilities: In the utilities sector, HART is employed for managing water and wastewater treatment processes, as well as monitoring power generation and distribution.

Manufacturing: Manufacturers use HART for process control, quality assurance, and monitoring production equipment.

HVAC and Building Automation: HART is used in heating, ventilation, and air conditioning (HVAC) systems and building automation to optimize energy usage and maintain environmental conditions.

Pulp and Paper: HART plays a crucial role in the pulp and paper industry for monitoring and controlling paper production processes.

Pharmaceuticals: In the pharmaceutical sector, HART ensures precise control and monitoring of critical processes, including chemical reactions and product handling.

Food and Beverage: HART is employed in the food and beverage industry to control and monitor various production and packaging processes.

Water and Wastewater: The water and wastewater industry uses HART for process control, water treatment, and environmental monitoring.

8. HART Versions and Evolutions

HART has gone through several revisions and updates to meet the evolving needs of industrial automation. The two primary versions are:

HART 5: This version introduced enhanced features, including expanded device status reporting and the ability to transmit multi-variable data. It also standardized support for the HART field device identification and revision number.

HART 6: HART 6 brought significant improvements in device diagnostics and the introduction of HART-IP, which allows HART communication over Ethernet networks. HART 6 also included support for additional field devices and more extensive device descriptions (DDs).

WirelessHART: In response to the growing demand for wireless communication, the WirelessHART protocol was introduced. It is based on the HART protocol and uses wireless technology to communicate with field devices. WirelessHART is particularly suitable for applications where running wires is impractical or cost-prohibitive.

9. HART Communication Challenges and Considerations

While HART communication offers numerous benefits, there are some challenges and considerations to be aware of:

Data Overhead: HART digital communication introduces additional data overhead on the analog current loop. This can impact the speed and accuracy of analog signal transmission in some cases.

Interference: HART communication may be susceptible to electromagnetic interference in certain industrial environments. Proper shielding and grounding are essential to mitigate this issue.

Configuration and Compatibility: Ensuring that HART-enabled devices and host systems are compatible and configured correctly is essential for successful communication.

Power Requirements: HART-enabled field devices typically require an external power supply, as they cannot draw power from the 4-20 mA loop. This consideration is important for installation planning.

Complexity: The integration of HART can introduce complexity in control systems, especially for those not accustomed to digital communication protocols. Training and expertise are crucial.

10. The Future of HART

HART remains a prevalent communication protocol in industrial automation, particularly in applications that rely on legacy 4-20 mA systems. The future of HART may involve continued enhancements in device diagnostics, expanded support for wireless communication, and improved integration with other industrial communication protocols.

As the Industrial Internet of Things (IIoT) and Industry 4.0 initiatives gain momentum, HART is likely to adapt to the changing landscape of industrial automation, potentially offering more seamless connectivity with higher-level systems and cloud-based platforms.

In conclusion, HART is a robust and versatile communication protocol that has played a significant role in advancing industrial automation and process control. Its ability to transmit both analog and digital data simultaneously, along with its compatibility with existing infrastructure, makes it an attractive choice for a wide range of industries. With ongoing developments and adaptations, HART is poised to continue serving as a fundamental technology in the industrial automation landscape.

DeviceNet

DeviceNet is a widely used industrial communication network protocol that has played a pivotal role in industrial automation and control systems. Developed by Allen-Bradley, now part of Rockwell Automation, DeviceNet is a part of the Common Industrial Protocol (CIP) family and is designed for efficiently connecting and communicating between industrial devices, sensors, actuators, and controllers. In this comprehensive article, we will explore the history, architecture, communication modes, applications, advantages, and considerations associated with DeviceNet.

1. History of DeviceNet

DeviceNet was first introduced in the early 1990s as a response to the growing need for a cost-effective and reliable communication protocol for industrial automation. Developed by Allen-Bradley, the protocol aimed to provide a standardized, open, and deterministic network for connecting a wide range of industrial devices in a factory environment. DeviceNet is part of a suite of protocols within the Common Industrial Protocol (CIP) family, which also includes ControlNet and EtherNet/IP.

DeviceNet has evolved over the years to adapt to the changing needs of industrial automation, offering improvements in performance, ease of use, and integration with other industrial networks.

2. DeviceNet Architecture

DeviceNet is designed around a master-slave architecture, where devices known as "masters" or "scanners" communicate with "slaves" or "devices." The architecture includes the following key components:

Scanner (Master Device): The scanner serves as the master device on the DeviceNet network. It is typically a programmable logic controller (PLC), industrial computer, or gateway device that manages and controls the communication on the network.

Devices (Slaves): Devices, or slaves, are the various industrial components connected to the network, such as sensors, actuators, motor drives, valves, and other field devices. Each device has a unique address and responds to requests from the scanner.

Network Cable: DeviceNet uses a linear network topology with a trunkline/dropline configuration. This means that the network cable runs along the trunkline with branches or "drop lines" where devices are connected. The communication is primarily based on a two-wire cable, typically shielded, with power and communication combined on the same wires.

Terminators: Terminators are resistors placed at each end of the network cable to terminate the signal properly and prevent reflections that can disrupt communication.

3. DeviceNet Communication Modes

DeviceNet offers several communication modes to support different types of interactions between the scanner and devices. The primary modes include:

Explicit Messaging: In explicit messaging, the scanner explicitly requests data from a specific device or sends data to a specific device. This mode is suitable for point-to-point communication, device configuration, and reading or writing specific data points.

I/O Messaging: I/O messaging is a cyclic, data-exchange mechanism that allows devices to transmit and receive data at specific intervals. This mode is well-suited for real-time control and monitoring of field devices. The scanner polls each device in a scheduled manner to gather data.

Polling: Polling is a method used by the scanner to request information from devices. The scanner cycles through each device to collect data, ensuring that every device has an opportunity to communicate.

Change of State (COS): COS messaging allows a device to transmit data only when there is a change in its state or data values. This minimizes network traffic and is particularly useful when dealing with devices that provide status updates infrequently.

4. DeviceNet Data Representation

DeviceNet utilizes the Common Industrial Protocol (CIP) for data representation and object modeling. CIP defines a structured way of organizing data within devices and a consistent way to access and manage that data. It allows for a broad range of data types and services, which include:

Data Types: DeviceNet supports various data types, such as boolean (on/off), integer (16-bit and 32-bit), floating-point, string, and more. These data types allow for the representation of different types of data, from discrete signals to complex process variables.

Objects: CIP defines objects as logical groupings of data within a device. Objects can represent parameters, control settings, or diagnostic information. For example, an object could represent the speed control parameters for a motor drive.

Services: CIP services encompass actions that can be performed on objects, such as reading, writing, configuring, or executing specific functions within a device.

5. DeviceNet Profiles

DeviceNet profiles are standardized templates that specify how specific types of devices should communicate and what data should be exchanged. These profiles facilitate interoperability between devices from different manufacturers. Some of the common DeviceNet profiles include:

Device Profile: A device profile defines the behavior and functionality of a specific type of device. For example, a motor drive device profile would specify the control parameters, status information, and methods for controlling a motor drive.

Communication Profile: A communication profile specifies how devices should communicate on the network. This includes the network configuration, communication rates, and message formats.

Application Profile: Application profiles define how devices with specific functions should interact within an application. For example, an application profile for a conveyor system would detail the communication requirements between the motor drives, sensors, and controllers.

DeviceNet profiles simplify device integration and configuration by providing a standardized structure for manufacturers to follow.

6. DeviceNet Object Dictionary

DeviceNet devices feature an object dictionary that serves as a catalog of all the data objects and services available within the device. The object dictionary allows the scanner to understand the capabilities of each device and how to interact with them. It provides detailed information on data types, object identifiers, services, and data access rights.

The object dictionary is essential for configuring, monitoring, and controlling devices on the network, as it guides the scanner in making the right requests and interpreting the device's responses.

7. DeviceNet in Industrial Applications

DeviceNet has a broad range of applications across various industrial sectors. Some of the key applications include:

Manufacturing: DeviceNet is commonly used in manufacturing environments for tasks like motor control, conveyor systems, and quality control. It allows for the efficient control and monitoring of production processes.

Process Control: In process industries, DeviceNet is employed to manage various field devices, such as flow meters, temperature sensors, and control valves. It enables real-time control and data acquisition in chemical, petrochemical, and pharmaceutical plants.

Automotive Industry: The automotive industry relies on DeviceNet for controlling robotic systems, assembly lines, and quality control processes. It plays a crucial role in automating production and ensuring precision.

Food and Beverage: DeviceNet is used in food and beverage processing to control and monitor equipment, ensuring the quality and safety of products. It aids in managing processes such as filling, packaging, and labeling.

Packaging and Material Handling: DeviceNet is well-suited for managing material handling systems, conveyors, and packaging equipment, enabling efficient and reliable operations.

Energy and Utilities: In energy and utilities, DeviceNet is employed for managing power distribution, water treatment, and wastewater processing. It ensures the reliable operation of critical infrastructure.

Building Automation: DeviceNet is utilized in building automation systems to control lighting, HVAC systems, security, and access control. It plays a role in optimizing energy usage and enhancing occupant comfort.

Pharmaceuticals: The pharmaceutical industry relies on DeviceNet for precise control and monitoring of chemical processes, such as mixing, heating, and drying.

Water and Wastewater: DeviceNet is crucial for managing water and wastewater treatment processes, controlling pumps, valves, and sensors.

8. Advantages of DeviceNet

DeviceNet offers several advantages that have contributed to its popularity in industrial applications:

Deterministic Communication: DeviceNet provides deterministic communication, ensuring that data is delivered reliably and in a predictable time frame. This is critical for real-time control and monitoring applications.

Interoperability: DeviceNet profiles and object dictionaries promote interoperability among devices from different manufacturers. This simplifies device integration and reduces compatibility issues.

Cost-Effective: The use of a two-wire communication system for both data and power simplifies cabling and reduces installation and maintenance costs.

Scalability: DeviceNet networks can be easily expanded by adding or removing devices without significant disruption. This scalability is vital for evolving industrial processes.

Real-Time Diagnostics: DeviceNet allows for real-time diagnostics and monitoring of devices, enabling proactive maintenance and minimizing downtime.

High Reliability: The deterministic nature of DeviceNet communication, along with its robust physical layer, makes it highly reliable even in harsh industrial environments.

Ease of Configuration: DeviceNet networks are typically easy to configure and maintain, with the ability to remotely configure and monitor devices.

9. DeviceNet Challenges and Considerations

While DeviceNet offers numerous benefits, there are some challenges and considerations to be aware of:

Bandwidth Limitations: DeviceNet may have limitations in handling a large number of devices or devices with high data transmission requirements. Careful network design is necessary to optimize performance.

Diagnostics Complexity: While DeviceNet provides excellent diagnostic capabilities, managing and interpreting diagnostic information from multiple devices can be complex.

Network Synchronization: In applications where tight synchronization is crucial, additional measures may be required to ensure precise coordination between devices.

Security: DeviceNet does not inherently provide robust security features. Implementing security measures to protect against unauthorized access is essential.

10. Future of DeviceNet

The future of DeviceNet is influenced by the broader trends in industrial automation, including the adoption of Industry 4.0 and the Industrial Internet of Things (IIoT). While DeviceNet has served well in traditional industrial settings, its evolution is likely to involve:

Integration with Ethernet-Based Protocols: DeviceNet networks may increasingly integrate with Ethernet-based industrial protocols to enable connectivity with higher-level systems and cloud-based platforms.

Wireless Communication: The adoption of wireless communication technologies, such as WirelessHART and ISA100.11a, may play a role in extending DeviceNet capabilities for applications where wired connections are impractical.

Enhanced Diagnostics and Predictive Maintenance: DeviceNet is likely to offer more advanced diagnostics and predictive maintenance features, leveraging the wealth of data it can provide to improve system reliability.

Cybersecurity Enhancements: With the growing importance of cybersecurity in industrial networks, DeviceNet may evolve to incorporate more robust security features to protect against cyber threats.

Increased Integration with IIoT Platforms: DeviceNet networks may become more tightly integrated with IIoT platforms, enabling seamless data exchange with enterprise-level systems and facilitating data analytics and optimization.

In conclusion, DeviceNet has been a cornerstone in industrial automation for decades, providing reliable and deterministic communication for a wide range of devices and applications. Its ability to interoperate across different manufacturers and its cost-effective, deterministic communication make it a valuable technology in industrial environments. As industrial automation continues to evolve, DeviceNet is expected to adapt to new challenges and opportunities, ensuring its relevance in the future of industrial communication.

Profibus

Profibus (Process Field Bus) is a widely used industrial communication protocol that has played a pivotal role in industrial automation and process control systems. Developed by a consortium of companies in the late 1980s, Profibus is known for its versatility in connecting and controlling a wide range of industrial devices, sensors, actuators, and controllers. In this comprehensive article, we will explore the history, architecture, communication modes, applications, advantages, and considerations associated with Profibus.

1. History of Profibus

Profibus was developed in the late 1980s as a response to the increasing need for a standardized and efficient communication protocol in industrial automation. The protocol was created by a consortium of companies, including Siemens, ABB, and other leading industrial automation manufacturers. Profibus aimed to provide a robust and versatile communication system that could facilitate the exchange of data and control information in a wide range of industrial applications.

Since its inception, Profibus has undergone several revisions and adaptations to meet the evolving needs of the industrial automation sector. It has evolved into different variants, such as Profibus-DP, Profibus-PA, and ProfiNet, each tailored for specific applications and requirements.

2. Profibus Architecture

Profibus communication typically follows a master-slave architecture, with one or more devices serving as masters and numerous devices acting as slaves. The architecture consists of the following key components:

Master Device: The master device is the central controller responsible for initiating communication on the Profibus network. It can be a programmable logic controller (PLC), a distributed control system (DCS), or a supervisory control and data acquisition (SCADA) system.

Slave Devices: Slave devices are the various industrial components connected to the network. These devices can include sensors, actuators, motor drives, and other field devices. Slave devices respond to commands and requests from the master device.

Profibus Cable: Profibus networks use shielded twisted-pair cables for communication. The cable type and specifications may vary depending on the Profibus variant (e.g., Profibus-DP, Profibus-PA) and the specific application requirements.

Terminators: Terminators are resistors placed at each end of the network cable to ensure signal integrity and prevent reflections that could disrupt communication.

3. Profibus Communication Modes

Profibus supports various communication modes to cater to different types of interactions between the master and slave devices. The primary communication modes include:

Cyclic Communication: Cyclic communication is a periodic exchange of data between the master and slave devices. The master device cyclically polls the slave devices for data updates or control commands. This mode is well-suited for real-time control and monitoring applications.

Acyclic Communication: Acyclic communication is used for non-periodic, event-driven messages. It allows the master device to send unscheduled messages to specific slave devices when needed. Acyclic communication is often used for diagnostic purposes and alarms.

Time-Triggered Communication: Time-triggered communication is a deterministic mode where data exchange occurs at predefined time intervals. This mode is used in applications that require precise synchronization and guaranteed data delivery times.

4. Profibus Data Representation

Profibus utilizes a structured approach to data representation and object modeling, which is essential for organizing and accessing data within devices. This approach includes:

Data Types: Profibus supports various data types, including binary (on/off), integer (16-bit and 32-bit), floating-point, string, and more. These data types enable the representation of different types of data, from discrete signals to complex process variables.

Objects: Profibus defines objects as logical groupings of data within a device. Objects represent specific parameters, control settings, or diagnostic information. For example, an object might represent the setpoint for a temperature controller.

Services: Profibus services encompass actions that can be performed on objects, such as reading, writing, configuring, or executing specific functions within a device.

5. Profibus Profiles

Profibus profiles are standardized templates that specify how specific types of devices should communicate and what data should be exchanged. These profiles facilitate interoperability between devices from different manufacturers. Some of the common Profibus profiles include:

Device Profile: A device profile defines the behavior and functionality of a specific type of device. For example, a device profile for a flow meter would specify the measurement parameters, status information, and communication methods.

Communication Profile: A communication profile specifies how devices should communicate on the network. This includes the network configuration, communication rates, and message formats.

Application Profile: Application profiles define how devices with specific functions should interact within an application. For example, an application profile for a pumping system would detail the communication requirements between the motor drives, sensors, and controllers.

Profibus profiles simplify device integration and configuration by providing a standardized structure for manufacturers to follow.

6. Profibus Object Dictionary

Profibus devices feature an object dictionary that serves as a catalog of all the data objects and services available within the device. The object dictionary allows the master device to understand the capabilities of each device and how to interact with them. It provides detailed information on data types, object identifiers, services, and data access rights.

The object dictionary is essential for configuring, monitoring, and controlling devices on the network, as it guides the master device in making the right requests and interpreting the device's responses.

7. Profibus Variants and Applications

Profibus comes in various variants, each designed for specific applications and requirements. Some of the common Profibus variants include:

Profibus-DP (Decentralized Periphery): Profibus-DP is used for high-speed communication in factory automation and process control. It is suitable for connecting sensors, actuators, motor drives, and other devices that require fast data exchange.

Profibus-PA (Process Automation): Profibus-PA is designed for process automation applications, particularly in the chemical, petrochemical, and pharmaceutical industries. It is used for process instrumentation, control valves, and hazardous areas.

Profibus-DL (Drive Link): Profibus-DL is optimized for motion control and drive applications. It allows for precise control and monitoring of motors, drives, and positioning systems.

Profibus-FMS (Fieldbus Message Specification): Profibus-FMS is used for data exchange in manufacturing and process control. It enables the exchange of larger data packets and is suitable for tasks like recipe management and production data acquisition.

Profibus-Safe: Profibus-Safe is an extension of Profibus that adds safety-related communication capabilities. It is used in applications where functional safety is critical, such as emergency shutdown systems and safety interlock devices.

ProfiNet: While not a Profibus variant, Profinet is a related industrial Ethernet protocol that is often considered in the Profibus family. Profinet is designed for high-performance applications and real-time communication over Ethernet networks.

Each Profibus variant serves specific industrial sectors and applications, providing solutions tailored to the unique demands of those domains.

8. Advantages of Profibus

Profibus offers several advantages that have contributed to its popularity in industrial applications:

Deterministic Communication: Profibus provides deterministic communication, ensuring that data is delivered reliably and in a predictable time frame. This is critical for real-time control and monitoring applications.

Interoperability: Profibus profiles and object dictionaries promote interoperability among devices from different manufacturers. This simplifies device integration and reduces compatibility issues.

High Data Throughput: Profibus is capable of high-speed data transmission, making it suitable for applications that require rapid data exchange.

Scalability: Profibus networks can be easily expanded by adding or removing devices without significant disruption. This scalability is vital for evolving industrial processes.

Real-Time Diagnostics: Profibus allows for real-time diagnostics and monitoring of devices, enabling proactive maintenance and minimizing downtime.

High Reliability: The deterministic nature of Profibus communication, along with its robust physical layer, makes it highly reliable even in harsh industrial environments.

Ease of Configuration: Profibus networks are typically easy to configure and maintain, with the ability to remotely configure and monitor devices.

Safety Integration: Profibus-Safe and related safety extensions allow for the integration of safety-related functions within the network, enhancing overall system safety.

9. Profibus Challenges and Considerations

While Profibus offers numerous benefits, there are some challenges and considerations to be aware of:

Complexity: Profibus networks can become complex, especially in large installations with numerous devices. Proper network design and configuration are essential to ensure efficient and reliable operation.

Limited Cable Length: The maximum cable length in Profibus networks can be limited, especially at higher data rates. Repeaters or signal amplifiers may be necessary for longer distances.

Environmental Considerations: Profibus networks may require shielding and grounding to mitigate the impact of electromagnetic interference (EMI) in industrial environments.

Diagnostics and Troubleshooting: Profibus diagnostics can be complex, and interpreting diagnostic information from multiple devices can be challenging. Adequate training and expertise are crucial for troubleshooting and maintenance.

Security: Profibus does not inherently provide robust security features. Implementing security measures to protect against unauthorized access and data breaches is essential.

10. Future of Profibus

The future of Profibus is influenced by the broader trends in industrial automation, including the adoption of Industry 4.0 and the Industrial Internet of Things (IIoT). While Profibus has served well in traditional industrial settings, its evolution is likely to involve:

Integration with Ethernet-Based Protocols: Profibus networks may increasingly integrate with Ethernet-based industrial protocols to enable connectivity with higher-level systems and cloud-based platforms.

Wireless Communication: The adoption of wireless communication technologies, such as WirelessHART and ISA100.11a, may play a role in extending Profibus capabilities for applications where wired connections are impractical.

Enhanced Diagnostics and Predictive Maintenance: Profibus is likely to offer more advanced diagnostics and predictive maintenance features, leveraging the wealth of data it can provide to improve system reliability.

Cybersecurity Enhancements: With the growing importance of cybersecurity in industrial networks, Profibus may evolve to incorporate more robust security features to protect against cyber threats.

Increased Integration with IIoT Platforms: Profibus networks may become more tightly integrated with IIoT platforms, enabling seamless data exchange with enterprise-level systems and facilitating data analytics and optimization.

In conclusion, Profibus has been a cornerstone in industrial automation for decades, providing reliable and deterministic communication for a wide range of devices and applications. Its ability to interoperate across different manufacturers and its cost-effective, deterministic communication make it a valuable technology in industrial environments. As industrial automation continues to evolve, Profibus is expected to adapt to new challenges and opportunities, ensuring its relevance in the future of industrial communication.

Fieldbus

Fieldbus is a family of industrial communication protocols designed to enable the exchange of data and control information among a wide range of industrial devices, sensors, actuators, and controllers. It has played a pivotal role in industrial automation and process control systems, offering advantages such as increased flexibility, reduced wiring, and improved diagnostics. In this comprehensive article, we will explore the history, architecture, communication modes, applications, advantages, and considerations associated with Fieldbus.

1. History of Fieldbus

The concept of Fieldbus emerged as a response to the need for more efficient and flexible communication between industrial devices in the 1980s. Prior to Fieldbus, traditional point-to-point wiring was the standard for connecting devices to a central control system, which was cumbersome and limited in terms of scalability. The initial development of Fieldbus protocols aimed to address these limitations by enabling multiple devices to share a common communication medium, reducing the amount of wiring required.

Fieldbus technology gained traction in various industries, including process automation, manufacturing, and utilities. Different Fieldbus protocols were developed to suit specific application needs and requirements. Fieldbus technology marked a significant shift in industrial automation by offering more versatile communication solutions.

2. Fieldbus Architecture

Fieldbus systems follow a networked architecture, where multiple devices are connected to a common communication network. The architecture comprises the following key components:

Field Devices: Field devices are the sensors, actuators, motor drives, valves, and other industrial components that are integrated into the Fieldbus network. Each field device is capable of communicating with other devices over the network.

Fieldbus Network: The Fieldbus network serves as the communication backbone, allowing devices to exchange data and control information. Various Fieldbus protocols define the network specifications and the rules for communication.

Fieldbus Controller: The Fieldbus controller is the central processing unit responsible for managing communication and data exchange on the Fieldbus network. It can be a programmable logic controller (PLC), distributed control system (DCS), or a supervisory control and data acquisition (SCADA) system.

Communication Medium: Fieldbus networks use different communication media, such as twisted-pair cables, fiber optics, or wireless connections, depending on the chosen Fieldbus protocol and the application's specific requirements.

3. Fieldbus Communication Modes

Fieldbus protocols support different communication modes to cater to various types of interactions between field devices and controllers. Some of the common communication modes include:

Cyclic Communication: Cyclic communication is a periodic exchange of data between the controller and field devices. In this mode, devices send data updates to the controller at predefined intervals. It is suitable for real-time control and monitoring applications.

Acyclic Communication: Acyclic communication is used for non-periodic, event-driven messages. Devices can send unscheduled messages to the controller or to other devices when specific events occur. Acyclic communication is often employed for alarms and diagnostic data.

Time-Triggered Communication: Time-triggered communication is a deterministic mode where data exchange occurs at predefined time intervals. This mode is used in applications that require precise synchronization and guaranteed data delivery times.

4. Fieldbus Data Representation

Fieldbus protocols typically define a standardized approach to data representation and object modeling. This structuring allows for the organization and access of data within field devices and controllers. It includes:

Data Types: Fieldbus protocols support various data types, including digital (on/off), analog (integer and floating-point), and string data types. These data types enable the representation of a wide range of data, from simple binary signals to complex process variables.

Objects: Fieldbus defines objects as logical groupings of data within a device. Objects represent specific parameters, control settings, or diagnostic information. For example, an object might represent the setpoint for a temperature controller.

Services: Fieldbus services encompass actions that can be performed on objects, such as reading, writing, configuring, or executing specific functions within a device.

5. Fieldbus Profiles

Fieldbus profiles are standardized templates that specify how specific types of devices should communicate and what data should be exchanged. These profiles facilitate interoperability between devices from different manufacturers. Some of the common Fieldbus profiles include:

Device Profile: A device profile defines the behavior and functionality of a specific type of device. For example, a device profile for a flow meter would specify the measurement parameters, status information, and communication methods.

Communication Profile: A communication profile specifies how devices should communicate on the network. This includes the network configuration, communication rates, and message formats.

Application Profile: Application profiles define how devices with specific functions should interact within an application. For example, an application profile for a pumping system would detail the communication requirements between the motor drives, sensors, and controllers.

Fieldbus profiles simplify device integration and configuration by providing a standardized structure for manufacturers to follow. They promote interoperability and ensure that devices from different manufacturers can work together seamlessly.

6. Fieldbus Variants and Applications

Fieldbus technology has given rise to several Fieldbus protocols, each tailored for specific industrial sectors and applications. Some of the common Fieldbus protocols and their applications include:

Foundation Fieldbus: Foundation Fieldbus is primarily used in process automation applications. It is well-suited for controlling and monitoring field devices in industries such as oil and gas, petrochemical, chemical, and pharmaceutical manufacturing.

Profibus: Profibus encompasses a family of protocols designed for various industrial applications. Profibus-DP (Decentralized Periphery) is suitable for factory automation, Profibus-PA (Process Automation) is used in process industries, and Profibus-DL (Drive Link) is optimized for motion control and drive applications.

DeviceNet: DeviceNet is a Fieldbus protocol widely used in manufacturing and industrial automation. It is particularly suited for connecting sensors, actuators, motor drives, and other devices that require fast data exchange.

CANopen: CANopen is an open Fieldbus protocol commonly used in automation, robotics, and vehicle applications. It is known for its flexibility and support for devices with different communication capabilities.

Modbus: Modbus is a widely used Fieldbus protocol that is often employed in industrial automation and building automation. It is simple and versatile, making it a popular choice for a wide range of applications.

EtherCAT: EtherCAT is a high-performance Fieldbus protocol suitable for applications that require fast communication and synchronization, such as motion control and robotics.

HART (Highway Addressable Remote Transducer): HART is a hybrid Fieldbus protocol that combines both analog and digital communication. It is widely used in process industries for connecting smart field devices.

AS-Interface (Actuator-Sensor Interface): AS-Interface is a simple and cost-effective Fieldbus protocol used for connecting binary sensors and actuators in applications such as material handling and conveyor systems.

ProfiNet: ProfiNet is a Fieldbus protocol that leverages Ethernet for communication. It is designed for high-performance applications and is often used in the automation of manufacturing processes.

Each Fieldbus protocol caters to specific industrial sectors and offers unique features that make it suitable for particular applications. The choice of protocol depends on the specific requirements and goals of the automation project.

7. Advantages of Fieldbus

Fieldbus technology offers several advantages that have contributed to its widespread adoption in industrial applications:

Reduced Wiring: Fieldbus networks eliminate the need for extensive point-to-point wiring, which leads to cost savings in cabling and installation.

Flexibility: Fieldbus allows for the easy addition or removal of devices without significant disruption to the network. It offers scalability and adaptability to changing automation requirements.

Enhanced Diagnostics: Fieldbus networks provide rich diagnostic information, allowing for real-time monitoring and proactive maintenance. This results in reduced downtime and increased system reliability.

Interoperability: Fieldbus protocols and profiles promote interoperability among devices from different manufacturers, ensuring that a diverse range of devices can work together seamlessly.

Deterministic Communication: Many Fieldbus protocols offer deterministic communication, ensuring that data is delivered reliably and within a predictable time frame. This is essential for real-time control and monitoring applications.

Cost Savings: Fieldbus technology can lead to cost savings in terms of cabling, installation, and maintenance. It also allows for more efficient use of resources.

Energy Efficiency: Fieldbus networks often support energy-saving features, enabling devices to operate in an energy-efficient manner and contributing to sustainability goals.

8. Fieldbus Challenges and Considerations

While Fieldbus technology offers numerous benefits, there are some challenges and considerations to be aware of:

Complexity: Fieldbus networks can become complex, especially in large installations with numerous devices. Proper network design and configuration are essential to ensure efficient and reliable operation.

Network Redundancy: Ensuring network redundancy and fault tolerance is crucial to prevent disruptions in critical applications.

Data Security: Fieldbus protocols do not inherently provide robust security features. Implementing security measures to protect against unauthorized access and data breaches is essential, especially in today's interconnected world.

Cable Length Limitations: Some Fieldbus protocols may have cable length limitations, particularly at higher data rates. Repeaters or signal amplifiers may be necessary for longer distances.

Environmental Considerations: Fieldbus networks may require shielding and grounding to mitigate the impact of electromagnetic interference (EMI) in industrial environments.

9. Future of Fieldbus

The future of Fieldbus technology is influenced by the broader trends in industrial automation, including the adoption of Industry 4.0 and the Industrial Internet of Things (IIoT). While Fieldbus technology has served well in traditional industrial settings, its evolution is likely to involve:

Integration with Ethernet-Based Protocols: Fieldbus networks may increasingly integrate with Ethernet-based industrial protocols to enable connectivity with higher-level systems and cloud-based platforms.

Wireless Communication: The adoption of wireless communication technologies, such as WirelessHART and ISA100.11a, may play a role in extending Fieldbus capabilities for applications where wired connections are impractical.

Enhanced Diagnostics and Predictive Maintenance: Fieldbus networks are likely to offer more advanced diagnostics and predictive maintenance features, leveraging the wealth of data they can provide to improve system reliability.

Cybersecurity Enhancements: With the growing importance of cybersecurity in industrial networks, Fieldbus technology may evolve to incorporate more robust security features to protect against cyber threats.

Increased Integration with IIoT Platforms: Fieldbus networks may become more tightly integrated with IIoT platforms, enabling seamless data exchange with enterprise-level systems and facilitating data analytics and optimization.

In conclusion, Fieldbus technology has been a cornerstone in industrial automation for decades, providing reliable and versatile communication solutions for a wide range of devices and applications. Its ability to reduce wiring, enhance diagnostics, and offer interoperability makes it a valuable technology in industrial environments. As industrial automation continues to evolve, Fieldbus is expected to adapt to new challenges and opportunities, ensuring its relevance in the future of industrial communication.

RS232

RS-232 (Recommended Standard 232) is a widely used serial communication standard that has played a significant role in connecting and exchanging data between various devices, particularly in early computer systems and industrial applications. Developed by the Electronic Industries Association (EIA), RS-232 has a rich history and has evolved over the years to accommodate changing technology and communication needs. In this comprehensive article, we will explore the history, architecture, signaling, applications, advantages, and considerations associated with RS-232.

1. History of RS-232

RS-232, or Recommended Standard 232, was developed by the Electronic Industries Association (EIA) in the mid-20th century. Its primary purpose was to standardize the electrical characteristics of data communication equipment to ensure compatibility between different manufacturers' devices. RS-232 was introduced in the early 1960s and quickly became a widely adopted standard for serial communication.

The development of RS-232 was driven by the need to establish a common language for devices to communicate with each other, especially in the early days of computing. Before the standardization of RS-232, there was a lack of consistency in terms of voltage levels, signal timings, and connectors, which hindered the interoperability of equipment.

Over time, RS-232 became the de facto standard for connecting computers to peripherals such as modems, printers, and terminals. Its popularity extended beyond computing into various industries, including industrial automation, telecommunications, and laboratory instrumentation. RS-232 remained a prevalent standard for decades, and even as new communication technologies emerged, it continued to be used in legacy systems and specialized applications.

2. RS-232 Architecture

RS-232 is a simple, point-to-point serial communication standard that involves the exchange of data between two devices: a Data Terminal Equipment (DTE) and a Data Communications Equipment (DCE). The DTE and DCE can take various forms, including computers, modems, terminals, and other data communication devices.

The key components of RS-232 architecture include:

DTE (Data Terminal Equipment): The DTE is the device that generates or consumes data. This could be a computer, terminal, or any equipment that sends or receives data. In a computer context, the DTE's serial port (COM port) serves as the interface for connecting peripherals like modems or printers.

DCE (Data Communications Equipment): The DCE is responsible for establishing and maintaining the communication link. Common examples of DCE devices include modems, serial ports on communication servers, and other equipment that facilitates data transmission.

RS-232 Cable: RS-232 communication typically involves a cable with a minimum of three conductors: transmit (TX), receive (RX), and ground (GND). The TX and RX lines are used for data transmission in opposite directions, while the GND line provides a common reference point for electrical signals.

Connector: RS-232 connections use various connector types, such as the DE-9 (commonly referred to as DB-9) and the DB-25 connectors. The choice of connector depends on the specific application and equipment in use.

Voltage Levels: RS-232 defines voltage levels for logical "0" and logical "1" states. Traditionally, a logical "0" is represented by a voltage between -3V and -15V, while a logical "1" is represented by a voltage between +3V and +15V.

Signaling: RS-232 uses a specific signaling scheme where logical "0" is represented as a negative voltage, and logical "1" is represented as a positive voltage. The voltage transitions are used to signal the start and stop of data transmission, and data bits are transmitted serially.

3. RS-232 Signaling and Data Transmission

RS-232 defines the electrical characteristics of data transmission, including voltage levels, signal timing, and data format. The signaling specifications are crucial for the proper interpretation of data at both the sender and receiver sides. The key aspects of RS-232 signaling and data transmission include:

Voltage Levels: RS-232 uses voltage levels to represent binary data. A logical "0" is typically transmitted as a negative voltage, while a logical "1" is transmitted as a positive voltage. The voltage levels can vary within the specified range but must fall within the defined thresholds for reliable communication.

Start and Stop Bits: RS-232 uses start and stop bits to frame each data byte. The start bit indicates the beginning of a data byte, while the stop bit(s) indicate the end of the byte. Common configurations include 8 data bits, 1 start bit, and 1 stop bit (8N1), but other configurations are possible.

Data Rate (Baud Rate): The data rate, also known as the baud rate, specifies the speed at which data is transmitted over the RS-232 connection. It is measured in bits per second (bps). Common baud rates include 9600, 19200, and 115200 bps, but RS-232 supports a wide range of baud rates.

Parity Bit: RS-232 allows for the inclusion of a parity bit for error checking. Parity can be set to none, even, or odd. The parity bit is used to check for data integrity, and it can help detect errors in transmission.

Flow Control: RS-232 supports two types of flow control: hardware (RTS/CTS) and software (XON/XOFF). Flow control mechanisms help regulate the rate of data transmission, preventing data overflows and ensuring reliable communication between devices.

Full-Duplex Communication: RS-232 enables full-duplex communication, allowing data to be transmitted in both directions simultaneously. This means that two devices can exchange data independently without waiting for the other to finish transmitting.

4. RS-232 Applications

RS-232 has been a fundamental standard for connecting devices in a wide range of applications across various industries. Some of the key applications include:

Computer Peripherals: RS-232 was widely used to connect computers to peripherals such as modems, printers, mice, and external storage devices. It allowed for the expansion of computer capabilities and the exchange of data with external equipment.

Industrial Automation: RS-232 has been employed in industrial automation for connecting Programmable Logic Controllers (PLCs), Human-Machine Interfaces (HMIs), sensors, and other industrial equipment. It remains relevant in legacy systems and specialized industrial applications.

Telecommunications: In the early days of data communication, RS-232 was used for connecting computer terminals to mainframe computers and for interfacing with telecommunication equipment, such as modems and multiplexers.

Laboratory Instrumentation: RS-232 has been used in laboratory settings for connecting instruments, data loggers, and sensors to computers. It enables data acquisition and control in scientific research and experimentation.

Point-of-Sale (POS) Systems: RS-232 has been used in POS systems to connect cash registers, barcode scanners, and receipt printers, facilitating retail and transactional processes.

Telemetry and Remote Sensing: RS-232 has been employed in telemetry systems and remote sensing applications to collect and transmit data from remote locations to central control centers or data collection points.

Legacy Systems: RS-232 remains a vital standard in legacy systems and equipment that continue to serve their intended purposes. Many industrial and scientific devices, even with the availability of more modern communication standards, still use RS-232 for connectivity.

5. Advantages of RS-232

RS-232 offers several advantages that have contributed to its enduring popularity in various applications:

Simplicity: RS-232 is straightforward to implement and use. It provides a simple and reliable means of connecting devices and exchanging data.

Widespread Adoption: RS-232 was a widely adopted standard, ensuring interoperability among devices from different manufacturers. This made it a go-to choice for connecting equipment in various industries.

Versatility: RS-232 can be used for connecting a wide range of devices, making it suitable for diverse applications in computing, industrial automation, telecommunications, and more.

Point-to-Point Communication: RS-232's point-to-point communication model simplifies the setup, as it involves a single sender and receiver. This model is suitable for many applications where only two devices need to communicate.

Full-Duplex Operation: RS-232 supports full-duplex communication, enabling simultaneous transmission in both directions. This feature is advantageous for real-time data exchange.

Legacy Support: RS-232 remains relevant for connecting with legacy systems and equipment, ensuring continued operation of older technology.

6. RS-232 Challenges and Considerations

While RS-232 has numerous advantages, there are also challenges and considerations associated with its use:

Limited Distance: RS-232 communication is typically limited to relatively short distances, often around 50 feet (15 meters). Beyond this distance, signal degradation can occur, necessitating signal amplification or the use of other communication standards.

Voltage Levels: RS-232 signaling involves voltage levels that can vary between devices. Ensuring that devices conform to the same voltage standards is critical for reliable communication.

Cable Configuration: RS-232 cables must be correctly configured with the appropriate connectors, pinouts, and grounding to ensure proper communication. Different devices may require different cable configurations.

Lack of Network Topology: RS-232 is a point-to-point communication standard and does not inherently support networked topologies. Expanding RS-232 communication to multiple devices often involves complex cabling.

Limited Speed: RS-232's data rate (baud rate) is typically limited compared to more modern communication standards, making it less suitable for high-speed data transfer applications.

Error Handling: RS-232 has limited error detection and correction capabilities. While it provides parity checking, it may not offer the robust error-handling features found in other communication standards.

7. Future of RS-232

The future of RS-232 is influenced by the ongoing developments in technology, communication standards, and the increasing demand for faster and more versatile data exchange. While RS-232 remains relevant in specific applications, its use is gradually waning in favor of more modern and capable communication technologies. The future of RS-232 may involve the following:

Transition to Modern Interfaces: Many modern devices and equipment now feature USB, Ethernet, or wireless interfaces, which offer higher data rates and greater versatility. As a result, RS-232 is gradually being replaced in new equipment designs.

Legacy Support: RS-232 will continue to be relevant for the foreseeable future due to the large number of legacy systems and equipment that rely on it. Manufacturers and industries will need to support RS-232 interfaces for these legacy systems.

Serial-to-Ethernet Adapters: To extend the life of RS-232 devices and integrate them into modern networked environments, serial-to-Ethernet adapters are commonly used. These adapters enable RS-232 devices to communicate over Ethernet networks.

Industrial Automation: RS-232 may still be used in specific industrial automation applications, particularly when connecting to older industrial equipment or interfacing with legacy control systems.

Specialized Use Cases: RS-232 will remain relevant in specialized use cases, such as laboratory instrumentation, where legacy equipment is still in use and the cost of replacement is prohibitive.

In conclusion, RS-232 has a rich history and has served as a foundational standard for connecting devices in a wide range of applications. Its simplicity and versatility have made it a go-to choice for serial communication for many years. While its use has declined in favor of more modern communication standards, RS-232 continues to play a vital role in legacy systems and specialized applications, ensuring the continued operation of older technology. Its future lies in maintaining legacy support and coexisting with newer communication technologies as they continue to advance.

RS485

RS-485, or Recommended Standard 485, is a widely used serial communication standard that has been a cornerstone in industrial automation and data communication for decades. Developed by the Electronic Industries Association (EIA), RS-485 is known for its robustness, noise immunity, and versatility in connecting devices, sensors, and controllers over long distances. In this comprehensive article, we will explore the history, architecture, signaling, applications, advantages, and considerations associated with RS-485.

1. History of RS-485

RS-485, like its predecessor RS-232, was developed by the Electronic Industries Association (EIA) to standardize serial communication protocols. The standardization aimed to facilitate the interoperability of communication equipment and to address the limitations of RS-232, which was primarily designed for point-to-point communication over short distances.

RS-485 was introduced in the late 1970s and early 1980s as an improved and more robust solution for data communication over longer distances and in noisy industrial environments. Its development was driven by the growing demand for reliable data exchange in industrial automation, process control, and remote monitoring applications.

The key feature that sets RS-485 apart from RS-232 is its differential signaling, which allows it to tolerate common-mode noise and provide long-distance communication capabilities. As a result, RS-485 quickly gained popularity in industrial settings where data integrity and noise immunity were critical.

Over the years, RS-485 has seen numerous revisions and adaptations to accommodate changing technology and communication needs. It remains a prominent and versatile standard for serial communication, with applications spanning industrial automation, building management, automotive systems, and more.

2. RS-485 Architecture

RS-485 is a balanced, differential serial communication standard that enables the exchange of data between multiple devices over a shared communication medium. It features a networked architecture that can connect numerous devices, including sensors, controllers, motor drives, and data acquisition equipment. The core components of RS-485 architecture include:

RS-485 Transceivers: RS-485 transceivers are integrated circuits (ICs) or chips responsible for converting electrical signals into RS-485-compliant differential signals and vice versa. These transceivers ensure that data is transmitted in a balanced, noise-immune manner.

RS-485 Cable: RS-485 communication typically uses twisted-pair cables with a minimum of two conductors (A and B). These twisted-pair cables help mitigate electromagnetic interference (EMI) and noise, ensuring reliable communication.

Terminators: Terminators are resistors placed at each end of the RS-485 cable to absorb signal reflections and ensure signal integrity. Proper termination is essential for the reliable operation of the RS-485 network.

Connectors: RS-485 networks can use various types of connectors, such as RJ-45 connectors or terminal blocks, depending on the specific application and industry requirements.

Network Topology: RS-485 networks can be configured in different topologies, including point-to-point, multi-drop, and multidrop/bus configurations. These topologies determine how devices are connected and how data flows within the network.

Voltage Levels: RS-485 defines voltage levels for logical "0" and logical "1" states. Differential signaling ensures that a logical "0" is represented by a voltage difference between the A and B conductors, and a logical "1" is represented by the opposite voltage difference.

Signaling: RS-485 employs differential signaling, where data is transmitted as the voltage difference between the A and B conductors. The receiver interprets the voltage difference to decode the binary data.

3. RS-485 Signaling and Data Transmission

RS-485 signaling and data transmission are fundamental to its noise immunity and long-distance communication capabilities. Understanding how RS-485 signaling works is crucial for reliable data exchange. Key aspects of RS-485 signaling and data transmission include:

Differential Signaling: RS-485 uses differential signaling to transmit data. A logical "0" is represented by a positive voltage on the A conductor and an equal negative voltage on the B conductor. A logical "1" is represented by the opposite voltage levels. The voltage difference between A and B determines the state of the data.

Half-Duplex and Full-Duplex Operation: RS-485 supports both half-duplex and full-duplex communication. In half-duplex mode, data transmission occurs in one direction at a time, with devices taking turns to send and receive data. In full-duplex mode, devices can simultaneously transmit and receive data.

Data Rate (Baud Rate): The data rate, measured in bits per second (bps), specifies the speed at which data is transmitted over the RS-485 connection. Common baud rates for RS-485 communication include 9600, 19200, 38400, and 115200 bps, but RS-485 can support a wide range of data rates.

Data Frame Format: RS-485 data frames typically include a start bit, data bits (usually 8 bits), an optional parity bit for error checking, and one or more stop bits. The inclusion of parity and stop bits helps ensure data integrity.

Flow Control: RS-485 communication can implement various flow control mechanisms, such as hardware flow control (RTS/CTS) and software flow control (XON/XOFF). Flow control regulates the data flow between devices, preventing data overflows and ensuring smooth communication.

Error Detection and Correction: While RS-485 offers noise immunity, it may not include built-in error detection and correction features. Error detection mechanisms, such as CRC (Cyclic Redundancy Check), can be implemented at higher protocol layers to ensure data integrity.

4. RS-485 Applications

RS-485 is widely used in various applications across industries where robust and noise-immune data communication over long distances is essential. Some of the key applications of RS-485 include:

Industrial Automation: RS-485 is a backbone for industrial automation and process control systems. It connects sensors, actuators, Programmable Logic Controllers (PLCs), Human-Machine Interfaces (HMIs), and other devices in manufacturing, factory automation, and industrial process control.

Building Management Systems (BMS): RS-485 is used in building management systems to connect environmental sensors, lighting controls, HVAC (Heating, Ventilation, and Air Conditioning) equipment, and access control systems.

Automotive Systems: RS-485 is employed in automotive applications for connecting various subsystems, such as airbag control modules, engine control units, and body control modules. It supports reliable data exchange in the harsh automotive environment.

Telecommunications: In telecommunications, RS-485 connects equipment in Central Office (CO) applications and in the field, such as Digital Subscriber Line Access Multiplexers (DSLAMs) and remote terminals.

Data Acquisition Systems: RS-485 is used in data acquisition systems to connect sensors, data loggers, and instrumentation devices. It provides a reliable means of collecting and transmitting data from remote locations.

Electric Power Distribution: RS-485 is used in electric power distribution systems to connect smart meters, power monitoring equipment, and energy management systems.

Security Systems: RS-485 connects components in security systems, including access control panels, surveillance cameras, and alarm systems, enabling real-time monitoring and control.

Long-Range Communication: RS-485 is ideal for long-range communication in applications where traditional serial communication standards like RS-232 cannot reach. It is well-suited for communication between devices that are situated at considerable distances from each other.

5. Advantages of RS-485

RS-485 offers several advantages that have contributed to its widespread adoption in various industries:

Noise Immunity: RS-485's differential signaling minimizes the impact of common-mode noise, making it highly resistant to electromagnetic interference (EMI) and noise in industrial environments.

Long-Distance Communication: RS-485 supports long-distance communication, making it suitable for applications where devices are situated meters or even kilometers apart.

Robustness: RS-485 is known for its robustness and reliability in harsh industrial settings. It can withstand temperature variations, humidity, and other environmental challenges.

Multi-Drop Configuration: RS-485 allows for multi-drop configurations, where multiple devices can be connected to the same bus, enabling efficient data exchange among devices.

Full-Duplex and Half-Duplex Operation: RS-485 provides the flexibility to operate in both full-duplex and half-duplex modes, accommodating different communication needs and traffic patterns.

Versatility: RS-485 can be used in various industries and applications, offering a versatile solution for connecting a wide range of devices and sensors.

Cost-Effective: RS-485 offers a cost-effective means of communication, especially in applications that require long-distance communication over twisted-pair cabling.

6. RS-485 Challenges and Considerations

While RS-485 provides many advantages, there are also challenges and considerations to keep in mind when deploying RS-485 networks:

Termination: Proper termination is essential for RS-485 networks to minimize signal reflections and ensure data integrity. The absence of proper termination can lead to signal degradation.

Voltage Levels: Ensuring that RS-485 devices conform to the same voltage levels is crucial for successful communication. Inconsistent voltage levels can result in communication errors.

Data Rate Limitations: While RS-485 can support a range of data rates, it may not be suitable for extremely high-speed applications. Higher data rates can result in shorter maximum communication distances.

Network Topology: Designing RS-485 networks requires consideration of the network topology, termination points, and the distribution of devices to maintain signal quality and minimize reflections.

Error Handling: RS-485 may not inherently provide advanced error handling features. Error detection mechanisms should be implemented at higher protocol layers to ensure data integrity.

Security: RS-485 networks are generally not encrypted, and data on the bus is accessible to all connected devices. If security is a concern, additional measures may be necessary to protect data.

7. Future of RS-485

The future of RS-485 is influenced by the ongoing developments in technology and communication standards. While RS-485 remains a prominent communication standard in specific applications, its role is evolving in the context of modern communication technologies. The future of RS-485 may involve the following trends:

Integration with Ethernet and Wireless: RS-485 is likely to continue integrating with Ethernet and wireless technologies to accommodate modern networked environments and IIoT (Industrial Internet of Things) applications.

Higher Data Rates: RS-485 may evolve to support higher data rates to meet the demands of more data-intensive applications in industrial automation, data acquisition, and telecommunications.

Enhanced Protocol Layers: The development of higher-level protocols for RS-485 may introduce advanced error detection, correction, and security features to further improve data integrity and reliability.

Legacy Support: RS-485 will continue to be relevant for many years, especially for connecting with legacy systems and equipment in industrial and automation settings. Manufacturers will need to maintain support for RS-485 interfaces.

Smart Grids: RS-485 will play a role in the development of smart grids, where it connects smart meters, sensors, and energy management systems to enable more efficient power distribution and management.

Industrial Automation: RS-485 will continue to be essential for connecting sensors, PLCs, HMIs, and other devices in industrial automation and process control systems, facilitating real-time data exchange.

In conclusion, RS-485 is a robust and versatile communication standard that has stood the test of time in industrial automation and data communication. Its ability to provide long-distance, noise-immune communication has made it invaluable in various applications. While its use has evolved alongside modern communication technologies, RS-485 remains a crucial part of many industries and will continue to adapt to the changing communication landscape.

TCP/IP

TCP/IP is a fundamental suite of protocols that forms the backbone of the internet and plays a crucial role in data communication. Let's break down the key components and concepts of TCP/IP.

1. Introduction to TCP/IP:

TCP/IP, which stands for Transmission Control Protocol/Internet Protocol, is a set of communication protocols used for the internet and other similar networks. Developed in the 1970s by the U.S. Department of Defense, TCP/IP has become the standard protocol suite for networking.

2. Protocol Stack:

TCP/IP is organized into a layered architecture, with each layer responsible for specific tasks. The architecture consists of four layers:

a. Link Layer (or Network Interface Layer): This layer deals with the physical connection between devices on the same network. It includes protocols for Ethernet, Wi-Fi, and other hardware-specific technologies.

b. Internet Layer: The Internet layer is primarily responsible for routing packets between different networks. The Internet Protocol (IP) is a crucial component of this layer.

c. Transport Layer: This layer ensures end-to-end communication, providing reliable, error-checked data delivery. TCP and UDP (User Datagram Protocol) are the main protocols at this layer.

d. Application Layer: The top layer includes protocols that support specific network applications and services, such as HTTP for web browsing, SMTP for email, and FTP for file transfer.

3. Internet Protocol (IP):

The Internet Protocol (IP) is a central component of the TCP/IP suite. It provides the addressing and routing mechanism to facilitate packet switching across networks. IP has two versions in common use: IPv4 and IPv6. IPv4 uses a 32-bit addressing scheme, while IPv6 uses a 128-bit scheme to accommodate the growing number of devices connected to the internet.

4. Transmission Control Protocol (TCP):

TCP is a connection-oriented protocol that ensures reliable and ordered delivery of data between devices. It establishes a connection, manages data flow, and handles retransmission of lost packets. TCP is widely used for applications that require error-free and sequenced delivery, such as web browsing and file transfer.

5. User Datagram Protocol (UDP):

UDP is a connectionless protocol that operates at the transport layer. Unlike TCP, it does not establish a connection before transmitting data and does not guarantee delivery or order. UDP is suitable for real-time applications like video streaming and online gaming, where low latency is more critical than perfect data delivery.

6. Addressing and Subnetting:

IP addresses uniquely identify devices on a network. IPv4 addresses are written in the format xxx.xxx.xxx.xxx, where each "xxx" can range from 0 to 255. Subnetting allows the division of a larger IP network into smaller, more manageable sub-networks.

7. Domain Name System (DNS):

DNS is a crucial application layer protocol that translates human-readable domain names into IP addresses. This translation allows users to access websites using easy-to-remember domain names instead of numerical IP addresses.

8. Dynamic Host Configuration Protocol (DHCP):

DHCP automates the assignment of IP addresses within a network. It dynamically allocates IP addresses to devices when they join the network, simplifying network administration and preventing address conflicts.

9. Internet Control Message Protocol (ICMP):

ICMP is an integral part of the Internet Layer and is used for error reporting and diagnostics. Ping, a commonly used network tool, relies on ICMP to test the reachability of a host on an Internet Protocol (IP) network.

10. Routing and Gateway:

Routing involves determining the optimal path for data packets to travel from the source to the destination. Routers, operating at the Internet layer, play a key role in this process. Gateways facilitate communication between networks with different communication protocols.

11. Security Protocols:

Security is a crucial aspect of network communication. Protocols like Secure Sockets Layer (SSL) and its successor, Transport Layer Security (TLS), ensure secure data transmission over the internet. IPsec provides a framework for secure communication at the network layer.

12. TCP/IP in Action:

Understanding TCP/IP is essential for comprehending how data is transmitted across the internet. When you enter a website's URL in a browser, the DNS resolves the domain name to an IP address, DHCP assigns your device an IP address, and TCP ensures reliable data transfer while HTTP or HTTPS facilitates web page retrieval.

13. Challenges and Future Developments:

IPv4 address exhaustion is a significant challenge, leading to the widespread adoption of IPv6. Security concerns, such as DDoS attacks and cyber threats, continue to evolve, requiring ongoing developments in security protocols.

14. Conclusion:

TCP/IP is the backbone of modern networking, facilitating seamless communication across diverse devices and networks. Its layered architecture, encompassing protocols like IP, TCP, and UDP, provides a robust foundation for internet communication. As technology advances, TCP/IP will likely continue to adapt to new challenges and support the ever-growing demands of the digital world.

Mechatrolink

Mechatrolink is a high-performance industrial network protocol designed for motion control applications. This communication protocol is specifically tailored to meet the demands of industrial automation systems, providing a reliable and efficient means of connecting various devices within a control system. In this detailed exploration, we'll delve into the key aspects of Mechatrolink, including its history, architecture, communication principles, applications, advantages, and future trends.

1. Introduction to Mechatrolink:

Mechatrolink is an open fieldbus protocol developed to enable communication between different types of devices in motion control systems. It was first introduced in 1993 by the Mechatrolink Association, a group of companies dedicated to the advancement of this communication standard. The protocol has since evolved through various versions, with each iteration introducing improvements and expanded capabilities.

2. History and Development:

The development of Mechatrolink can be traced back to the need for a standardized communication protocol in the field of industrial automation, particularly in systems involving motion control. Before Mechatrolink, various proprietary communication methods were employed, leading to interoperability issues and limiting the flexibility of automation systems. Mechatrolink aimed to address these challenges by providing a common platform for communication among devices such as servo drives, motors, and programmable logic controllers (PLCs).

3. Mechatrolink Architecture:

Mechatrolink follows a layered architecture, similar to the OSI (Open Systems Interconnection) model. The key layers include:

a. Physical Layer: This layer deals with the electrical and mechanical aspects of communication, specifying the physical medium, connectors, and transmission rates.

b. Data Link Layer: Responsible for error detection and correction, the data link layer ensures reliable communication between devices. Mechatrolink uses a token-passing method to control access to the network.

c. Network Layer: The network layer manages the addressing and routing of data packets within the Mechatrolink network. It provides the foundation for device identification and communication.

d. Application Layer: At the top of the stack, the application layer defines the specific communication protocols and data formats used by devices within the Mechatrolink network.

4. Communication Principles:

Mechatrolink employs a deterministic communication method, ensuring that devices can predictably exchange data within a predefined time frame. This deterministic nature is crucial for motion control applications, where precise timing and synchronization are essential. The protocol utilizes a token-passing scheme to control access to the network, preventing data collisions and ensuring reliable communication.

5. Device Profiles:

Mechatrolink supports different device profiles, each tailored to a specific type of device. Common profiles include servo drives, variable frequency drives (VFDs), and remote I/O devices. These profiles define the communication parameters, data formats, and functionality specific to each device type, promoting interoperability within a Mechatrolink network.

6. Mechatrolink Versions:

Over the years, Mechatrolink has evolved through multiple versions, each introducing enhancements and additional features. These versions include Mechatrolink-I, Mechatrolink-II, and Mechatrolink-III. Mechatrolink-III, the latest version at the time of this discussion, offers increased data transfer rates, improved noise immunity, and expanded network topology options.

7. Applications of Mechatrolink:

Mechatrolink finds widespread use in various industrial automation applications, particularly those involving motion control. Some key applications include:

a. Robotic Systems: Mechatrolink facilitates communication between robotic arms, servo drives, and controllers, ensuring precise and coordinated motion in industrial robots.

b. Machine Tools: In machining applications, Mechatrolink enables seamless communication between CNC (Computer Numerical Control) systems, motors, and sensors, enhancing the overall efficiency and accuracy of machine tools.

c. Packaging Machinery: Mechatrolink is employed in packaging equipment to control the movement of conveyor systems, servo motors, and other components, optimizing the packaging process.

d. Automated Assembly Lines: Mechatrolink plays a crucial role in automated assembly lines, where it ensures synchronized motion control and communication between different stations.

8. Advantages of Mechatrolink:

a. Deterministic Communication: The deterministic nature of Mechatrolink ensures precise timing and synchronization, making it suitable for applications that demand high accuracy in motion control.

b. Open Standard: Mechatrolink is an open standard, allowing devices from different manufacturers to communicate seamlessly within a Mechatrolink network.

c. Scalability: The protocol supports various network topologies, and its scalability allows for the addition of devices without significant disruption to the existing network.

d. Ease of Integration: Mechatrolink's standardized profiles simplify the integration of different devices, reducing configuration efforts and enhancing interoperability.

e. High Performance: Mechatrolink's high data transfer rates and efficient communication protocols contribute to the overall performance of industrial automation systems.

9. Challenges and Considerations:

While Mechatrolink offers numerous benefits, users should be aware of certain challenges, such as the need for specialized hardware and potential limitations in network size. Careful consideration of these factors is crucial for ensuring optimal performance in specific applications.

10. Future Trends:

As technology continues to advance, the evolution of Mechatrolink is likely to involve higher data transfer rates, enhanced security features, and increased support for the Industrial Internet of Things (IIoT). The Mechatrolink Association is expected to play a pivotal role in steering the protocol toward meeting the evolving needs of the industrial automation landscape.

11. Conclusion:

Mechatrolink has emerged as a vital communication protocol in the realm of industrial automation, particularly in applications requiring precise motion control. Its deterministic nature, open standard, and support for various device profiles make it a versatile choice for manufacturers seeking reliable and interoperable solutions. As industries continue to evolve, Mechatrolink is poised to play a crucial role in shaping the future of industrial communication protocols.

CAN

The Controller Area Network (CAN) is a widely used communication protocol in the field of automotive and industrial applications. Developed initially for automotive use, CAN has evolved into a versatile and robust protocol with applications in various industries. In this comprehensive exploration, we'll delve into the history, architecture, communication principles, applications, advantages, and future trends of the Controller Area Network.

1. Introduction to Controller Area Network (CAN):

The Controller Area Network, commonly referred to as CAN, is a robust and efficient communication protocol designed for real-time, high-integrity data transmission in environments with high electromagnetic interference. Originally developed by Bosch in the mid-1980s for in-vehicle networking, CAN has since found widespread adoption beyond the automotive industry due to its reliability, low cost, and deterministic communication capabilities.

2. History and Development:

The development of CAN was driven by the need for a reliable and efficient communication protocol in automotive systems. Traditional point-to-point wiring in vehicles was becoming impractical due to the increasing complexity of electronic systems. In 1986, Bosch introduced the first version of CAN (CAN 1.0), and subsequently, the protocol evolved through various versions, including CAN 2.0A and CAN 2.0B. These versions introduced improvements such as extended message identifiers and enhanced error detection.

3. CAN Architecture:

The CAN architecture is based on a multi-master, multi-drop network topology, allowing multiple electronic control units (ECUs) to communicate on the same bus. The key components of the CAN architecture include:

a. Controller (Node): Each device on the CAN network is referred to as a node. Nodes can be microcontrollers, sensors, actuators, or other electronic devices. Each node has a CAN controller responsible for managing communication.

b. CAN Bus: The physical medium for communication is the CAN bus, a two-wire twisted-pair cable consisting of a CAN High (CAN_H) and a CAN Low (CAN_L) line. The differential signaling on these lines enhances noise immunity.

c. Message: Communication on the CAN bus occurs through messages. Each message has an identifier that determines its priority. Lower identifier values represent higher priority, allowing for a deterministic and predictable communication scheme.

d. Frame: A CAN message is encapsulated within a frame, which includes the identifier, control bits, data, and error-checking information. There are two types of frames: Data Frame and Remote Frame.

e. Bit Timing: CAN uses a non-destructive bit-wise arbitration method, where nodes with higher-priority messages gain access to the bus. Bit timing is crucial for synchronization, and nodes adjust their timing based on the bit-wise arbitration process.

4. Communication Principles:

CAN uses a message-oriented communication model, where nodes on the network can send and receive messages. The non-destructive arbitration process ensures that the node with the highest priority message gains bus access. Collision resolution is inherent in the protocol, allowing for deterministic communication with low latency.

5. Types of CAN Frames:

a. Data Frame: The Data Frame is the most common frame type and carries actual data for control and monitoring purposes. It includes an identifier, control bits, data, and a cyclic redundancy check (CRC) for error detection.

b. Remote Frame: The Remote Frame is used to request data from a specific node. It contains an identifier and control bits but does not carry data.

6. CAN Versions:

CAN has undergone several revisions, with the most significant being CAN 2.0A and CAN 2.0B. These versions introduced extended identifiers, allowing for a larger address space, and improved error detection mechanisms. CAN FD (Flexible Data-rate) is a more recent development that enables higher data transfer rates and larger data payloads.

7. Applications of CAN:

CAN was initially developed for automotive applications, and it remains a cornerstone of in-vehicle networking. However, its reliability and efficiency have led to its adoption in various other industries, including:

a. Industrial Automation: CAN is used in industrial automation systems to connect sensors, actuators, and programmable logic controllers (PLCs). It facilitates real-time communication in manufacturing environments.

b. Medical Devices: CAN is employed in medical devices and equipment for communication between different modules and components. Its deterministic nature is crucial in medical applications where precise timing is essential.

c. Aerospace: In aerospace applications, CAN is used for communication between avionics systems, sensors, and control units. Its reliability makes it suitable for critical systems in aircraft.

d. Marine: CAN is utilized in marine systems for communication between navigation systems, engine control units, and various sensors on boats and ships.

e. Home Automation: CAN finds application in home automation systems, connecting smart devices, sensors, and controllers for seamless communication in smart homes.

8. Advantages of CAN:

a. Deterministic Communication: CAN offers deterministic communication, ensuring that messages are transmitted with low latency and predictable timing. This is crucial in applications where real-time responsiveness is paramount.

b. Reliability: The differential signaling on the CAN bus, coupled with error-checking mechanisms, enhances the reliability of communication, even in environments with high electromagnetic interference.

c. Scalability: CAN's multi-master, multi-drop architecture allows for the easy addition of nodes to the network without significant reconfiguration. This scalability is beneficial in systems that may undergo expansions or modifications.

d. Low Cost: CAN is a cost-effective communication solution, making it attractive for applications with budget constraints. The simplicity of the protocol contributes to the overall cost-effectiveness.

e. Versatility: While initially designed for automotive applications, CAN's versatility has led to its adoption in a wide range of industries, demonstrating its adaptability to different communication needs.

9. Challenges and Considerations:

Despite its advantages, CAN does have certain limitations. As data transfer rates increase, CAN's ability to handle large amounts of data may become a bottleneck. Additionally, CAN does not inherently provide security features, and while it has robust error-checking mechanisms, it may not be suitable for applications with extremely stringent reliability requirements.

10. Future Trends:

As technology continues to advance, the future of CAN involves developments such as higher data transfer rates, enhanced security features, and increased integration with emerging technologies like the Internet of Things (IoT). The evolution of CAN FD and the exploration of CAN in combination with Ethernet are among the trends that may shape the protocol's future.

11. Conclusion:

The Controller Area Network (CAN) has proven to be a pivotal communication protocol, initially designed for automotive applications but now widely adopted in various industries. Its deterministic communication, reliability, and versatility have contributed to its enduring popularity. As industries continue to advance, CAN is likely to evolve to meet the ever-growing demands of real-time, high-integrity communication in diverse applications, solidifying its place as a fundamental technology in the world of embedded systems and industrial automation.

EtherCAT

EtherCAT (Ethernet for Control Automation Technology) is a high-performance industrial communication protocol that has gained popularity in the realm of automation and control systems. Designed to provide real-time communication with low latency, EtherCAT enables the efficient exchange of data between devices in industrial networks. In this detailed exploration, we'll delve into the history, architecture, communication principles, applications, advantages, and future trends of EtherCAT.

1. Introduction to EtherCAT:

EtherCAT is an industrial Ethernet-based communication protocol developed to address the growing demand for high-performance, real-time communication in automation systems. It was introduced by Beckhoff Automation in 2003 and has since become a widely adopted standard in various industries, offering advantages such as low communication latency, high data throughput, and scalability.

2. History and Development:

The development of EtherCAT was motivated by the need for faster and more deterministic communication in industrial automation. Traditional fieldbus systems were facing limitations in terms of data transfer rates and real-time capabilities. Beckhoff Automation, a German company, introduced EtherCAT as a solution to these challenges, leveraging the speed and ubiquity of Ethernet technology.

3. EtherCAT Architecture:

EtherCAT's architecture is unique and contributes to its high-performance capabilities. The protocol utilizes a "processing on the fly" principle, allowing data to be processed at each node as it passes through the network. The key components of the EtherCAT architecture include:

a. EtherCAT Master: The master device initiates communication on the EtherCAT network. It sends a telegram, which contains data and instructions, to the slave devices. The master manages the synchronization and timing of the network.

b. EtherCAT Slave: Each device connected to the EtherCAT network is a slave. Slaves process the data on the fly, meaning they read, modify, or generate new data in real-time as the data passes through them. This processing capability contributes to EtherCAT's low communication latency.

c. EtherCAT Telegram: The telegram is the fundamental communication unit in EtherCAT. It contains the data for all the slaves, and as it passes through each slave, they extract or insert their specific data. The telegram is continuously cyclically transmitted on the network.

d. Distributed Clocks: EtherCAT employs a distributed clock mechanism for synchronization, ensuring that all devices in the network operate in a coordinated and synchronized manner. This is crucial for applications that demand precise timing.

4. Communication Principles:

EtherCAT's communication principles are designed to achieve real-time performance with minimal latency. The protocol uses a cyclic data exchange mechanism, where the master sends a telegram containing data for all slaves, and each slave processes its specific data on the fly. This ensures that the entire network operates with a deterministic and predictable timing cycle.

EtherCAT's "processing on the fly" approach allows for parallel data processing at each node, resulting in minimal communication delays. The distributed clock synchronization further enhances the accuracy of timing across all devices in the network.

5. Types of EtherCAT Devices:

EtherCAT supports various device types, each serving a specific purpose in industrial automation. Some common EtherCAT devices include:

a. EtherCAT Master Devices: These devices initiate and control communication on the EtherCAT network. They are responsible for sending telegrams, managing synchronization, and coordinating data exchange.

b. EtherCAT Slave Devices: Slaves are the devices that perform specific tasks in the industrial process. They can include sensors, actuators, drives, and other control devices. Each slave processes its assigned data in real-time as the telegram passes through.

c. Couplers/Gateways: Couplers or gateways allow the integration of EtherCAT networks with other fieldbus systems, enabling interoperability between different automation devices.

6. Application of EtherCAT:

EtherCAT finds application in a wide range of industrial automation scenarios where real-time communication is crucial. Some notable applications include:

a. Machine Control Systems: EtherCAT is commonly used in machine control systems for applications such as CNC machines, packaging machines, and printing presses. Its low latency and high-speed capabilities make it suitable for precise control.

b. Robotics: In robotic systems, EtherCAT facilitates communication between the robot controller, sensors, and actuators. Real-time control is essential for tasks that require precise movement and coordination.

c. Automotive Manufacturing: EtherCAT is employed in automotive manufacturing for tasks such as controlling assembly line robots, monitoring sensors, and managing conveyor systems. The protocol's speed and reliability contribute to the efficiency of production processes.

d. Process Automation: EtherCAT is utilized in process automation industries for applications like controlling valves, monitoring sensors, and managing data acquisition systems. Its real-time capabilities are beneficial in ensuring accurate and timely process control.

e. Test and Measurement Systems: In test and measurement applications, EtherCAT enables high-speed communication between testing equipment, sensors, and data acquisition devices. Its deterministic nature is crucial for obtaining precise measurement data.

7. Advantages of EtherCAT:

a. Real-time Performance: EtherCAT provides real-time communication with low latency, making it suitable for applications that demand precise and deterministic control.

b. High Data Throughput: The parallel processing capability of EtherCAT, combined with its high-speed communication, allows for efficient data exchange and high data throughput.

c. Scalability: EtherCAT networks can easily scale to accommodate a large number of devices without significant degradation in performance. This scalability is beneficial for expanding automation systems.

d. Deterministic Timing: The distributed clock mechanism ensures synchronized timing across all devices in the network, contributing to deterministic and coordinated operations.

e. Open Standard: EtherCAT is an open standard, allowing multiple vendors to implement the protocol in their devices. This openness promotes interoperability and flexibility in choosing automation components.

8. Challenges and Considerations:

While EtherCAT offers significant advantages, users should be aware of certain challenges. Configuration complexity and the need for specialized hardware can be considerations when implementing EtherCAT in a system. Additionally, the determination of optimal cycle times and careful network planning are crucial for achieving the desired performance.

9. Future Trends:

As industrial automation continues to advance, the future of EtherCAT may involve developments in areas such as higher data rates, enhanced security features, and increased integration with emerging technologies like the Industrial Internet of Things (IIoT). The protocol is likely to evolve to meet the evolving demands of Industry 4.0 and smart manufacturing.

10. Conclusion:

EtherCAT has established itself as a leading industrial communication protocol, offering real-time performance and high-speed data exchange capabilities. Its unique architecture, featuring distributed clock synchronization and processing on the fly, has contributed to its widespread adoption in various industrial automation applications. As industries continue to evolve, EtherCAT is poised to play a pivotal role in shaping the future of real-time communication protocols, particularly in the context of smart manufacturing and Industry 4.0 initiatives.

Introduction to Supervisory Control Systems

A Supervisory Control System (SCS) is a critical component of industrial automation that plays a pivotal role in monitoring, controlling, and optimizing complex processes. This system provides a higher-level oversight of various devices and subsystems within an industrial environment, ensuring efficient and safe operations. In this comprehensive exploration, we'll delve into the fundamental concepts, architecture, key components, applications, advantages, challenges, and future trends of Supervisory Control Systems.

1. Introduction to Supervisory Control Systems:

Supervisory Control Systems (SCS) are a type of control system that sits atop a hierarchy of control layers in industrial automation. These systems are designed to monitor, manage, and supervise lower-level processes and devices, providing a centralized interface for operators to interact with and control the industrial processes. SCS plays a critical role in enhancing the efficiency, safety, and reliability of complex industrial systems.

2. Hierarchy of Control Systems:

In industrial automation, control systems are often organized into a hierarchical structure comprising multiple layers. The hierarchy typically includes:

a. Field Level: At the lowest level, field devices such as sensors, actuators, and instruments interact directly with the physical processes.

b. Control Level: The control level involves controllers, programmable logic controllers (PLCs), and distributed control systems (DCS) responsible for real-time control and coordination of processes.

c. Supervisory Level: Above the control level is the supervisory level, which houses the Supervisory Control System. This layer provides a higher-level overview, coordination, and decision-making capability.

d. Enterprise Level: The top layer, the enterprise level, integrates the industrial control system with business systems, enabling data analysis, reporting, and strategic decision-making.

3. Architecture of Supervisory Control Systems:

The architecture of a Supervisory Control System is designed to facilitate effective monitoring, control, and coordination of industrial processes. Key components of the architecture include:

a. Human Machine Interface (HMI): The HMI is the user interface through which operators interact with the Supervisory Control System. It provides a graphical representation of the industrial processes, real-time data, and control options.

b. Data Acquisition System: This component collects data from various sensors and field devices in the industrial processes. The data is then processed and made available for analysis and control at the supervisory level.

c. Communication Infrastructure: Supervisory Control Systems rely on a robust communication infrastructure to exchange data with lower-level control systems and field devices. Communication protocols, networks, and interfaces are essential components.

d. Control Logic and Algorithms: The supervisory level often incorporates advanced control logic and algorithms for decision-making and process optimization. This includes functions such as alarm management, trend analysis, and predictive maintenance.

e. Database System: A database system is often employed to store historical data, configuration settings, and other relevant information. This data repository supports analytics, reporting, and troubleshooting.

4. Key Components of Supervisory Control Systems:

a. Human Machine Interface (HMI): The HMI is a crucial component that provides a visual representation of the industrial processes. It includes features such as real-time monitoring, alarm displays, and control interfaces for operators.

b. Data Acquisition System (DAS): The DAS is responsible for gathering data from sensors, instruments, and other field devices. It ensures that relevant information is available for analysis and decision-making at the supervisory level.

c. Communication Protocols: Various communication protocols facilitate the exchange of data between different layers of the control hierarchy. Common protocols include OPC (OLE for Process Control), Modbus, and Profibus.

d. Supervisory Control Logic: This encompasses the control algorithms and logic implemented at the supervisory level. It includes strategies for process optimization, coordination of lower-level controllers, and response to abnormal situations.

e. Database System: A database system stores and manages data collected from the industrial processes. It supports historical analysis, trend monitoring, and reporting.

5. Applications of Supervisory Control Systems:

Supervisory Control Systems find applications in a wide range of industries and processes. Some notable examples include:

a. Manufacturing: In manufacturing environments, SCS can oversee and coordinate production lines, ensuring efficient utilization of resources, monitoring quality, and responding to deviations in real-time.

b. Energy Management: SCS is employed in energy management systems to monitor and control the operation of power plants, ensuring optimal performance, efficiency, and reliability.

c. Water and Wastewater Treatment: In water treatment plants, Supervisory Control Systems help manage the treatment process, monitor water quality, and control the distribution of treated water.

d. Transportation Systems: SCS plays a crucial role in managing transportation systems such as traffic control, railway operations, and airport logistics.

e. Building Automation: In large facilities, SCS can be used for building automation, overseeing HVAC (Heating, Ventilation, and Air Conditioning) systems, lighting, and security.

f. Oil and Gas Industry: Supervisory Control Systems are employed in oil and gas facilities for monitoring and controlling extraction, refining, and distribution processes.

6. Advantages of Supervisory Control Systems:

a. Centralized Monitoring: SCS provides a centralized interface for monitoring the entire industrial process, allowing operators to have a comprehensive overview of the system.

b. Efficient Control: The supervisory level facilitates efficient control and coordination of lower-level controllers and devices, ensuring optimal performance and resource utilization.

c. Real-time Decision Making: With real-time data acquisition and processing, SCS enables operators to make informed decisions promptly, reducing response times to abnormal situations.

d. Process Optimization: Supervisory Control Systems often include advanced algorithms for process optimization, contributing to increased efficiency and reduced resource consumption.

e. Scalability: SCS is designed to be scalable, allowing for the addition of new devices or subsystems without significant reconfiguration.

7. Challenges and Considerations:

Despite the advantages, the implementation of Supervisory Control Systems comes with certain challenges and considerations:

a. Cybersecurity: As industrial systems become more interconnected, the risk of cybersecurity threats increases. Protecting Supervisory Control Systems from unauthorized access and cyberattacks is a paramount concern.

b. Integration Complexity: Integrating a Supervisory Control System with existing control layers and devices may pose challenges, especially in systems with diverse legacy components.

c. Human Factors: Operator training and the design of the HMI are critical factors. Effective training programs and user-friendly interfaces are essential for ensuring operators can respond appropriately to various scenarios.

d. System Reliability: Ensuring the reliability of the entire system, including communication networks and devices, is crucial for preventing downtime and maintaining continuous operations.

8. Future Trends:

As technology continues to advance, several trends are shaping the future of Supervisory Control Systems:

a. Artificial Intelligence and Machine Learning: The integration of AI and machine learning algorithms in Supervisory Control Systems is expected to enhance decision-making capabilities, enabling predictive maintenance and process optimization.

b. Edge Computing: The adoption of edge computing allows for more distributed and decentralized decision-making, reducing latency and improving the responsiveness of Supervisory Control Systems.

c. IoT Integration: The integration of the Internet of Things (IoT) technologies enables enhanced data collection from a multitude of sensors and devices, providing richer information for analysis and control.

d. Cloud-based Solutions: Cloud computing offers scalability and flexibility, allowing organizations to deploy and manage Supervisory Control Systems more efficiently.

e. Cybersecurity Measures: With an increasing focus on industrial cybersecurity, future Supervisory Control Systems are likely to incorporate advanced cybersecurity measures to protect against evolving threats.

9. Conclusion:

Supervisory Control Systems represent a critical layer in the hierarchical structure of industrial automation, providing centralized oversight, control, and coordination. These systems contribute to the efficiency, safety, and reliability of complex industrial processes across various industries. As technology evolves, Supervisory Control Systems are expected to integrate advanced features, such as AI, machine learning, and IoT, to further enhance their capabilities. Cybersecurity measures will remain a priority as industries strive to ensure the integrity and resilience of their Supervisory Control Systems in the face of evolving challenges.

SCADA

Supervisory Control and Data Acquisition (SCADA) is a comprehensive control system used in various industries to monitor, control, and manage complex processes and infrastructures. SCADA systems play a crucial role in enhancing efficiency, ensuring safety, and facilitating decision-making by providing real-time data and control capabilities. In this detailed exploration, we'll delve into the history, architecture, components, communication protocols, applications, advantages, challenges, and future trends of SCADA systems.

1. Introduction to SCADA:

Supervisory Control and Data Acquisition, commonly known as SCADA, is a control system architecture that utilizes computers, networked data communications, and graphical user interfaces for high-level process monitoring and control. SCADA systems are employed in various industries, including manufacturing, utilities, transportation, and infrastructure, to gather and analyze real-time data, enabling operators to make informed decisions and control processes remotely.

2. History of SCADA:

The roots of SCADA can be traced back to the 1960s when the need for centralized control and monitoring of industrial processes became evident. Early SCADA systems were based on simple telemetry systems that transmitted data over long distances using wired or radio communication. Over the decades, advancements in computing technology, communication protocols, and graphical interfaces have led to the evolution of SCADA into sophisticated and highly integrated systems.

3. SCADA Architecture:

The architecture of a SCADA system is designed to facilitate effective monitoring, control, and data acquisition. Key components of the architecture include:

a. Supervisory Computers: These computers run the SCADA software and serve as the central control unit. They receive real-time data from field devices and send control commands to the controlled processes.

b. Remote Terminal Units (RTUs) and Programmable Logic Controllers (PLCs): RTUs and PLCs are field devices responsible for acquiring data from sensors and actuators in the field. They send this data to the supervisory computers and execute control commands received from the SCADA system.

c. Communication Infrastructure: SCADA systems rely on a robust communication infrastructure to facilitate the exchange of data between supervisory computers and field devices. Communication protocols such as Modbus, DNP3 (Distributed Network Protocol), and OPC (OLE for Process Control) are commonly used.

d. Human Machine Interface (HMI): The HMI provides operators with a graphical representation of the monitored processes. It displays real-time data, alarms, and control options, allowing operators to interact with the SCADA system.

e. Historian: The historian is responsible for storing and managing historical data collected by the SCADA system. This data is crucial for trend analysis, reporting, and compliance purposes.

4. Components of SCADA Systems:

a. Supervisory Computers: These are the central processing units that run the SCADA software. They collect and process data from field devices, issue control commands, and provide a human-readable interface for operators.

b. Remote Terminal Units (RTUs): RTUs are field devices that interface with sensors and actuators. They collect data from the field and send it to the supervisory computers. RTUs also execute control commands received from the SCADA system.

c. Programmable Logic Controllers (PLCs): PLCs are similar to RTUs but are more commonly used in discrete manufacturing processes. They are responsible for automating the control of machines and processes.

d. Communication Infrastructure: The communication infrastructure includes networks, protocols, and interfaces that enable data exchange between supervisory computers and field devices. Common communication protocols include Modbus, DNP3, and OPC.

e. Human Machine Interface (HMI): The HMI is the user interface that allows operators to interact with the SCADA system. It provides real-time data visualization, control options, and alarms.

f. Historian: The historian component stores and manages historical data collected by the SCADA system. This data is essential for analysis, reporting, and compliance.

5. Communication Protocols in SCADA:

Communication protocols are essential for the seamless exchange of data between different components of a SCADA system. Several protocols are commonly used in SCADA systems, each serving specific purposes:

a. Modbus: Modbus is a widely used serial communication protocol that allows communication between SCADA systems and field devices such as RTUs and PLCs.

b. DNP3 (Distributed Network Protocol): DNP3 is designed for the reliable exchange of data between SCADA systems and remote devices in utility automation.

c. OPC (OLE for Process Control): OPC is a set of standards that define the interface between SCADA systems and process control devices, enabling interoperability.

d. IEC 61850: This standard is specifically designed for the communication requirements of power utility automation. It defines protocols for intelligent electronic devices (IEDs) in substations.

e. EtherNet/IP: EtherNet/IP is an industrial network protocol commonly used in SCADA systems for communication between devices over an Ethernet network.

6. Applications of SCADA:

SCADA systems find applications in a diverse range of industries and processes where real-time monitoring and control are essential. Some notable applications include:

a. Energy Management: SCADA systems are used in the energy sector to monitor and control power generation, transmission, and distribution. They help optimize energy production and ensure grid stability.

b. Water and Wastewater Treatment: SCADA systems play a crucial role in monitoring and controlling water treatment processes, ensuring water quality, and managing the distribution of treated water.

c. Manufacturing: In manufacturing, SCADA systems are employed to monitor and control production processes, manage inventory, and optimize overall efficiency.

d. Oil and Gas Industry: SCADA is used in the oil and gas sector to monitor and control drilling operations, pipeline infrastructure, and refineries.

e. Transportation Systems: SCADA systems are utilized in transportation for monitoring and controlling traffic signals, railway operations, and other critical infrastructure.

f. Building Automation: SCADA systems contribute to building automation by monitoring and controlling HVAC systems, lighting, and security.

g. Telecommunications: SCADA is used in the telecommunications industry for monitoring and controlling network infrastructure, ensuring optimal performance and reliability.

7. Advantages of SCADA:

a. Real-time Monitoring: SCADA systems provide real-time monitoring of industrial processes, allowing operators to have an up-to-date view of the system.

b. Remote Control: SCADA systems enable remote control of processes, allowing operators to make adjustments or issue commands from a central location.

c. Efficiency Optimization: SCADA systems contribute to the optimization of industrial processes, leading to increased efficiency and reduced operational costs.

d. Data Analysis: SCADA systems collect and store historical data, allowing for in-depth analysis of trends, performance, and potential issues.

e. Alarm Management: SCADA systems provide real-time alarms and notifications, enabling operators to respond promptly to abnormal situations and prevent downtime.

8. Challenges and Considerations:

a. Cybersecurity: With increased connectivity, SCADA systems are vulnerable to cybersecurity threats. Implementing robust cybersecurity measures is crucial to protect against unauthorized access and attacks.

b. Integration Complexity: Integrating SCADA systems with existing infrastructure can be complex, especially in environments with diverse legacy components. Careful planning is required to ensure seamless integration.

c. Human Factors: Operator training and the design of the HMI are critical considerations. Effective training programs and user-friendly interfaces are essential for ensuring operators can respond appropriately to various scenarios.

d. Reliability: Ensuring the reliability of the entire SCADA system, including communication networks and devices, is crucial for preventing downtime and maintaining continuous operations.

9. Future Trends:

a. Edge Computing: The adoption of edge computing in SCADA systems allows for more distributed and decentralized processing, reducing latency and improving the responsiveness of the system.

b. Artificial Intelligence and Machine Learning: The integration of AI and machine learning in SCADA systems is expected to enhance predictive analytics, anomaly detection, and overall system optimization.

c. Cloud-based Solutions: Cloud computing offers scalability and flexibility, allowing organizations to deploy and manage SCADA systems more efficiently.

d. 5G Technology: The deployment of 5G technology can enhance communication speeds and reliability in SCADA systems, enabling faster and more responsive data exchange.

e. Advanced Human-Machine Interaction: The development of advanced HMIs with features such as augmented reality (AR) and virtual reality (VR) can enhance operator visualization and interaction.

10. Conclusion:

Supervisory Control and Data Acquisition (SCADA) systems have become integral to modern industrial processes, providing real-time monitoring, control, and data acquisition capabilities. As technology continues to advance, SCADA systems are expected to evolve with the integration of edge computing, artificial intelligence, and cloud-based solutions. Ensuring robust cybersecurity measures and addressing integration complexities will be crucial as industries strive to leverage the full potential of SCADA systems for efficient and secure operations across diverse sectors.

Distributed Control System

A Distributed Control System (DCS) is a sophisticated control system used in various industries to monitor and control complex processes. Unlike centralized control systems, DCS distributes control functions across multiple processors, enabling efficient management of large-scale industrial processes. In this detailed exploration, we'll delve into the history, architecture, components, communication protocols, applications, advantages, challenges, and future trends of Distributed Control Systems.

1. Introduction to Distributed Control Systems:

A Distributed Control System (DCS) is a type of control system used in industrial processes to monitor and control equipment and processes. Unlike traditional centralized control systems, where control functions are concentrated in a single location, DCS distributes control tasks across multiple processors. This distributed architecture enables the efficient management of complex and large-scale industrial processes, providing real-time control, monitoring, and optimization.

2. History of Distributed Control Systems:

The development of Distributed Control Systems can be traced back to the late 20th century when the need for more efficient and flexible control systems in industrial processes became apparent. Early DCS implementations emerged in industries such as chemical processing, power generation, and manufacturing. Over the years, advancements in computing technology, communication protocols, and software engineering have contributed to the evolution and widespread adoption of DCS across various sectors.

3. DCS Architecture:

The architecture of a Distributed Control System is characterized by the distribution of control functions across multiple processors, typically organized in a hierarchical or networked structure. Key components of DCS architecture include:

a. Processors/Controllers: DCS employs multiple processors or controllers, distributed strategically throughout the industrial process. These controllers are responsible for executing control algorithms, collecting data from field devices, and making real-time decisions.

b. Input/Output (I/O) Modules: I/O modules interface with field devices such as sensors and actuators. They convert analog or digital signals from the field into a format that can be processed by the controllers and vice versa.

c. Communication Network: A robust communication network connects the controllers, I/O modules, and other components of the DCS. The network facilitates the exchange of data and commands in real-time, enabling seamless coordination among distributed elements.

d. Human Machine Interface (HMI): The HMI provides operators with a user-friendly interface to monitor the industrial process, view real-time data, and interact with the DCS. It serves as a central control point for operators to make decisions and adjustments.

e. Engineering Station: The engineering station is used for configuring, programming, and maintaining the DCS. Engineers use this station to design control strategies, set parameters, and troubleshoot the system.

4. Components of Distributed Control Systems:

a. Controllers/Processors: Controllers or processors form the core of the DCS architecture. They execute control algorithms, process real-time data, and coordinate the overall control strategy. Multiple controllers work in tandem to distribute the processing load.

b. Input/Output (I/O) Modules: I/O modules interface with field devices and sensors to collect and send data to the controllers. They play a crucial role in converting signals between the analog or digital domain and the DCS.

c. Communication Network: The communication network facilitates the exchange of data and commands between controllers, I/O modules, and other components. Common communication protocols include Profibus, Foundation Fieldbus, and Ethernet/IP.

d. Human Machine Interface (HMI): The HMI provides a graphical representation of the industrial process, real-time data visualization, and control options for operators. It is the primary interface for human interaction with the DCS.

e. Engineering Station: The engineering station is used for system configuration, programming, and maintenance. Engineers use this station to design control strategies, set parameters, and troubleshoot the DCS.

f. Redundancy Systems: Redundancy systems ensure system reliability by providing backup components in case of a failure. This includes redundant controllers, communication pathways, and power supplies.

5. Communication Protocols in DCS:

Communication protocols are critical for the seamless exchange of data between different components of a DCS. Various protocols are employed in DCS systems, each serving specific purposes:

a. Profibus: Profibus is a widely used fieldbus communication protocol in industrial automation. It supports high-speed data exchange between controllers, I/O modules, and field devices.

b. Foundation Fieldbus: Foundation Fieldbus is a digital communication protocol designed for real-time control in process automation. It enables communication between field devices and controllers in a distributed environment.

c. Ethernet/IP: Ethernet/IP is an industrial network protocol that allows communication between devices over an Ethernet network. It is commonly used in DCS for high-speed data exchange.

d. Modbus: Modbus is a simple and widely used serial communication protocol in industrial automation. It facilitates communication between controllers and field devices.

e. HART (Highway Addressable Remote Transducer): HART is a hybrid communication protocol that enables digital communication with field devices while maintaining compatibility with existing analog systems.

6. Applications of Distributed Control Systems:

DCS systems find applications in a variety of industries where large-scale, complex processes require efficient monitoring and control. Some notable applications include:

a. Chemical Processing: DCS is extensively used in chemical plants for monitoring and controlling various processes such as reaction vessels, distillation columns, and mixing systems.

b. Power Generation: In power plants, DCS systems monitor and control the operation of turbines, boilers, and electrical distribution systems to ensure reliable and efficient power generation.

c. Oil and Gas Industry: DCS is employed in oil and gas facilities for the control of drilling operations, refining processes, pipeline transportation, and offshore platforms.

d. Water and Wastewater Treatment: DCS systems play a vital role in water treatment plants, managing processes such as filtration, chemical dosing, and distribution to ensure clean and safe water.

e. Manufacturing: DCS is used in manufacturing industries for controlling production processes, managing inventory, and ensuring quality control in areas such as automotive, pharmaceuticals, and food production.

f. Pharmaceuticals: In the pharmaceutical industry, DCS systems control and monitor processes involved in drug manufacturing, ensuring precise control and adherence to quality standards.

g. Mining: DCS is utilized in mining operations for the control of excavation, transportation, and processing of minerals and ores.

7. Advantages of Distributed Control Systems:

a. Scalability: DCS systems are highly scalable, allowing for the expansion or modification of control functions without significant reconfiguration.

b. Redundancy: Redundancy features in DCS systems enhance system reliability by providing backup components and communication pathways in case of failures.

c. Real-time Control: DCS systems offer real-time control capabilities, enabling operators to respond promptly to changes in the industrial process.

d. Centralized Monitoring: While control functions are distributed, DCS provides centralized monitoring through a unified HMI, providing operators with a comprehensive overview of the entire system.

e. Flexibility: DCS systems are flexible and adaptable to changes in the industrial process, making them suitable for dynamic and evolving environments.

8. Challenges and Considerations:

a. Integration Complexity: Integrating DCS systems with existing infrastructure can be complex, especially in environments with diverse legacy components. Careful planning is required to ensure seamless integration.

b. Cybersecurity: With increased connectivity, DCS systems are vulnerable to cybersecurity threats. Implementing robust cybersecurity measures is crucial to protect against unauthorized access and attacks.

c. Training Requirements: Operators and maintenance personnel need specialized training to operate and maintain DCS systems effectively. Training programs should be comprehensive to ensure the proficient use of the system.

d. Initial Cost: The initial cost of implementing a DCS system can be substantial. However, the long-term benefits, including increased efficiency and reliability, often justify the investment.

9. Future Trends:

a. Integration with Industrial IoT (IIoT): The integration of DCS with IIoT technologies enables enhanced data collection, analytics, and connectivity, paving the way for more intelligent and data-driven industrial processes.

b. Edge Computing: The adoption of edge computing in DCS systems allows for more distributed and decentralized processing, reducing latency and improving the responsiveness of the system.

c. Advanced Analytics and Machine Learning: DCS systems are likely to incorporate advanced analytics and machine learning algorithms for predictive maintenance, anomaly detection, and optimization of industrial processes.

d. Cloud-based Solutions: Cloud computing offers scalability and flexibility, allowing organizations to deploy and manage DCS systems more efficiently. This trend may lead to increased adoption of cloud-based DCS solutions.

e. Advanced Human-Machine Interaction: The development of advanced HMIs with features such as augmented reality (AR) and virtual reality (VR) can enhance operator visualization and interaction in DCS systems.

10. Conclusion:

Distributed Control Systems (DCS) have revolutionized industrial automation by providing a scalable, flexible, and efficient solution for monitoring and controlling complex processes. The distributed architecture of DCS enables real-time control, centralized monitoring, and seamless integration with various industries, including chemical processing, power generation, and manufacturing. As technology continues to advance, the integration of Industrial IoT, edge computing, and advanced analytics is expected to shape the future of DCS, making industrial processes more intelligent, adaptive, and responsive. Addressing challenges such as cybersecurity and ensuring continuous training for personnel will be essential as industries leverage the benefits of DCS for improved efficiency and reliability.

Safety Systems

Safety systems play a crucial role in industrial environments by safeguarding personnel, equipment, and the environment from potential hazards. These systems are designed to prevent accidents, mitigate the impact of incidents, and ensure the safe operation of processes. In this comprehensive exploration, we'll delve into the key concepts, types, components, standards, applications, challenges, and future trends of safety systems.

1. Introduction to Safety Systems:

Safety systems are integral components of industrial processes aimed at managing and mitigating risks to ensure the well-being of personnel, protect equipment, and prevent environmental harm. These systems employ a combination of technologies, protocols, and procedures to identify, assess, and address potential hazards in a proactive manner.

2. Importance of Safety Systems:

The significance of safety systems in industrial settings cannot be overstated. They serve several critical functions:

a. Personnel Safety: Protecting the health and well-being of workers is a primary objective of safety systems. These systems are designed to prevent accidents, injuries, and fatalities in the workplace.

b. Asset Protection: Safety systems help safeguard industrial assets, including machinery, equipment, and infrastructure, by preventing damage or destruction caused by accidents or incidents.

c. Environmental Protection: Industrial processes can have environmental implications. Safety systems aim to prevent spills, leaks, and emissions that could harm the environment and surrounding ecosystems.

d. Regulatory Compliance: Adherence to safety standards and regulations is a legal requirement for industries. Safety systems ensure compliance with these standards, avoiding legal consequences and penalties.

e. Operational Continuity: By mitigating risks and preventing incidents, safety systems contribute to the continuity of operations, reducing downtime and maintaining productivity.

3. Types of Safety Systems:

Safety systems can be categorized into several types, each serving specific purposes in industrial environments:

a. Emergency Shutdown Systems (ESD): ESD systems are designed to rapidly and safely shut down an industrial process in the event of an emergency, preventing the escalation of incidents.

b. Fire and Gas Detection Systems: These systems employ sensors to detect the presence of fires or hazardous gases, triggering alarms and initiating response measures to mitigate the risk.

c. Process Safety Systems: Process safety systems focus on preventing accidents and incidents during the normal operation of industrial processes. They include measures such as pressure relief systems, interlocks, and alarms.

d. Occupational Safety Systems: These systems address hazards related to the work environment, including personal protective equipment (PPE), safety signage, and training programs to promote safe practices among personnel.

e. Safety Instrumented Systems (SIS): SIS are designed to take specific actions to prevent or mitigate the impact of hazardous events. They include instruments, sensors, and logic solvers to initiate safety measures.

4. Components of Safety Systems:

Safety systems consist of various components, each playing a specific role in ensuring the effectiveness of the overall system:

a. Sensors: Sensors are critical components that detect changes in the environment, such as temperature, pressure, gas concentration, or the presence of flames. These sensors provide input to the safety system to trigger appropriate responses.

b. Logic Solvers: Logic solvers process the inputs from sensors and make decisions based on predefined logic. They determine the appropriate actions to be taken in response to detected hazards.

c. Actuators: Actuators are responsible for implementing the actions determined by the logic solvers. This may include shutting down equipment, activating fire suppression systems, or releasing pressure in the case of an overpressure event.

d. Communication Systems: Communication systems facilitate the exchange of information between various components of the safety system. This ensures that data from sensors reaches the logic solvers, and commands from logic solvers are communicated to actuators.

e. Human Machine Interface (HMI): The HMI provides a user-friendly interface for operators to monitor the status of the safety system, receive alerts, and take manual control if necessary. It serves as a critical link between the system and human operators.

f. Alarms and Notifications: Alarms and notifications alert operators and personnel to potential hazards or incidents. These can be visual or auditory warnings designed to grab attention and prompt immediate action.

5. Safety Standards and Regulations:

The development and implementation of safety systems are guided by a multitude of standards and regulations to ensure consistency, effectiveness, and compliance. Some key standards include:

a. Occupational Safety and Health Administration (OSHA): In the United States, OSHA sets and enforces safety and health regulations to protect workers. OSHA standards cover a wide range of industries and hazards.

b. International Electrotechnical Commission (IEC): IEC standards, particularly IEC 61508 and IEC 61511, provide guidelines for functional safety in the design and operation of safety instrumented systems.

c. American National Standards Institute (ANSI): ANSI standards cover various aspects of safety, including safety colors, labels, and signs, to promote consistency and clarity in safety communication.

d. National Fire Protection Association (NFPA): NFPA standards, such as NFPA 72 for fire alarm and signaling systems, provide guidelines for the design, installation, testing, and maintenance of safety systems.

e. European Union (EU) Directives: The EU has directives, such as the Machinery Directive and the ATEX Directive, that mandate safety requirements for machinery and equipment operating in potentially explosive atmospheres.

6. Applications of Safety Systems:

Safety systems find applications across diverse industries where there are inherent risks associated with industrial processes. Some notable applications include:

a. Chemical Processing: Safety systems are critical in chemical plants to prevent incidents such as chemical spills, fires, and explosions. They include measures to control pressure, temperature, and chemical reactions.

b. Oil and Gas Industry: In the oil and gas sector, safety systems are employed on drilling rigs, refineries, and pipelines to prevent incidents like blowouts, fires, and gas leaks.

c. Power Generation: Safety systems play a vital role in power plants to ensure the safe operation of turbines, boilers, and electrical distribution systems, preventing incidents that could lead to power outages or equipment damage.

d. Manufacturing: Safety systems are integral in manufacturing processes to protect personnel from machinery-related hazards, prevent equipment failures, and ensure the quality of manufactured products.

e. Mining: In the mining industry, safety systems are deployed to manage risks associated with excavation, transportation, and processing of minerals, reducing the likelihood of accidents and injuries.

f. Transportation: Safety systems in transportation include features such as collision avoidance systems, emergency braking, and airbag deployment in vehicles, as well as safety measures in railway and aviation systems.

g. Construction: Safety systems in construction focus on preventing accidents such as falls, equipment collisions, and material handling incidents. This includes the use of personal protective equipment (PPE) and safety signage.

7. Advantages of Safety Systems:

a. Accident Prevention: The primary advantage of safety systems is their ability to prevent accidents and incidents, thereby reducing the risk of injuries, fatalities, and damage to equipment.

b. Compliance: Safety systems help industries comply with regulatory standards and guidelines, avoiding legal consequences and ensuring a safe working environment.

c. Operational Continuity: By mitigating risks and preventing incidents, safety systems contribute to the continuous operation of industrial processes, reducing downtime and maintaining productivity.

d. Environmental Protection: Safety systems help prevent environmental harm by controlling and mitigating incidents that could lead to chemical spills, emissions, or other forms of pollution.

e. Personnel Well-being: The implementation of safety systems prioritizes the well-being of personnel, creating a safer and healthier work environment.

8. Challenges and Considerations:

a. Integration Complexity: Integrating safety systems with existing infrastructure can be complex, especially in environments with diverse legacy components. Careful planning is required to ensure seamless integration.

b. False Alarms: False alarms can lead to complacency and a lack of response when genuine incidents occur. Ensuring the accuracy and reliability of safety system alarms is crucial.

c. Maintenance Requirements: Regular maintenance of safety systems is essential to ensure their continued effectiveness. This includes testing, calibration, and replacement of components as needed.

d. Human Factors: Operator training and awareness are critical for the successful operation of safety systems. Human error or lack of understanding can impact the system's performance.

e. Cybersecurity: With the increasing connectivity of industrial systems, cybersecurity is a growing concern. Safeguarding safety systems from cyber threats is essential to prevent unauthorized access or tampering.

9. Future Trends:

a. Integration with Industrial IoT (IIoT): Safety systems are likely to integrate with IIoT technologies for enhanced monitoring, data analytics, and predictive maintenance, providing a more comprehensive approach to risk management.

b. Artificial Intelligence (AI) and Machine Learning: The incorporation of AI and machine learning in safety systems can improve incident prediction, anomaly detection, and decision-making, enhancing the overall effectiveness of these systems.

c. Advanced Sensing Technologies: Advancements in sensing technologies, such as advanced gas detectors, wearable sensors, and imaging systems, will contribute to more accurate and comprehensive hazard detection.

d. Remote Monitoring and Control: The use of remote monitoring and control capabilities, facilitated by advancements in communication technologies, allows for real-time assessment and response to incidents from a centralized location.

e. Augmented Reality (AR) and Virtual Reality (VR): AR and VR technologies can be employed for training purposes, allowing personnel to simulate emergency scenarios and practice response procedures in a virtual environment.

10. Conclusion:

Safety systems play a pivotal role in ensuring the well-being of personnel, protecting assets, and preventing environmental harm in industrial settings. By employing a combination of sensors, logic solvers, actuators, and communication systems, these systems proactively identify and address potential hazards. Adherence to safety standards and regulations, along with continuous maintenance and operator training, is essential to the effectiveness of safety systems. As industries embrace advancements in technology, the integration of IIoT, AI, and advanced sensing technologies is expected to shape the future of safety systems, making them more intelligent, responsive, and capable of providing a comprehensive approach to risk management. Addressing challenges such as integration complexity, false alarms, and cybersecurity will be crucial as industries strive to create safer and more resilient industrial environments.

Human Machine Interfaces

Human-Machine Interface (HMI) is a critical component in various technological systems that facilitate interaction between humans and machines. HMIs encompass a broad spectrum of interfaces, ranging from physical buttons and switches to graphical user interfaces (GUIs) on computer screens. In this comprehensive exploration, we'll delve into the history, types, components, design principles, applications, challenges, and future trends of Human-Machine Interfaces.

1. Introduction to Human-Machine Interfaces (HMI):

A Human-Machine Interface (HMI) serves as the point of interaction between humans and machines, enabling users to control, monitor, and communicate with a system. The design and functionality of HMIs play a crucial role in user experience, efficiency, and overall system performance. HMIs are integral to a wide range of industries, including manufacturing, process control, healthcare, transportation, and consumer electronics.

2. Evolution of Human-Machine Interfaces:

The evolution of HMIs can be traced through various stages, reflecting advancements in technology and design:

a. Manual Controls: Early machines and systems featured manual controls such as levers, knobs, and switches, requiring direct physical interaction.

b. Analog and Digital Displays: The advent of analog and digital displays introduced visual feedback, allowing users to monitor system parameters and receive information in a more comprehensible format.

c. Text-Based Interfaces: Text-based interfaces, including command-line interfaces (CLIs), provided a more interactive and efficient means of communication with computers and systems.

d. Graphical User Interfaces (GUIs): The introduction of GUIs revolutionized HMIs by incorporating graphical elements, icons, and menus. This shift made systems more user-friendly and accessible.

e. Touchscreens and Gesture Controls: The integration of touchscreens and gesture controls further enhanced user interaction, offering intuitive and tactile interfaces in devices such as smartphones and tablets.

f. Voice and Natural Language Interfaces: Recent advancements include voice recognition and natural language interfaces, enabling users to interact with systems using spoken commands and conversational language.

3. Types of Human-Machine Interfaces:

HMIs come in various types, each tailored to specific applications and user requirements:

a. Physical Interfaces: These include traditional buttons, switches, knobs, and levers that users physically manipulate to control a system. Physical interfaces are common in machinery, appliances, and industrial control panels.

b. Touchscreen Interfaces: Touchscreens allow users to interact with systems by tapping, swiping, or gesturing on a display. This type of interface is prevalent in smartphones, tablets, information kiosks, and industrial control systems.

c. Graphical User Interfaces (GUIs): GUIs present information and controls through graphical elements such as icons, buttons, and menus. They are widely used in computers, software applications, and embedded systems.

d. Voice and Speech Interfaces: Voice interfaces enable users to interact with systems using spoken commands. This technology is found in virtual assistants, smart speakers, and automotive infotainment systems.

e. Augmented Reality (AR) and Virtual Reality (VR) Interfaces: AR and VR interfaces provide immersive experiences by overlaying digital information onto the physical world (AR) or creating entirely virtual environments (VR). These interfaces find applications in gaming, training, and simulations.

f. Brain-Computer Interfaces (BCIs): BCIs establish a direct communication link between the brain and a computer or device, allowing users to control systems through neural signals. BCIs hold promise for applications in healthcare, assistive technology, and gaming.

4. Components of Human-Machine Interfaces:

The components of an HMI system depend on its type and complexity, but common elements include:

a. Input Devices: Input devices capture user commands and interactions. Examples include keyboards, mice, touchscreens, voice recognition systems, and gesture sensors.

b. Output Displays: Output displays present information, feedback, and visualizations to users. These can be traditional monitors, LED displays, touchscreens, heads-up displays (HUDs), or virtual reality headsets.

c. Control Elements: Control elements, such as buttons, sliders, and switches, enable users to manipulate and adjust settings. In digital interfaces, these may be represented as on-screen controls.

d. Processing Unit: The processing unit, often part of the overall system or device, interprets user inputs, manages the interface logic, and generates appropriate outputs. It may include microcontrollers, CPUs, or dedicated processing units.

e. Communication Interfaces: Communication interfaces facilitate the exchange of data between the HMI system and the controlled device or system. These interfaces can include wired connections (USB, Ethernet) or wireless connections (Bluetooth, Wi-Fi).

f. Feedback Mechanisms: Feedback mechanisms, such as haptic feedback (vibrations), audible alerts, or visual indicators, inform users about the system's status or the result of their actions.

5. Design Principles for Human-Machine Interfaces:

Effective HMI design is crucial for creating user-friendly, intuitive, and efficient interfaces. Key design principles include:

a. User-Centered Design: Prioritize the needs, preferences, and capabilities of the end-users throughout the design process. Consider user feedback and conduct usability testing to refine the interface.

b. Consistency: Maintain consistency in design elements, layout, and interaction patterns to create a cohesive and predictable user experience. Consistency enhances learnability and reduces user errors.

c. Feedback and Affordance: Provide clear feedback to users about the result of their actions. Affordances, visual or tactile cues, should indicate how users can interact with elements and what actions are possible.

d. Simplicity and Clarity: Keep the interface simple and avoid unnecessary complexity. Use clear language, concise labels, and straightforward navigation to enhance user comprehension.

e. Hierarchy and Organization: Organize information hierarchically, emphasizing important elements and grouping related functions. Clear organization facilitates efficient navigation and task completion.

f. Minimize Cognitive Load: Reduce cognitive load by presenting information in a digestible manner, avoiding information overload, and prioritizing essential details. Minimizing cognitive load enhances user decision-making and task performance.

g. Flexibility and Customization: Allow users to customize the interface based on their preferences and needs. Providing flexibility accommodates diverse user requirements and enhances overall usability.

6. Applications of Human-Machine Interfaces:

HMIs are pervasive in various industries and applications, contributing to enhanced user interaction and system control. Some notable applications include:

a. Manufacturing and Industrial Automation: HMIs are integral to control panels and systems in manufacturing environments, enabling operators to monitor production processes, adjust settings, and respond to alarms.

b. Process Control Systems: Industries such as chemical processing, power generation, and oil and gas utilize HMIs for monitoring and controlling complex processes, ensuring operational efficiency and safety.

c. Consumer Electronics: Smartphones, tablets, smart TVs, and other consumer electronics heavily rely on touchscreens and graphical interfaces to provide users with intuitive control and access to features.

d. Automotive Interfaces: Automotive HMIs include dashboards, infotainment systems, and heads-up displays. These interfaces provide drivers and passengers with information, entertainment, and control over various vehicle functions.

e. Healthcare Systems: In healthcare, HMIs are used in medical devices, patient monitoring systems, and diagnostic equipment. These interfaces assist healthcare professionals in managing and interpreting medical data.

f. Aviation and Aerospace: Cockpit interfaces in aircraft feature advanced HMIs to assist pilots in navigation, communication, and system control. Aerospace applications also include control interfaces for unmanned aerial vehicles (UAVs).

g. Smart Homes: Smart home devices utilize HMIs for user control and interaction. Voice-activated assistants, touchscreens, and mobile apps enable users to manage connected devices and home automation systems.

7. Advantages of Human-Machine Interfaces:

a. Improved User Experience: Well-designed HMIs enhance the overall user experience by providing intuitive controls, clear feedback, and efficient navigation.

b. Increased Efficiency: User-friendly interfaces contribute to increased efficiency by reducing the time and effort required to interact with and control systems.

c. Enhanced Safety: In industrial settings, effective HMIs contribute to operational safety by providing operators with real-time information, alarms, and control capabilities.

d. Accessibility: HMIs can be designed to accommodate diverse user needs, including accessibility features for individuals with disabilities, making technology more inclusive.

e. Reduced Training Time: Intuitive interfaces reduce the learning curve for users, minimizing the time and resources needed for training.

8. Challenges and Considerations:

a. Complexity: Designing HMIs for complex systems or applications requires careful consideration to avoid overwhelming users with information and options.

b. Adaptability: Interfaces need to be adaptable to various user preferences, devices, and contexts, posing challenges in creating universally effective designs.

c. Cybersecurity: As interfaces become more connected, ensuring the security of HMIs against cyber threats becomes a critical consideration to prevent unauthorized access and data breaches.

d. Usability Testing: Conducting thorough usability testing is essential to identify potential issues and refine the design. However, it can be resource-intensive and time-consuming.

e. Interoperability: HMIs must often interact with diverse systems and devices, requiring compatibility and interoperability considerations during design and implementation.

9. Future Trends in Human-Machine Interfaces:

a. Gesture Recognition: Advancements in gesture recognition technology will enable users to interact with systems through natural hand movements, expanding the range of input options.

b. Brain-Computer Interfaces (BCIs): BCIs hold promise for direct communication between the brain and machines, opening up possibilities for enhanced control and accessibility.

c. Augmented Reality (AR) and Virtual Reality (VR): The integration of AR and VR technologies in HMIs will provide immersive and interactive experiences, especially in gaming, training, and simulations.

d. Voice and Natural Language Processing: Continued improvements in voice recognition and natural language processing will enhance the accuracy and versatility of voice-controlled interfaces.

e. Biometric Authentication: Biometric authentication features, such as facial recognition and fingerprint scanning, will play a larger role in ensuring secure access to devices and systems.

10. Conclusion:

Human-Machine Interfaces (HMIs) play a pivotal role in shaping how humans interact with technology and systems across diverse industries. From physical controls and touchscreens to voice recognition and augmented reality, the evolution of HMIs reflects the ongoing quest for more intuitive, efficient, and user-friendly interfaces. Design principles focused on user-centered design, consistency, and simplicity contribute to positive user experiences, while ongoing challenges, such as cybersecurity and adaptability, require careful consideration. As technology continues to advance, incorporating trends like gesture recognition, brain-computer interfaces, and augmented reality, the future of HMIs holds exciting possibilities for more immersive, accessible, and intelligent interactions between humans and machines.

Total Integrated Automation

Total Integrated Automation (TIA) is a concept within the realm of industrial automation that emphasizes the comprehensive integration of various automation components and systems. It encompasses the convergence of control systems, communication networks, sensors, actuators, and other elements to create a unified and interconnected automation infrastructure. The goal of TIA is to streamline processes, enhance efficiency, and improve overall system performance in industrial settings.

1. Components of Total Integrated Automation:

a. Control Systems: TIA involves the integration of different types of control systems, such as Programmable Logic Controllers (PLCs), Distributed Control Systems (DCS), and Supervisory Control and Data Acquisition (SCADA) systems. These systems work in harmony to control and monitor industrial processes.

b. Sensors and Actuators: The integration of sensors and actuators is fundamental in TIA. Sensors collect data from the environment, while actuators execute control commands based on that data. These devices play a crucial role in providing real-time information for decision-making.

c. Communication Networks: Robust communication networks, including Ethernet, industrial communication protocols (e.g., Profibus, Modbus), and wireless technologies, are essential for seamless data exchange between various components in a TIA setup.

d. Human-Machine Interface (HMI): TIA often involves the implementation of a unified Human-Machine Interface that provides operators with a comprehensive view of the entire industrial process. This allows for efficient monitoring, control, and troubleshooting.

e. Information Technology (IT) Systems: Integration with IT systems, such as enterprise resource planning (ERP) and data analytics platforms, is part of TIA. This integration aligns automation with broader business objectives and facilitates data-driven decision-making.

f. Robotics: TIA may include the integration of robotic systems, enabling collaborative work between robots, human operators, and other machines. This integration is particularly relevant in advanced manufacturing environments.

2. Benefits of Total Integrated Automation:

a. Operational Efficiency: TIA eliminates silos and optimizes processes, leading to improved operational efficiency. The seamless integration of components ensures a smooth flow of information and actions.

b. Cost Savings: By minimizing downtime, reducing errors, and optimizing resource utilization, TIA contributes to cost savings in industrial operations.

c. Data-Driven Decision Making: The integration of data from various sources enables better-informed decision-making processes. Real-time data analytics within a TIA framework can provide valuable insights.

d. Flexibility and Scalability: TIA systems are designed to be flexible and scalable, allowing organizations to adapt to changing requirements and easily expand their operations.

e. Enhanced Product Quality: TIA ensures consistency in processes, contributing to enhanced product quality and reduced variability.

f. Improved Safety: TIA systems can include safety features and protocols, reducing the risk of accidents and enhancing overall workplace safety.

3. Challenges and Considerations in Total Integrated Automation:

a. Interoperability Issues: Different automation components may use diverse communication protocols or standards, leading to challenges in achieving seamless interoperability within a TIA framework.

b. Security Concerns: As systems become more interconnected, there's an increased risk of cybersecurity threats. TIA requires robust security measures to protect against unauthorized access and data breaches.

c. Legacy System Integration: Many industries have existing legacy systems that might be challenging to integrate with modern automation technologies. Legacy systems may require upgrades or specialized interfaces for seamless integration within a TIA framework.

d. Data Standardization: Integrating data from different sources may involve dealing with varied data formats and standards. Establishing standardized data formats is crucial for efficient data exchange within a TIA framework.

e. Training and Skill Development: Employees need training to operate and maintain TIA systems. Skill development is essential to keep up with the evolving technology.

4. Applications of Total Integrated Automation:

a. Manufacturing: TIA is widely used in manufacturing processes, including assembly lines, quality control, and material handling. It optimizes production workflows for increased efficiency.

b. Process Industries: Industries such as chemical, petrochemical, and pharmaceuticals leverage TIA for the efficient control and monitoring of complex processes. TIA ensures precision and reliability in process control.

c. Energy Management: TIA is applied in energy management systems, optimizing the generation, distribution, and consumption of energy in industrial and commercial facilities.

d. Building Automation: In smart buildings, TIA controls heating, ventilation, air conditioning (HVAC), lighting, and security systems for energy efficiency and occupant comfort.

e. Supply Chain and Logistics: TIA is utilized in supply chain and logistics for inventory management, order processing, and distribution. It ensures smooth and synchronized operations in the supply chain.

f. Healthcare: In healthcare settings, TIA helps in managing patient records, medical equipment, and overall hospital operations. It enhances efficiency in healthcare delivery.

5. Future Trends in Total Integrated Automation:

a. Internet of Things (IoT) Integration: The integration of IoT devices with TIA systems will provide more data points for analysis, enabling predictive maintenance and better decision-making.

b. Artificial Intelligence (AI) and Machine Learning (ML): The incorporation of AI and ML algorithms in TIA systems will enhance the ability to analyze data, predict trends, and optimize processes.

c. Edge Computing: Edge computing brings processing capabilities closer to the data source, reducing latency and enabling faster decision-making in TIA setups.

d. Digital Twins: The concept of digital twins involves creating virtual replicas of physical processes or systems. TIA can leverage digital twins for simulation, analysis, and optimization.

e. Augmented Reality (AR) and Virtual Reality (VR): AR and VR technologies can be integrated into TIA systems for enhanced visualization, training, and troubleshooting.

f. Blockchain Technology: Blockchain can be utilized to enhance the security and transparency of data exchange in TIA systems, particularly in sensitive industries.

6. Conclusion:

Total Integrated Automation (TIA) represents a holistic approach to industrial automation, emphasizing the seamless integration of various components and systems. By creating a unified infrastructure that connects control systems, sensors, communication networks, and other elements, TIA aims to optimize processes, enhance efficiency, and improve overall performance in industrial settings. The benefits of TIA include operational efficiency, cost savings, data-driven decision-making, flexibility, scalability, enhanced product quality, and improved safety. However, challenges such as interoperability issues, security concerns, legacy system integration, data standardization, and the need for continuous training and skill development must be carefully addressed. As technology continues to advance, trends like IoT integration, AI and ML applications, edge computing, digital twins, and immersive technologies such as AR and VR are poised to shape the future landscape of Total Integrated Automation. Organizations that effectively navigate these trends and challenges stand to gain significant advantages in their industrial operations.

Industry 4.0

Industry 4.0 is a transformative concept in the realm of manufacturing and industrial processes. It represents the fourth industrial revolution and is characterized by the integration of digital technologies, data-driven insights, and advanced automation to create smart, interconnected, and highly efficient production systems. In this detailed exploration, we will delve into the history, key principles, technologies, applications, challenges, and future trends of Industry 4.0.

1. Introduction to Industry 4.0:

Industry 4.0, also known as the fourth industrial revolution, builds upon the advancements of the previous three industrial revolutions. It represents a paradigm shift in manufacturing, leveraging digital technologies to create "smart factories" and interconnected systems. The term "Industry 4.0" was first introduced at the Hannover Fair in 2011 in Germany, reflecting the country's commitment to technological innovation in manufacturing.

2. Historical Context:

a. First Industrial Revolution (Late 18th to Early 19th Century): The first industrial revolution marked the transition from agrarian and manual labor-based economies to mechanized production powered by water and steam. The introduction of the spinning jenny and the steam engine revolutionized manufacturing.

b. Second Industrial Revolution (Late 19th to Early 20th Century): The second industrial revolution brought about mass production through the use of electricity and the assembly line. Innovations such as the telegraph, telephone, and the internal combustion engine further transformed industries.

c. Third Industrial Revolution (Late 20th Century): The third industrial revolution, often referred to as the Digital Revolution, introduced computerization and automation. The widespread use of computers, electronics, and the internet significantly impacted manufacturing and communication.

d. Fourth Industrial Revolution (21st Century - Present): Industry 4.0 is characterized by the fusion of physical systems with digital technologies. It involves the integration of the internet of things (IoT), artificial intelligence (AI), big data analytics, and other advanced technologies to create intelligent, self-optimizing production systems.

3. Key Principles of Industry 4.0:

a. Interconnectivity: Industry 4.0 emphasizes the seamless connectivity of machines, devices, and systems. This enables real-time data exchange and communication between different components of the production process.

b. Information Transparency: Data transparency is a crucial principle, involving the availability of relevant information for all stakeholders in the production process. This transparency allows for better decision-making and process optimization.

c. Technical Assistance: Industry 4.0 systems provide technical assistance through advanced technologies such as augmented reality (AR) and virtual reality (VR). These technologies assist operators in tasks like maintenance, troubleshooting, and training.

d. Decentralized Decision-Making: Industry 4.0 promotes decentralized decision-making by enabling individual components and systems to make autonomous decisions based on real-time data. This leads to more agile and responsive production processes.

4. Technologies Driving Industry 4.0:

a. Internet of Things (IoT): IoT involves connecting physical devices, sensors, and machines to the internet, enabling them to collect and exchange data. In Industry 4.0, IoT plays a central role in creating interconnected and intelligent systems.

b. Big Data Analytics: Big data analytics involves the processing and analysis of large volumes of data to extract meaningful insights. In Industry 4.0, big data analytics is used to optimize processes, predict maintenance needs, and improve overall efficiency.

c. Artificial Intelligence (AI): AI technologies, including machine learning and deep learning, are employed in Industry 4.0 to enable machines to learn from data, make decisions, and continuously improve performance.

d. Augmented Reality (AR) and Virtual Reality (VR): AR and VR technologies provide immersive experiences and assist in various aspects of manufacturing, including maintenance, training, and design.

e. Additive Manufacturing (3D Printing): Additive manufacturing is used in Industry 4.0 for rapid prototyping, customized production, and the creation of complex and lightweight structures.

f. Cyber-Physical Systems (CPS): CPS involves the integration of physical processes with computational capabilities. In Industry 4.0, CPS enables the real-time monitoring and control of physical processes.

g. Blockchain Technology: Blockchain ensures secure and transparent transactions in Industry 4.0. It is applied in supply chain management, quality assurance, and secure data sharing.

5. Applications of Industry 4.0:

a. Smart Factories: Industry 4.0 transforms traditional factories into smart factories where machines, devices, and systems communicate and collaborate autonomously. This leads to increased efficiency, reduced downtime, and optimized production processes.

b. Predictive Maintenance: Industry 4.0 enables predictive maintenance by using sensors and data analytics to monitor the condition of equipment. This allows for timely maintenance, reducing the risk of unplanned downtime.

c. Digital Twins: Digital twins create virtual replicas of physical systems or products. In Industry 4.0, digital twins are used for simulation, analysis, and optimization, providing a digital representation of the real-world counterpart.

d. Supply Chain Optimization: Industry 4.0 optimizes supply chain management by enhancing visibility, traceability, and efficiency. This includes real-time monitoring of inventory, demand forecasting, and efficient logistics.

e. Customized Production: Industry 4.0 facilitates customized and on-demand production. Smart manufacturing systems can adapt to individual customer requirements, leading to more flexible and responsive production processes.

f. Energy Management: Smart energy management is a key application of Industry 4.0. By integrating sensors and automation, industries can optimize energy consumption, reduce waste, and improve overall sustainability.

6. Benefits of Industry 4.0:

a. Increased Efficiency: Industry 4.0 leads to improved operational efficiency through the integration of advanced technologies and data-driven insights.

b. Cost Savings: Predictive maintenance, optimized processes, and reduced downtime contribute to significant cost savings in smart factories.

c. Enhanced Product Quality: The use of data analytics and real-time monitoring ensures consistent product quality and reduces defects.

d. Flexibility and Customization: Industry 4.0 enables flexible and customized production, allowing manufacturers to adapt to changing market demands.

e. Improved Decision-Making: Access to real-time data and analytics empowers decision-makers to make informed and timely decisions.

f. Workplace Safety: Automation and robotics in Industry 4.0 contribute to improved workplace safety by handling hazardous tasks and reducing human exposure to dangerous environments.

7. Challenges and Considerations in Industry 4.0:

a. Security Concerns: With increased connectivity, the risk of cyber threats and data breaches becomes a major concern. Ensuring the cybersecurity of interconnected systems is crucial.

b. Interoperability: Integrating diverse technologies and systems from different vendors can lead to interoperability challenges. Standardization efforts are essential to address this issue.

c. Workforce Skills: The implementation of Industry 4.0 requires a skilled workforce capable of managing and maintaining advanced technologies. Workforce training and education are crucial considerations.

d. Data Privacy: The collection and analysis of vast amounts of data raise concerns about data privacy. Organizations must implement robust data protection measures to address these concerns.

e. Initial Implementation Costs: The upfront costs associated with implementing Industry 4.0 technologies can be significant. Organizations must carefully evaluate the return on investment over the long term.

f. Cultural Change: Embracing Industry 4.0 often requires a cultural shift within organizations. Resistance to change and lack of awareness among employees can pose challenges.

8. Future Trends in Industry 4.0:

a. 5G Technology: The rollout of 5G technology will further enhance connectivity and enable faster and more reliable communication between devices in Industry 4.0.

b. Edge Computing: Edge computing involves processing data closer to the source, reducing latency. It is expected to play a crucial role in Industry 4.0, especially in real-time applications.

c. Autonomous Systems: The development of autonomous systems, including autonomous robots and vehicles, will contribute to increased automation in manufacturing and logistics.

d. AI and Machine Learning Advancements: Ongoing advancements in AI and machine learning will lead to more sophisticated and intelligent manufacturing systems in Industry 4.0.

e. Sustainable Manufacturing: Industry 4.0 will increasingly focus on sustainable and environmentally friendly manufacturing practices, contributing to overall sustainability goals.

f. Human Augmentation: The integration of wearable devices and technologies that augment human capabilities will become more prevalent in smart factories.

9. Conclusion:

Industry 4.0 represents a groundbreaking shift in the way industries approach manufacturing and production processes. By leveraging advanced technologies such as IoT, AI, big data analytics, and robotics, Industry 4.0 aims to create smart, connected, and efficient manufacturing ecosystems. The benefits of increased efficiency, cost savings, enhanced product quality, and flexibility are compelling, but organizations must navigate challenges related to security, interoperability, workforce skills, and cultural change.

As Industry 4.0 continues to evolve, it is essential for businesses to stay abreast of technological advancements, invest in workforce training, and adopt a strategic approach to implementation. The ongoing trends of 5G technology, edge computing, autonomous systems, AI advancements, and sustainable manufacturing are indicative of the dynamic nature of Industry 4.0. Embracing these trends and addressing challenges will position organizations to thrive in the era of smart manufacturing and contribute to the ongoing evolution of industrial processes.